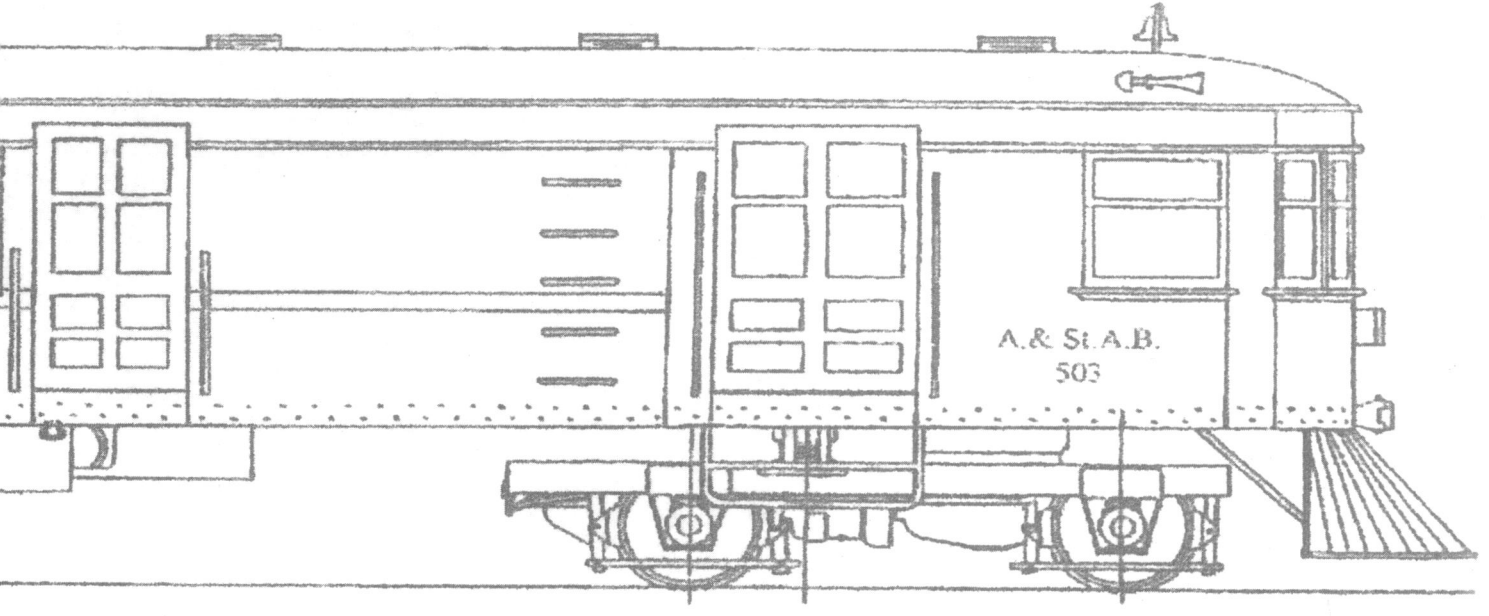
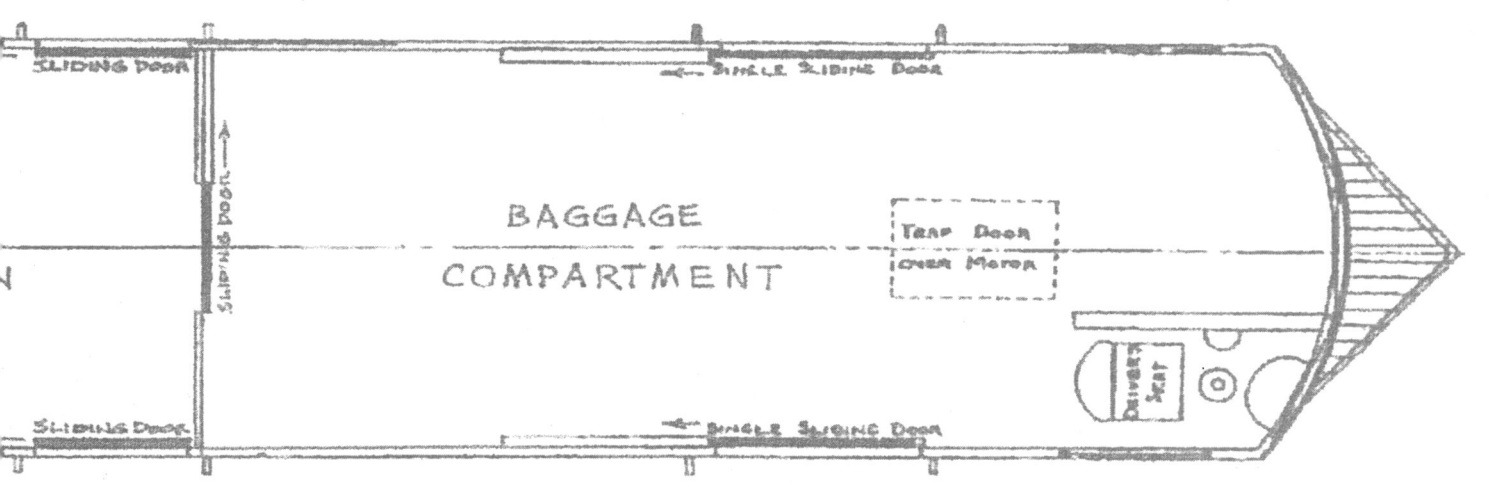

The Edwards Railway Motor Car Company

The Edwards Railway Motor Car Company

And its Visionary Founder, H.P. Edwards, "The Doctor of Sick Shortlines"

Cary Franklin Poole

www.HotBoxPress.com

The Edwards Railway Motorcar Company - And its Visionary Founder, H.P. Edwards, "The Doctor of Sick Shortlines."

Copyright © 2006 by Cary Franklin Poole. All rights reserved. Printed in the United States of America. No part of this book may be used or reproduced in any manner whatsoever without written permission except in the case of brief quotations embodied in critical articles or reviews. For information contact Hot Box Press at info@HotBoxPress.com, or PO Box 161078, Mobile, AL 36616

First Edition

Layout and design by Mark S. Vandercook

Library of Congress control number: 2005934615

ISBN: 0-9703544-0-1

Frontispiece - An original mixed-media work by Tony Howe depicts Birmingham & Southeastern no. 500 making the rounds on a leisurely but sweltering afternoon outside of Milstead, Alabama in 1948.

Hot Box Press
info@HotBoxPress.com
www.HotBoxPress.com
PO Box 161078, Mobile, AL 36616

Dedication

This volume is dedicated to the late Claude Franklin Poole, Jr. Known as Frank or "C.F." to his family, he passed at age sixty-eight after battling cancer for several months. He began his career as a telegrapher with the Central of Georgia Railway, then worked for the Southern Railway and eventually retired from the Norfolk Southern Railway after thirty-seven years of service. His family was both gratified and surprised by the large number of current and retired railroaders who attended his memorial and funeral services in September 2003.

In addition, this volume is dedicated to the many men and women who had the pleasure of working with Mr. Harry Powell Edwards over several years and over several railroads. May their exacting standards and craftsmanship continue to be enjoyed by future generations. Little did they know that their achievements and accomplishments would help write an important chapter of U.S. railroad history. They may be surprised to know several of their products are now treasured possessions by museums across the United States.

Contents

Acknowledgments *viii*
Introduction *1*

Part One: Edwards Railway Motor Car Company
1. 1912-1942 *11*
2. Rebirth *83*

Part Two: H.P. Edwards, "The Doctor of Sick Shortlines"
3. Management of the Atlantic & Western *113*
4. Management of the Atlanta & St. Andrews Bay *121*
5. Consulting on the Marianna & Blountstown *129*
6. Consulting on the Watauga & Yadkin River *141*
7. Consulting on the Georgia, Florida & Alabama *145*
8. Management of the Atlantic & East Carolina *149*

Appendixes:
A. Abbreviations Used in the Text, Maps & Rosters. *161*
B. Edwards Railway Motor Car Company Roster *162*
C. Atlantic & Western Roster *169*
D. Atlanta & St. Andrews Bay Roster *171*
E. Marianna & Blountstown Roster *175*
F. Watauga & Yadkin River Roster *176*
G. Georgia, Florida & Alabama Roster *177*
H. Atlantic & North Carolina/Atlantic & East Carolina Roster *179*

Bibliography: *181*
Index: *185*

Acknowledgments

There are many people to recognize for their untiring efforts in helping get the story of Harry P. Edwards onto the print page for posterity. This project, almost ten years in the making, began when I first heard about the Edwards Railway Motor Car Company along with the man who designed and built the cars. With this long journey in mind, I would like to thank the following for their efforts: My wife Carole and family members for giving me encouragement when writing lulls appeared. To Tom Sink and M. B. "Mac" Connery for first telling me about the Edwards Motor Car Company on that initial trip to Durham, North Carolina. Mac also pushed me to keep doing research when I needed some motivation. To William "Bill" Edwards for sharing his memories about his father, and also for relating his own experiences on the Atlantic & East Carolina. To Steven Torrico and the new Edwards Rail Car Company for preserving the physical legacy of Harry Edwards for future generations. Steven is now restoring and preserving several Edwards motor cars, as well as building new products to Harry's exacting standards.

John Porter and Bill Parrish of Sanford, North Carolina provided photographs, clippings and a chronological corporate history of the Edwards factory in Sanford. Both of them had worked at this facility. R. Douglas Walker helped immensely with the Watauga & Yadkin River Railroad and furnished critically-needed photographs. Dave Minor of the Fort Madison, Farmington & Western Railroad provided a wealth of information on the Chicago, Burlington & Quincy cars, which constituted Edwards' largest single order, while Louis Saillard provided details on Harry P. Edwards' life during the Great Depression.

William Irving and the Duke University Library staff allowed me access to the preserved records of Harry P. Edwards, while Ken Ardinger and Paul Copeland helped with proofing the locomotive rosters. Pat Trammell of Tallahassee, Florida provided information and photos on the Marianna & Blountstown Railroad. Lowell McManus of the MexList electronic bulletin board played a key role in forwarding my requests for information to Central and South American contacts, who could provide information on Edwards cars. In particular, Gustavo Arias supplied critical information on Colombian cars. In this phase, Daniel Lewis helped get my story out through Latin Rails.

Marvin Black, Russell Tedder and Parker Lamb assisted me with key photographs and information over the last few years, while David LeNoir, Associate Professor of English at Western Kentucky University once again served as the copy editor.

Introduction
Harry Powell Edwards - The Man and his Times

Noted American pop-culture philosopher Andy Warhol is given credit for the popularized phrase that, "everyone will have fifteen minutes of fame." Occasionally we are introduced to individuals whose entire lives have been a series of contributions to society, and it is difficult to identify their fifteen minutes of fame. Only by reviewing the entirety of their lives do we begin to understand these individuals' achievements. Harry Edwards was one of those rare persons who made many such marks in his life, and this book is an attempt to chronicle them.

Edwards was born in Laurinburg, North Carolina on November 7, 1885, and his professional life would leave a significant imprint on the Southern economy for over four decades. The son of Katherine Magleen and William Joseph Edwards, Harry's illustrious career benefited many communities in the United States, as well as in Central and South America. While he often referred to himself simply as a "transportation consultant," his overall influence included many other aspects, such as his early recognition of developing local Chambers of Commerce to benefit entire communities in which he resided. Although the majority of Edwards's career centered on the railroad industry, he took an active interest in promoting public transportation and interstate commerce as well.

The life and times of Harry Edwards are closely related with those of his father, William Joseph, who was a native of Greene County, North Carolina and a well-known figure in both railroading and banking. A native of Snow Hill, William moved to nearby Sanford, and soon founded the Bank of Sanford, later the Page Trust Company. William also founded both the First National Bank of Fayetteville and the Bank of Maxton, and served as chairman of all three for over twenty years.

In 1881, Harry's father moved to Laurinburg to become official storekeeper for the Carolina Central Railway, which later joined the Seaboard Air Line Railroad. From there he moved to Raleigh as the road's general purchasing agent. Three years later he returned to Sanford, to contemplate where this railroad background would lead him.

Some time later, William developed a deeper interest in railroads, which he passed on to his son. For example, he founded the Atlantic & Western Railroad (A&W) in 1899, and later became receiver of the Carolina & Northern Railroad, also serving as president of the Gulf Line Railway headquartered in Sylvester, Georgia. His service to the latter road included many improvements and even extensions to its route. While on the Board of the A&W, he also organized the Carolina Railroad Company, through which he hoped to construct a coastal connection between the A&W at Lillington, North Carolina and Swannsboro.

William Edwards was also prominent in local politics in Sanford, serving as an early mayor and successfully leading the community through its first bond issue. This revenue was used to attract industries and to establish a water system. It took an epidemic costing many lives, coupled with William's perseverance, but the bond issue was passed overwhelmingly and Edwards spent the next several months supervising the water project. In 1900, through tireless hours of seeing to every minute detail, he was able to not only see the completion of the original artesian well, but also supervised the

Harry Powell Edwards seen in his trademark Homburg hat. *Collection of W.J. Edwards.*

construction of a water line which linked the city with a new water source located at Lick Creek, four miles away.

William was also noted for his attempts at modernizing and diversifying local farms by hiring agricultural agents to assist local growers to add berries, melons and peaches to their crop base. At Edwards's suggestion, 250 acres were converted into growing peaches and 20,000 young peach trees were brought in simultaneously with the opening of the A&W Railway.

William's other noted accomplishment was the construction of the Commercial Building in Sanford, at the corner of Moore and Wicker Streets. His Bank of Sanford was located on the first floor and, with other downtown buildings, gradually became the trading and commercial center for Harnett County. Thus much of the county's prosperity was linked directly to Edwards's insight and forward thinking. Williams' wife, the former Kate Magleen of Laurinburg, whom he had married in 1884, was credited with founding the first Catholic Church in Sanford.

William contracted pneumonia and died on April 14, 1916, but not before watching Harry launch a distinguished career in railroading. William died while visiting his sister, Mrs. S. M. Warren, in Washington, D.C. The body was shipped home to Sanford via the Seaboard Air Line Railroad, where it was met by hundreds of locals wishing to pay their last respects. Funeral services were held at the city's largest auditorium, First Presbyterian Church, though the funeral mass was celebrated by Father Dillon, a priest from Southern Pines. William was survived by his wife, Katie, three sons, Harry P., Glenn and Darden Edwards, and four as yet unmarried daughters, Nannie, Katie, Marie and Julia May Edwards. Katie Edwards lived until July 7, 1951.

Harry was educated primarily in public schools, first in Raleigh and later in Sanford. He graduated from Sanford High School in 1900 and headed to Belmont Abbey College, Belmont, North Carolina, from which he received a Bachelor of Arts degree in 1903.

Having chosen a career in railroading, Harry had to learn from the bottom up. His first job, as a general laborer with the railroad his father had founded, began a life-long association with the A&W. From 1903 to 1919, Edwards served a minimum of six months in each of the following railroad positions: locomotive engineer, fireman, conductor, freight agent, shop mechanic, auditor and traffic manager. He eventually became the road's general manager.

Edwards was married in January 1916 to the former May Cross, daughter of T. M. and Mamie Cross. The marriage produced two children: Winslow, born in November 1916, and William Joseph, born in March 1919. Both sons would follow in the footsteps of their father, with numerous stints as railroad men.

While serving as the A&W's general manager, Edwards took note of the national interest involving the use of internal combustion engines for mass transportation. As early as 1915, Edwards converted a bus for rail use by modifying the wheel spacing (gauge) and replacing the tires and wheels with steel flanged wheels. Though successful on the A&W, the prototype was not placed into production until 1922, when Edwards founded the Edwards Railway Motor Car Company.

Edwards's full-time position on the A&W was suspended temporarily in 1919 when he joined the United States Railroad Administration (USRA). During World War I, President Woodrow Wilson had nationalized most Class I railroads to facilitate war production and transportation. From 1919 through 1921, Edwards worked for the USRA under the supervision of W. H. Harrihan, federal manager of the Seaboard Air Line Railroad and all shortlines connecting with the Seaboard system from Virginia to Florida. Edwards worked directly under W. H. King, who was responsible for shortline operations. While in this federal position, Edwards continued serving as general manger of the A&W, yet was able to absorb much information about other shortline operations under the tutelage of King.

In 1920, the United States returned all railroads to their owners, and Edwards returned to the A&W on a full-time basis. However, he was given an added responsibility as manager of an A&W-owned lumber company. He was also able to return to his interests in transportation using internal combustion engines. By 1922, he began experimenting with a coach powered by such an engine. After building a prototype car, he tested it on the A&W and then placed it in regular service. To prepare for marketing, Edwards received a U. S. patent for his design of the engine, transmission and drive mechanism. With his patents and his expanded knowledge of shortline operations, Edwards began an aggressive marketing campaign to demonstrate his "self-propelled coach" to railroads around the country.

After receiving positive feedback in his initial marketing efforts, Edwards organized the Edwards Railway Motor Car Company (ERwyMCC), serving as both president and general sales manager. He soon built a plant for constructing the cars adjacent to the A&W's line, and began doing detailed studies of typical operating conditions on several railroads in both the United States and overseas. He used these results to customize his sales pitch to each railroad, assuring them that his car could operate satisfactorily on their line.

As the general level of technology of such cars improved, Edwards incorporated the improvements on his models. For example, on September 27, 1924, Edwards applied for a patent for mounting the drive-motor directly on the power truck. The patent was awarded on August 25, 1925 and allowed Edwards's company to actively market this refinement in brochures and catalogues. Eventually, his motor cars were sold to over fifty railroads in the United States, Mexico, Canada, Panama, Colombia, Argentina, Ecuador, Peru and Guatemala.

In July 1927, Edwards set forth on a new venture, which took him for the first time outside his native state. The occasion was a vote by the A&W Board of Directors to ask for his resignation. This decision was brought about by his marketing strategies rather than any mismanagement issues, of which there was never any doubt. For example, Edwards preferred keeping the A&W's roadbed at a standard commonly associated with Class 1 lines, but this meant that the road was often delinquent in some of its payments to suppliers.

However, family members noted that Edwards was extremely fastidious in his business dealings. His son Bill remembered that his father kept a personal ledger of all expenses, both personal and company related. He would go as far as to account for a soft drink purchased at the local drug store by noting its cost in his ledger book. Literally, every cent that Edwards possessed could be accounted for, as he was constantly reviewing invoices. For example, he was once reviewing bills when he noted an invoice showed that he was billed $2.02 per hundred weight for Buda gasoline engines shipped from Harvey, Illinois. However, another invoice listed the cost as $2.54 per hundred weight. From research, Edwards was able to document that "Jones' Tariff 1514" and "Epsiden's Tariff 883" stated the correct rate to apply to these shipments was $1.56 per hundred-weight. Thus, he politely but firmly insisted that he be reimbursed for a miscalculation of tariff rates.

Even Edwards's business attire was dictated by his personal modesty. His most widely known photograph displays his trademark Homburg hat, tie and vest with an overcoat, quite a contrast with the flamboyant fashions of the flapper era. His sons remember that, even on family fishing trips, his father insisted on wearing a tie and long sleeved shirts.

A year after leaving the A&W, he lost control of the car company, and began a search for other railroad employment. Through his many sales contacts, he learned of an opening on the Atlanta & St. Andrews Bay Railway. Soon he was appointed to the positions of executive vice president and general manager by Minor C. Keith, founder and CEO of the United Fruit Company (world's largest banana supplier), which owned the "Bay Line." When Edwards assumed the general manager's position, the line consisted of ninety miles of main line and branch line track stretching from Panama City, Florida to Dothan, Alabama. It had been a chronic money loser, but Edwards's dedicated efforts turned the road around in eighteen months. Improvements were made to solicit new business as well as to increase traffic from existing on-line businesses. After his second year on the railroad, it did not have to borrow money to maintain its operations.

In addition to many improvements to the railroad itself, Edwards developed other revenue sources, such as the St. Andrews Bay Transportation Company, a subsidiary of the railroad that served as both a passenger bus line and local truck freight company. The bus portion served the local community for mass transportation, but the truck freight line served the communities of Marianna and Pensacola, Florida, and Dothan, Alabama.

Edwards was president and general manager of this company as well. With his A&SAB successes and in subsequent efforts, he gained a widespread reputation as "The Doctor of Sick Shortlines."

Although a successful corporate manager, Edwards inventiveness was always active, as illustrated by his work in designing and building the first steel-bulkhead pulpwood car in 1930. While with the A&SAB, he purchased fifty secondhand flatcars from the Gulf, Mobile & Northern Railroad and, after a few weeks in the road's Panama City shops, they emerged with steel end-bulkheads. They were promptly placed into logging service.

By 1932, with the Great Depression gripping the country, another personal disappointment struck Harry Edwards when, after Kieth was killed in an auto accident in 1929, the Bay Line was placed on the auction block by the executor of his estate. Eventually the executor found a buyer in the International Paper Company (IP). The IP brought in its own management, and dismissed Harry. Ironically, it was Edwards who, as a leader of the local Chamber of Commerce, had helped persuade the paper company to locate in Panama City.

Edwards's next job was as a consulting engineer, beginning in the early 1930s, with Florida's Marianna & Blountstown Railroad (M&B), a struggling shortline which ran twenty-nine miles between its namesake towns, and connected with the Louisville and Nashville Railroad at Marianna. Edwards' job was to prepare and present a convincing case before the Interstate Commerce Commission (ICC) for the M&B to acquire the Alabama, Florida & Gulf Railroad (AF&G). In addition to the acquisition, the M&B would need to build a line northward from Marianna to connect with the AF&G and also connect the AF&G to Dothan.

A permanent position with the M&B Railroad would have been a natural choice for Edwards, considering the proximity to Panama City, where he resided at the time. However, the line to Dothan was never constructed, and the M&B never extended farther than its origination points, except for a few isolated logging spurs. During this period Edwards participated in heated ICC hearings. He was required to argue against his former employer, which was opposed to the proposed merger of the M&B and the AF&G. In his testimony, Edwards pointed out to the mediator that there was a direct connection between the managements of the A&SAB and the International Paper Company.

Later in 1932, Edwards was called upon to investigate the possibility of reviving the Watauga & Yadkin River Railroad. Employed again as a consulting engineer, he developed plans and estimates for rebuilding the line in Caldwell County, North Carolina that had been abandoned in 1918 after extensive flood damage destroyed twenty-nine trestles and several miles of track. However, the costs of the rebuilding plan far exceeded the amount stockholders could raise, and so all locomotives and rolling stock were scrapped in 1933.

A year later, Harry was employed by the Freeman & Company Investment Bankers of New York City. He was charged with the task of reorganizing the Georgia, Florida, & Alabama Railway. The 226-mile line had been leased to the Seaboard Air Line Railroad, which had defaulted on rental agreements. Edwards's task was to develop an operating model for the bondholders, under Freeman & Company's leadership, and to operate the railroad as an independent regional carrier. As Edwards perfected the plan and was nearing submission for acceptance, the Seaboard Air Line Railroad suddenly paid all back rents and made assurances to continue rent payments. The bondholders felt this was a better alternative than trying to operate the line as an independent railroad during the Great Depression.

During the middle 1930s, Edwards worked as comptroller for the Miami-based L&L Truck Company that provided direct freight service between Atlanta and Miami. Based first out of Jacksonville, Florida, and then later Miami, his total period of employment with L&L was less than two years.

As the depression deepened in 1935, and work in the rail industry became increasingly difficult to find, Edwards took one of his few non-transportation related jobs when he was employed by the federal government. He was placed in charge of planning rehabilitation farm-colony payments. His position consisted of supervising, engineering, landscaping, construction, soil survey and management details. With his experience in banking, Edwards was soon placed in charge of the loan department of the North

Carolina Resettlement Administration, where he helped approve loans to farmers and cooperative farm groups.

This job no doubt led him to develop 128 acres of farmland he owned a few miles north of Sanford. This plot was surveyed and divided into 10-acre plots, which Edwards planned to sell for further development. He had a house built on the property in 1936 and lived there for nearly three years. As a demonstration project for area farmers, he built several chicken houses in which he planned to raise birds for sale. Harry's two sons often rode the A&W's Edwards motor cars for local trips. Bill recalled many runs from Sanford to Lillington to bring back watermelons. The melons would be loaded into the baggage compartment, and the boys would eat a few on the way back.

Bill Edwards remembers his father as being many things, but not a farmer. Since few had money to purchase land, Edwards leased out the 10-acre parcel adjacent to his place in exchange for tenant farm labor. The tenant had a player-piano that wouldn't fit in his house, so Mrs. Edwards allowed him to store it in the Edwards's living room. Being bored one summer, Bill and his older brother Winslow, both having their father's hankering to figure out how machines worked, disassembled the piano. Instead of playing the "William Tell Overture" as expected, the piano sounded as if it were playing a funeral dirge. The boys had just disassembled the piano when the tenant's wife came to the door asking for some shortening. Mrs. Edwards met the woman at the door and, through very fast talking, convinced her it was not a good time to come in.

The boys hastily reassembled the piano after finding the problem and correcting it with a few well-aimed squirts from an oil can. Such experiences convinced the boys, and their father, that maybe it was best the family stuck to the railroad business. Bill Edwards firmly believed his father to be very good in dealing with problems such as leasing a railroad, but he was not so good at the little problems around a farm house.

As the U.S. economy began to recover, Edwards left for his true calling, a vice president for sales for his former car company. From 1937 through 1939, Harry used contacts he had established through Minor Keith and the United Fruit Company to promote sales throughout South and Central America. As the U. S. economy still had room for a full recovery, the economies of this region were in need of new equipment, including modernized transportation. With their highway infrastructure far behind that of the U. S., many of these countries were eager to invest in gasoline-powered rail systems.

In April 1938, Edwards began a nearly two-decade stint as head of the Atlantic & East Carolina Railway (A&EC - the former Atlantic & North Carolina Railroad). It took Edwards eight months to win the state bid to operate the A&EC in association with his two sons. During this period, the A&EC was often referred to as the "Mullet Line," due to the numerous fish processing plants in the area. But Edwards decided to call it the "Tobacco Route," since that was the main cash crop along the eastern coast. This would become his most consistent period of employment, stretching over eighteen years, seventeen of which turned a profit for both the railroad and the state of North Carolina. Besides the longevity of his employment, it can be argued that this period was also his crowning jewel of railroad management. The Doctor had completely cured his patient!

Early in his railroad career Edwards had embraced the idea of internal combustion engines supplanting steam power, well before most other railroad managements arrived at the same conclusion. As Edwards dieselized the A&EC to make it one of the first regional railroads to completely replace steam, it was obvious he was not drawn to any one particular locomotive builder. He purchased three 44-ton switchers from General Electric (GE); a GP-7, an SW-1 and two F-2As from General Motors Electro-Motive Division (EMD), and an RS-1 from American Locomotive Company (ALCO). These choices would later turn A&EC engines into an interesting footnote to diesel locomotive history. For example, the F-2As were the first two orders placed for this particular model, while his RS-1 was the only one to ever be on the Southern Railway roster. Even in the Southern's black, silver and gold "penguin scheme," it retained the A&EC reporting marks after its sale to the Southern. Harry's management tenure lasted until 1957, when the ICC issued an order authorizing the Southern Railway to assume operations and management over the line.

Retired after the sale of the A&EC, Edwards continued to serve in community life. Being active in various chapters of the Knights of Columbus, and in the Catholic Church. From 1920 to 1921, he served as president of the Sanford Chamber of Commerce, later being vice president of the Panama City Chamber of Commerce in 1930. When he gained control of the A&EC, one of his duties was to move the corporate headquarters to New Bern. As a member of their Chamber of Commerce, he was active in promoting and marketing the local businesses. Shortly after his retirement in 1959, Edwards was elected president of the New Bern Chamber, replacing his son, Bill. As president, the elder Edwards was a natural fit, as he had helped sway 82 new industries to locate adjacent to the tracks of the A&EC.

Harry Powell Edwards lived the remainder of his life in New Bern. His wife, Mary, died on January 31, 1968 while Harry died three years later on October 11, 1971, at the age of eighty-five. A Requiem Mass was held following his death at St. Paul's Catholic Church. Interment was at the New Bern Memorial Cemetery. Winslow Magleen Edwards, the oldest child, died in 1996. H. P. Edwards is survived in his immediate family by his youngest son, William Joseph "Bill" Edwards of New Bern.

Part One: The Edwards Railway Motor Car Company

...ng from 140 to 150 Horse Power, Especially Adapted for Heavy Duty Work.

...ACITY 100 PASSENGERS AND 10,000 POUNDS OF BAGGAGE.

...is car will pull load of from fifty to three hundred tons, according to conditions and speed desired. It is designed to pull one standard 25-ton, wooden ...ssenger coach, with capacity load, at speed forty miles per hour, or will pull ...o specially constructed, Edwards Trailers of fifty passenger capacity each, at ...me speed. Can be used efficiently and economically for switching purposes.

COMBINATION BAGGAGE CAR AND LOCOMOTIVE

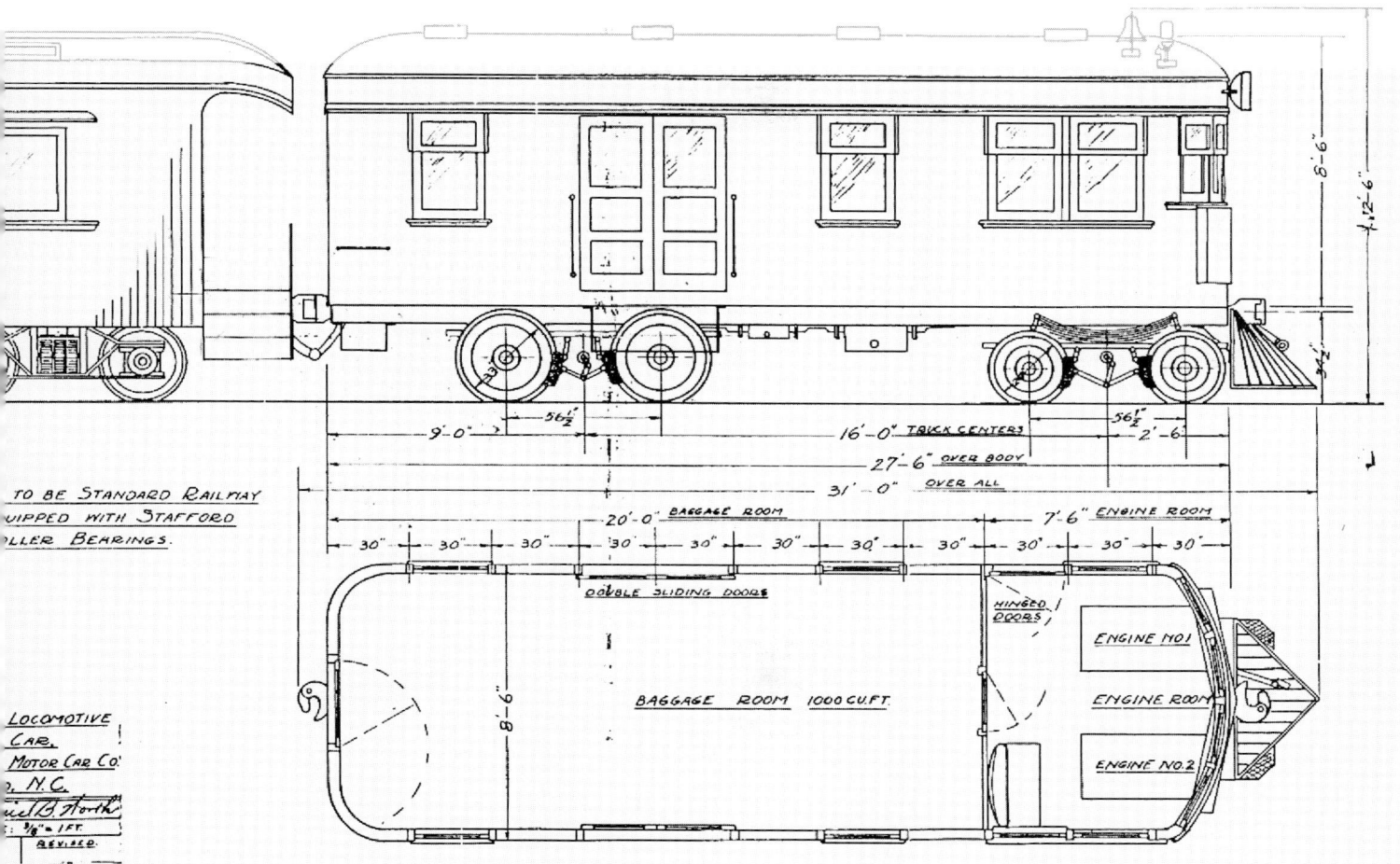

...RY OF SPECIFICATIONS ON COMBINATION GASOLINE LOCOMOTIVE AND BAGGAGE CAR.

...r is designed so that the entire power unit consti... ...s the driver's, the baggage, mail and express com... ...ment. All passengers are carried in a trailer, ...ch is to be a regular standard wooden railway passenger coach. The railroad company can, therefore, ...ze equipment it already has in service.

The power plant consists of two seventy-one ...se power motors, one motor driving each truck and ...arranged that both can be used together or separ... ...y. In starting, and ascending grades both motors ...be used, but after the train develops a maximum ...ed, or ascends the grade, one motor can be cut off,

radiators, magneto, carburetor, electric system, etc., are manufactured by old established motor truck concerns, which will insure the obtaining of repair parts at all times regardless of the existence of the car builder. All the vital parts that enter into the construction of this car will be of standard motor truck design now being manufactured in production quantities, such as Midwest Motors, Stromberg Carburetors, Eisemann Magneto, Cotta Transmissions, Westinghouse Electric System, etc.

5. This car will be equipped with standard M. C. B. auto-

1. 1915-1942

Since the introduction of the steam engine to railway transportation in the United States during the late 1830s, railway officials have sought ways and means to develop cost effective transportation. Beginning in the late 1860s with the widespread application of the streetcar, or trolley car, it was proven that lightweight cars could be used very successfully for mass transit. While standard steam railways ran lines into major cities, electric streetcars, with their overhead wire, stretched their vast network of track for miles throughout metropolitan and outlying neighborhoods. Stringing wires for more than fifteen or twenty miles, however, was cost prohibitive.

In the earliest days of railroad building, thousands of small railroad companies sprang up, creating a vast network of branch lines connecting small towns to each other and to the main lines of the larger railroads. Over the years these branch lines became costly to maintain and operate relative to the small amount of revenue-producing traffic. The railroads were obliged to operate these lines due to conditions of their original charters and heavy federal regulation. The government was not very inclined to allow abandonment either. Early on, branch lines established themselves as the life's blood of many small towns, not only for the movement of goods but also as a means of transporting the population.

Beginning in the early twentieth century, many railroads began searching for a cost effective alternative to the steam engine for use on branch lines. The United States found itself in a great period of industrial revolution at this same time. The internal combustion gasoline engine was starting to make progress with the "horseless carriage" and it was also developed for use in industrial and agricultural applications. As a number of engine builders began to demonstrate that the internal combustion engine could be improved upon, and reliability increased, the idea to apply the use of these gas engines to railway work naturally followed.

In the quest to improve efficiencies over steam powered passenger transportation, the self propelled rail car brought to light the internal combustion possibilities years—if not decades—before the dieselization of American railroads took place.

As a number of well established streetcar builders and coach manufacturers started to research and develop the self propelled rail car, the new contraption began to develop a variety of nicknames, such as "rail bus" and "motor rail coach." One nickname which seemed to catch on across the country was the moniker "doodlebug."

The typical doodlebug was essentially a specially built, self propelled, lightweight railway coach, which could also contain a baggage compartment. As the race to develop the doodlebug gained momentum after World War I, a variety of propulsion and mechanical drive combinations developed. Although the earliest doodlebugs were mechanically driven by means of chains and drive systems, eventually some builders equipped their cars with generators and electrical motors and transmissions, and others later experimented with diesel engines to power their cars.

The doodlebug brought the initial exposure of the internal combustion engine to railroad management. From the 1920s through the late 1930s, the doodlebug was improved and tested and became larger in size and its ability to haul heavy tonnage increased. This helped lead directly to the development of the diesel electric locomotive as a replacement for the steam locomotive.

One of the first attempts to tackle the internal combustion replacement of steam was the McKeen Car Company of Omaha, Nebraska. The McKeen car had a peculiar look: an extremely "knife shaped" front end. The sides of the coach came to a tapered point towards the front of the vehicle, giving it an extremely aerodynamic shape. Coupled with the windows resembling ship portholes, the car had a distinctive look. The car was a fair success, partly due to the aggressive salesmanship of William R. McKeen, Jr. While affiliated with E. H. Harriman, McKeen was able to use the connection to get his foot in the door while another salesperson might not. The car helped introduce the idea of internal combustion engine use to many railroads, but the car itself had several problems which could not be overcome. One of the major problems with the McKeen car was that its steel construction provided an extremely rough ride. On a positive note, however, the usefulness of the internal combustion engine was proven with some of the cars, when kept up to Union Pacific maintenance standards, turning in runs of 390 miles per day. Sales were generally limited to the larger Class 1 railroads, and shortlines were not able to invest in this new form of transportation. Most shortlines found the new technology too expensive to experiment with and chose to remain with steam power. The Atchison, Topeka & Santa Fe Railroad took possession of their first McKeen cars in 1906, a full twenty-six years before that railroad received its first diesel locomotive.

One of the unique features of the McKeen car was the mounting of the prime mover directly upon the front truck. The 100 hp marine engine was connected to the drive mechanism through a drive belt. The drive to the wheels was made by connecting the large belt from the motor to a flywheel mounted on the truck. Harry P. Edwards would later perfect this technique of mounting the prime mover directly on the front truck with the Model 20 Edwards car.

A second major builder of self propelled coaches was the J. G. Brill Company of Philadelphia, Pennsylvania. The Brill Company entered the motor car/railbus business in 1921 when it mounted a 2 ½ ton Mack bus chassis on flanged wheels. The railbus could travel up to 30 MPH and could carry thirty-one passengers. Brill's first product looked eerily like the second phase of the evolutionary process of Edwards's first product. The railbus had the truck front axle removed, and a double-axle pivoting truck was substituted. The Brill development came approximately four years after Edwards had experimented with a truck body frame; at a time when several companies were arriving at the same solution at the same time. The Mack Truck Company, Four-Wheel Drive Auto Company, and the White Motor Company were all arriving at their own versions of a motor car or railbus. In addition to these established companies, independents and shortlines were also racing to develop and build an inexpensive motor car.

Norfolk Southern no. 90 was a McKeen car built in 1910. The car was later rebuilt into a trolley in 1925. The unit was seventy feet long and weighed thirty-nine tons. **Collection of Tom Sink.**

A year later, in 1922, Brill had already understood that the railbus was only a small part of the solution to passenger transportation and had begun developing much larger motor cars. Brill's most popular design was the Model 55, which came with a standard six cylinder, 68 hp engine. The unit could seat forty-one passengers and could be ordered in 92 hp, 100 hp and 175 hp models, depending on the customer's preference. Brill would later produce a much larger, sixty foot, 250 hp motor car, which weighed in at 37 tons.

A third competitor in the self propelled coach was the Electro-Motive Company, or EMC. The company was purchased by General Motors in 1930 and remained a subsidiary of that corporation until being sold in 2005 to Greenbriar Equity LLC and Berkshire Partners LLC. Through its development of the self propelled coach, EMC was able to increase its technological advantage over other companies to become one of the leading locomotive builders in the later part of the twentieth century. EMC entered the market in 1924 and established itself very early on as having built a reliable, durable, and fuel efficient product. The EMC coach was produced in an unusual manner: the Winton Engine Company built the engine, and either the St. Louis Car Company, Pullman, or Osgood Bradley Company built the car components and produced the final assembly. In this manner, EMC saved itself from having to invest in a large physical plant or having a large payroll.

A fourth early competitor was the Wason car, built by the Wason Manufacturing Company, itself a subsidiary of Brill. Wason cars utilized General Electric components. While sales were limited in number, GE utilized the experience to increase its technological advances, and its research eventually led to the launching of its own line of locomotives in the 1960s.

In a very straightforward manner, the development of the self propelled rail car or "doodlebug" laid the groundwork for EMD and GE to become the two most dominant diesel-electric locomotive builders in North America. In the year 2005, EMD and GE remain the only major locomotive builders to provide motive power to the railroads of North America.

H. P. Edwards and the Atlantic & Western Railway

Harry P. Edwards received his initial railroad management training on the Atlantic & Western, a line his father, Joseph Edwards, founded on March 7, 1899. The line was originally to run from Sanford, North Carolina to Goldsboro, North Carolina a distance of seventy miles, though only twenty-five miles of track were ever lain.

As general manager he was concerned with the rising cost of providing passenger service powered by steam locomotives. As early as 1914, Edwards was interested in the idea of replacing his unprofitable steam powered passenger train with a gasoline powered, self propelled rail car. Edwards understood that savings were realized when the crew size was reduced. The typical steam train required an engineer, fireman, conductor, and one or two brakeman as needed. The typical self propelled rail car only required a motorman and conductor. These lower crew costs, coupled with the much lower costs of maintenance and operation, created additional savings.

During the period from 1914 to 1915, motor bus, truck and jitney competition—together with the high operating costs of steam trains—was threatening the very existence of branch and suburban railways, particularly the A&W.

One of the life long traits of Edwards was his fastidious attention to records of expense. He was convinced that along with using top notch materials, a firm had to pay strict attention to its expenses. Edwards was keenly adept at tracking the performance records of his equipment This served him well when he eventually went into the manufacturing and marketing of self propelled rail cars.

Records indicate that when motor car service was introduced on the twenty-five miles of line on the Atlantic & Western Railway, the A&W was operating a steam train two round trips per day, except Sunday, in mixed service. Their passenger revenues were constantly decreasing, as the travel along this line was also being handled by motor busses and jitneys which paralleled the line. Their operating cost (circa. 1921) with the steam train under this service was as follows:

OPERATING COSTS PRIOR TO USE OF MOTOR CAR
EXPENSES FOR TWELVE MONTHS (35,760 miles train service)

Crew of 4 men:	Engineer	3130 hours	$1500.00
	Fireman	3130 hours	1020.00
	Conductor	3130 hours	1320.00
	Brakeman	3130 hours	624.00
		Total:	$4,464.00

35,760 miles @ 12.48 cents per train mile	$ 4,464.00
Fuel, 1110 tons coal @ $5.75 per ton @ 17.85 cents per train mile	6,382.50
Maintenance of Locomotive and one coach @ 8 cents per mile	2,860.80
Water (1/2 cents per train mile)	178.80
Oil, waste etc., (1/4 cent per train mile)	89.40
Depreciation (Locomotive and coach) 4 cents per train mile	1,430.40
Total cost (per train mile 43.08 cents)	$15,405.90

OPERATING COSTS AFTER MOTOR CAR WAS PUT IN SERVICE

A steam train was operated only every other day to handle freight and a motor car was operated three round trips on each day the steam was layed off and two round trips on days the train was operated. This schedule provided three trains each way every day, and this arrangement resulted in a reduction in use of the steam train of 13,560 miles per year. The cost of the new schedule was as follows:

EXPENSES FOR TWELVE MONTHS (Steam train miles 12,360)

Crew for steam train	12,360 miles at 12.48 cents	$1,542.53
Fuel	12,360 miles at 17.85 cents	2,206.26
Maintenance	12,360 miles at 8.00 cents	988.80
Depreciation	12,360 miles at 4.00 cents	494.40
Oil, Waste, Water, etc.		92.70
Total		$5,324.69

EXPENSE OF MOTOR CAR OPERATING FOR TWELVE MONTHS (30 passenger capacity, 43,800 miles)

Crew for motor car, one man	$1,260.00
Fuel, 3,128 gallons gasoline @ 25 cents per	782.00
Oil, grease, etc.	114.00
Maintenance	438.98
Depreciation 2.25 cents per mile	985.50
Total cost (per motor car mile 8.18 cents)	$3,580.48

SUMMARY

Total operating cost before motor car was put in service	$15,405.90
Total operating cost after motor car was put in service: Steam train......$5,324.69 Motor Car......3,580.48 total	8,905.17
Net savings in operating expenses, per annum	$ 6,500.73
Increase in passenger revenue	6,420.00
Total savings and revenue increase, 12 months	$12,920.73

The first Edwards motor car, A&W no. M-1, in a rare action shot, "Hauling ten thousand pounds of freight and passengers on the Atlantic & Western Railroad at a total cost of ten cents a mile" according to the original caption of this photograph. Opposite page, showing the comparative operating cost (circa 1921) of steam train vs. Edwards car. **Collection of Billy Page.**

The competition presented by bus lines and jitneys ceased to be worthy of notice with the advent of frequent and dependable rail service, and passenger revenues immediately increased to an average of $535.00 per month.

On days when the steam train was laid off, the train crews were required to work in the shops on maintenance of equipment, thus making a corresponding reduction in payroll of shop forces.

Such operating costs would of course vary on different roads, but they show what the Edwards motor car equipment had initially done on the A&W and why such companies were interested in developing motor cars further.

Early Years 1915 to 1920

With all the competition in the self propelled rail car business, Edwards had noticed one major omission: the lack of shortline participation. Not finding a suitable model of car at an affordable price, Edwards looked to the highway motor bus and trucking business for development of his own car, to be built by his Atlantic & Western shop crew.

In the 1960s Edwards sat down to write a brief history of his company and its beginnings. This is what he recalled:

I conceived the idea of building a self propelled passenger car to replace the steam propelled train we were then operating on the Atlantic & Western Railroad.

A few highway trucks were then being built for use in the cities and in a few places where highways had been paved. I purchased a Kelly-Springfield highway truck which I believe was made in Springfield, Ill. I then built a passenger car body in my railroad shops and then put on this highway truck chassis and then put on four flanged railroad type wheels to replace the highway type wheels. When completed it looked very much like the present day highway bus, with the exception of the wheels. I took off the steam passenger train and began to operate this passenger motor car in its place, with a few exceptions, it worked out very well. Because of the long wheel base this motor car would not negotiate sharp curves very well, so I replaced the two front wheels with a four wheel pivoting truck, similar to all railway cars, this enabled this motor car to go around curves more easily and smoothly. Later I put a four wheel truck in the rear, and from time to time, I added more improvements as the need developed from our operating experience.

One unique feature of these first cars built from truck chassis was the use of what had been the steering wheel. This was modified to become a hand brake. It had a ratchet mechanism mounted on the floor at the base of the staff, and the motorman could bring the unit to a halt and tie it down by turning the steering wheel until the brakes were set or released. For an additional price the cars could be equipped with the more expensive Westinghouse air brake equipment; however, it was not long before all Edwards cars came standard with this air brake equipment. Edwards's reminiscence of the start of his company continues:

Many railroad officials came to Sanford to see this motor car perform and were impressed with its money saving possibilities and said there was a big market for this type of railroad equipment. I built four of these cars with a Kelly-Springfield truck chassis namely; Atlantic & Western Railroad, Maxton Alma & Southbound Railroad, Chicago Burlington & Quincy Railroad and the Baltimore & Ohio Railroad. After these cars were put into operation, they all reported satisfactory operation, but two said these cars were not large enough and should be made more stream lined and attractive in appearance. I organized a company in 1921, to build these cars and a plant was built for that purpose in Sanford, N.C. I was made President of the company and the corporate name of the company was "Edwards Railway Motor Car Company." We discontinued using a highway truck chassis and built an entirely new car which was stream lined and beautiful in appearance.

This first car was built for the A&W in 1917 in that railroad's shops with Road Number M-1. The car body was of all wooden construction and resembled something more like a highway jitney with a seating capacity of twenty-two. This car posed a unique problem for the company. Since it was built utilizing a truck chassis, the federal government made the natural assumption that the vehicle would be used for highway revenue service. After the sale was completed, Edwards received a bill for Federal tax to be assessed on the truck. Edwards had to demonstrate that the new rail car was not being used for road use, in order to have the federal tax assessment reversed. His effort to fight the tax assessment was emblematic of his personality; he was extremely fastidious with both his personal and corporate funds.

The earliest version of an ERwyMCC car was modified from a Kelly-Springfield truck body. Seen here posed with a matching trailer. **Collection of Bill Parrish.**

In 1920 the second unit was built for the A&W, as a two car unit consisting of a combination passenger and baggage motor car, seating eighteen passengers, and a trailer car, seating thirty-two for a total passenger capacity of fifty. The motor car was built on a Kelly-Springfield chassis and was known as the K-50 Edwards Special. The Model K-50 weighed 12,000 lbs. and the trailer car weighed 8,300 lbs. The total weight of the train was 20,300 lbs.

This motor car and trailer were much more advanced than the first car built. The motor car and trailer coach bodies were made of all steel construction, except for the roofs and floors. With this unit began the founding principles of coach construction for the Edwards firm, which quickly developed as the need for larger and heavier duty equipment increased.

This unit was also a bit unusual in that the motor car had no entrance for passengers, only a train door on the rear end, facing the trailer. Entrance to the motor unit was from open platforms placed on the ends of the trailer car. Clearly, this two car unit was designed to be used in tandem for passenger service. At least once, however, via photographic evidence from the November 1921 Edwards Bulletin No. 1, the motor car was used alone to pull a standard freight boxcar.

In the early days Edwards and his staff thought that their cars should be marketed for use in mixed freight and passenger service. However, it was soon found that the diminutive cars were really more practical for use in passenger service. There seems to have been very little interest in the application of Edwards cars for use in heavy freight service.

This second Edwards unit was used in the first major promotional campaign for the new Edwards Company. Unlike many other builders, Edwards spared no expense in the exploitation of his products. Extensive and elaborate sales bulletins, sales brochures and catalogs were to become a trademark of the Edwards firm.

Although this second unit was built in 1920, its specifications and photographs were used to promote the Edwards line of rail cars for the next few years. The following (beginning on page 19) is the detailed description, printed in an Edwards sales bulletin, of this second product built under Edwards's supervision at the A&W shops:

Atlantic & Western no. 5 shows the characteristic "bus on wheels" look **(top)** of the first handful of units from the ERwyMCC. No. 5 is thought to be the very first Edwards unit and was constructed in the A&W shops, which would have been located just to the left of the car. Eventually, no. 5 lost its single rear axle and a double axle was installed. As the Edwards cars continued to develop, Virginia & Carolina Southern no. 303 **(above)** was one of the strangest evolutions. The body of the unit was taken from a Birney street car and the engine compartment was built in the A&W shops. **Top, collection of John D. Porter. Above, photo by John B. Allen, collection of Mac Connery.**

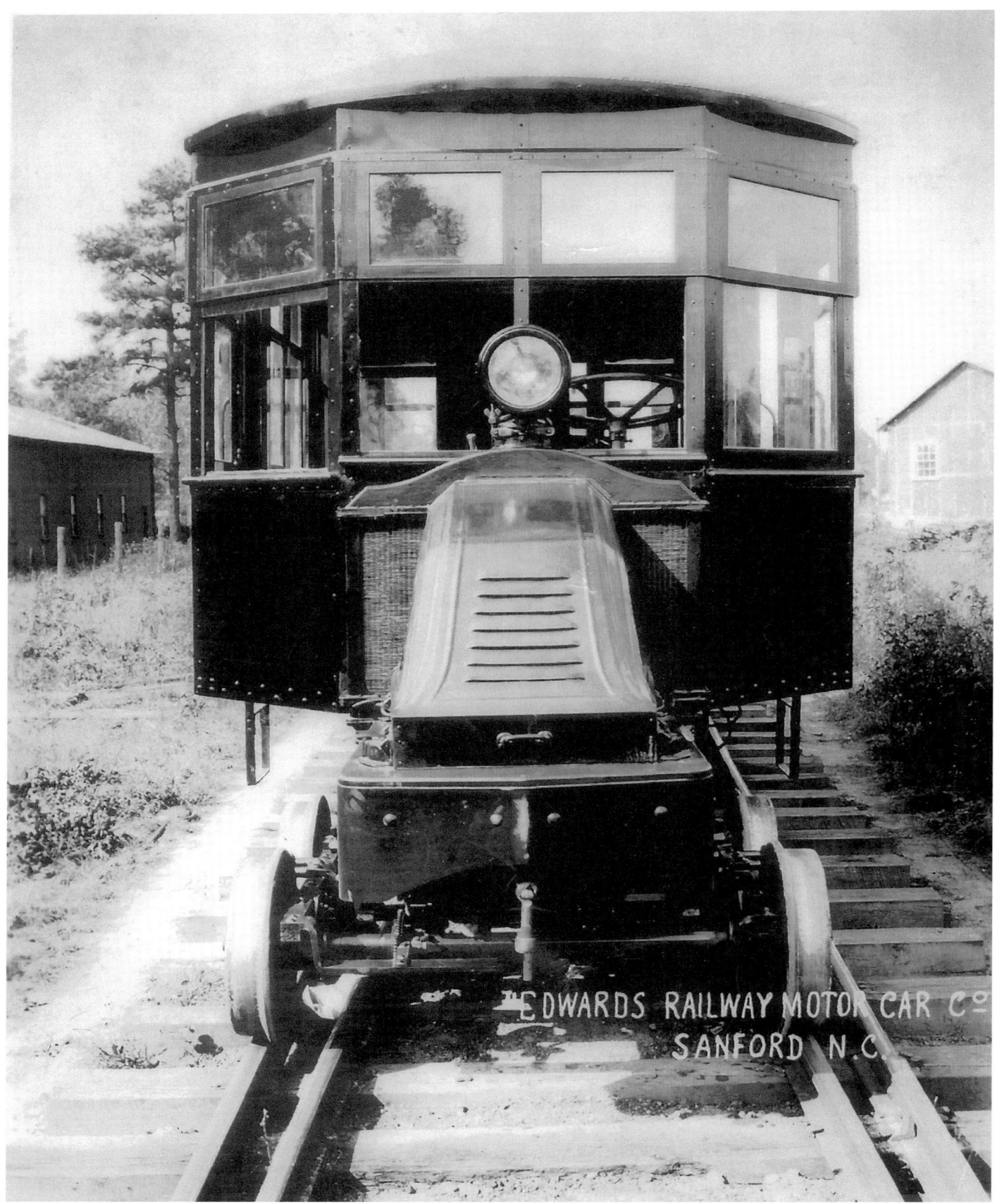

A front-end shot of an early Kelly-Springfield chassis supplied unit. The unit is not the B&O unit, which had a "cow-catcher" grill attached, but rather is believed to be either the A&W or the Maxton, Alma and Southbound unit. The steering wheel was used to lock down the brakes. *Collection of Stella B. Mashburn, Courtesy of the Edwards Rail Car Co.*

EDWARDS RAILWAY MOTOR CAR CO.

November 1921
Bulletin No.1

Sanford, N.C.

GENERAL DESCRIPTION OF EQUIPMENT

With four years of practical service as a guide for further development the company has produced a new model, which is beyond question the best type Railway Motor Car Equipment on the market today. Unlike the great majority of railway motor cars it is not an experiment, neither is it a converted truck, a motorbus on rails, or a fancy body on flanged wheels. It is real railroad equipment developed by railroad men working in conjunction with the best engineers in the automotive industry. In order that repair parts may be secured without difficulty we use in conjunction of our cars standard motor truck parts, such as the steel underframe, motor, transmission etc. These parts are manufactured by the Kelly-Springfield Motor Truck Co., Springfield, Ohio.

The car is supported on four driving wheels, in the rear and a four wheel pivoted pony truck in the front. The wheels are all arranged similar to those on an American Type locomotive. Power is applied to all four driving wheels by three chains one of which is enclosed. Our rear four-wheel drive is the Edwards design and construction. (Patents Applied for)

A body of steel construction is used on all our cars and they are most substantially constructed and present a very attractive appearance.

SPECIAL FEATURES

There are a number of converted highway trucks now being offered for railway use but the principal change they make in the rear end is merely to put steel tires on the regular highway wheels and they have the same final drive in the rear axle consisting of numerable gears and parts which are subject to the direct shock of the pounding wheels against the rails. Our experience has proven that this kind of drive will not stand up in railroad service. In our car we have a four wheel truck in the rear which has steel or cast iron wheels and solid axles (the same type construction as standard railway passenger coaches). Power is transmitted to these wheels with chains, and these chains serve the purpose of cushioning and absorbing the rail shocks before they reach the driving mechanism. Chains are the simplest and most satisfactory method of transmitting power. It is the next best thing to driving rods. On the cars we have in operation 25,000 miles of service is obtained from one set of chains and sprockets which represent a cost of one-fourth cent per mile.

The braking system is very efficient. These brakes are applied by turning a wheel at the driver's seat, which applies brakes to all wheels both motor car and trailer. Regular cast iron brake shoes are used on all wheels. Our braking system is a continuous brake system which applies cast iron shoes against all the wheels of the car and trailer, application of all these brake shoes is made by the driver at the drivers seat. We will apply Westinghouse Air Brakes to this car if desired by purchaser.

The body is built with superior arrangement for the comfort of the passengers, including ample electric lights, comfortable upholstery, curtains, roof ventilators, exhaust or hot water heat for cold weather, windows raise up as in regular steam railway coaches. They do not drop down in pockets as in most bus bodies.

The motor is equipped with self-starter, storage battery and generator. The motor in our K-50 model is a large 4 cylinder heavy duty type, bore 4 ½", stroke 6 ½" developing over 50 horsepower, built by Kelly-Springfield Motor Truck Co.

This car can be geared to make a speed as high as 45 miles per hour. When the grades are as high as 4 per cent, we gear the car for 30 miles per

An early photograph **(above left)** of B&O's no. 6000 showing the motorman's controls in the Kelly-Springfield supplied drive-train and chassis. The original truck controls remained on the left side of the cab. Top view **(above right)** of a Model 10 LMG narrow gauge chassis built sometime after 1926. Note that the controls were installed before the addition of the body. Chassis, drive-mechanism and engine placement of an early Model 10 **(below)**. This particular unit is thought to be either the Cape Fear or the CB&Q no. 500 car. *Top left & bottom, courtesy of The Railroad House Collection, collection of Calvin Harward. Top right, Collection of the Edwards Rail Car Co.*

hour. The car will make the same speed backward as forwards and has a transmission of four speeds in either direction.

MAINTENANCE AND DEPRECIATION

One of our model-K-35 thirty passenger capacity cars was put in operation on the Atlantic & Western Railroad in September 1917 and up to date (1921) has made 120,000 miles. The entire maintenance cost during this period was as follows:

788 machinist hours, 588 machinist helper hours....
..........................$ 812.00
Material used... $ 791.04
$1603.04

This makes an average maintenance cost of 1.33 cents per mile. Judging from the present condition of the car which has made 120,000 miles, we estimate that its life will be about 180,000 miles additional, based on this estimate the depreciation on this equipment will be about 2 ¼ cents per mile

GRADES

This equipment will operate over grades as high as ten per cent, but a grade that steep would have to be taken in low gear. Grades as much as four per cent can be negotiated in high gear, and by the large car, with trailer attached.

SNOW AND ICE CONDITIONS

It has been our experience that a two wheel driven motor car will not give satisfactory service in snow and ice conditions when we were experimenting with this type of drive it was always necessary to send a locomotive over the track to break the ice or snow before this type of motor car could be operated. The very lightest kind of snow or ice gave it trouble. With our four wheel drive we have a rear truck weighing 1700 lbs. and twice the tractive effort, which gives our car a decided advantage when operating under such conditions. This car will, therefore, break through a much heavier ice and grip the rail more easily than the two wheel type of drive.

WE HAVE PASSED THE EXPERIMENTAL STAGE

The Edwards Railway Motor Car Company has not experimented at the expense of the ultimate buyer. To be frank, we have had no intention of becoming manufactures until the pressure of interest from other railway companies showed us the opportunity to take the lead in a new industry and at the same time render a great service to every railroad with the problem of a nonproductive short line. We are the only company in the field who has demonstrated the success of its product from the railroad man's point of view exclusively. We offered nothing for sale until we had a proven success to offer, and one which we could back up with actual figures.

SPECIFICATIONS

CHASSIS: Engine, clutch, transmission, differential universal joints, frame, operating controls, springs, spring shackles, etc., are manufactured by the Kelly-Springfield Motor Truck Co., Springfield, Ohio, and are known as "Edwards Type Chasses." These chasses are made of 2 ½ ton and 5 ton chassis parts, and both capacities are made in various lengths to enable us to meet the railroad requirements of different railroads.

ENGINE: Model K-35 3 ¾ bore, stroke 5 ¼"Model K-50 4 ½ bore, stroke 6 ½" These engines will develop 30 and 50 actual horse-power respectively.

IGNITION: Eisemann waterproof high tension magneto, with impulse starter.

TRANSMISSION: 4 speeds forwards and 4 speeds reverse permitting running backwards at high speed, speed being same in either direction.

BRAKES: Cast iron brake shoes on all wheels, operated by wheel at driver's seat. Westinghouse Air Brakes can be used if desired.

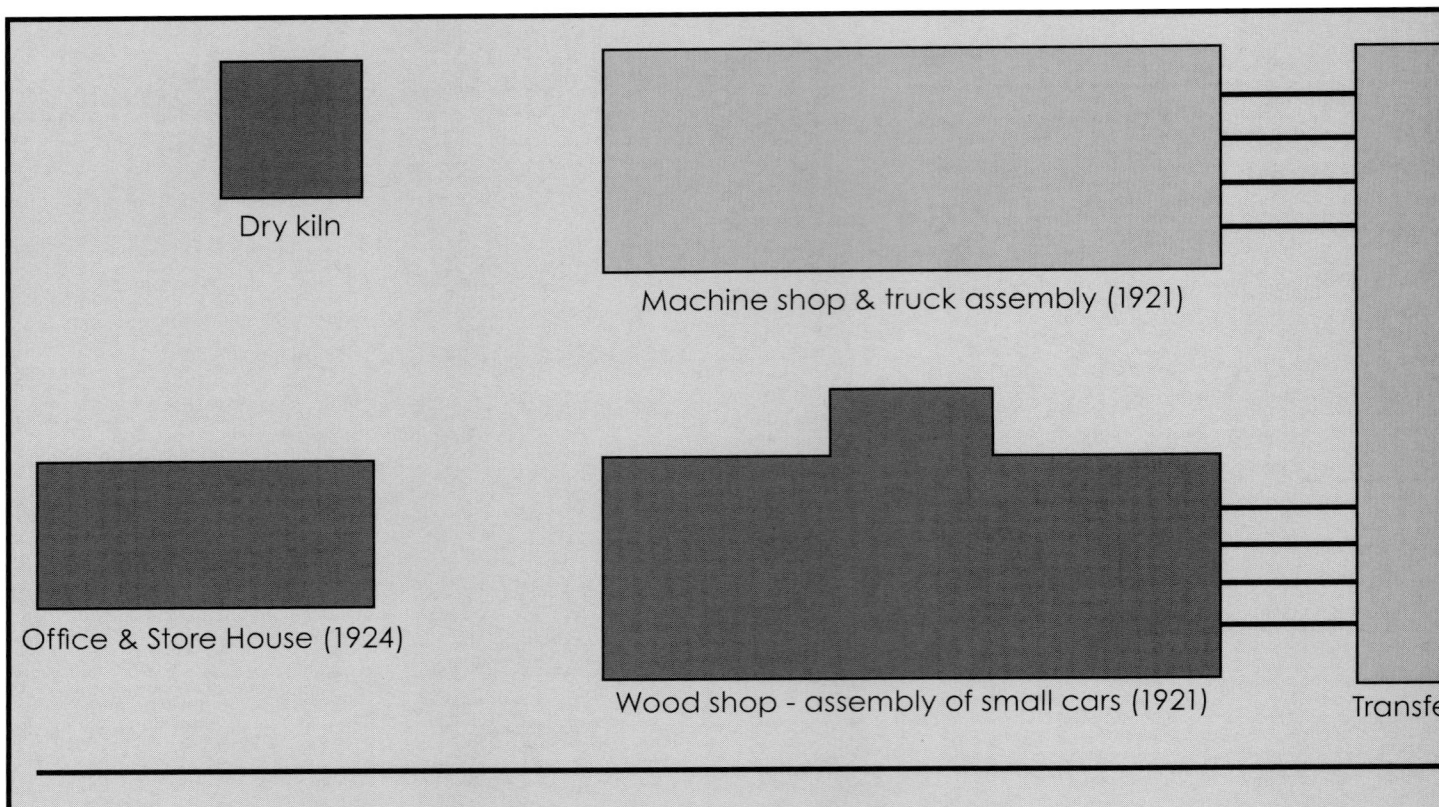

SPRINGS: Front and rear semi-elliptic.

WHEELS: The four front wheels are cast iron 20" diameter weighing 220 lbs. each. The four rear wheels are cast iron 24" diameter weighing 227 lbs. each, steel wheels are supplied if desired.

WHEEL BASE: Center of front truck to center of rear truck is made in lengths of 14 feet to 20 feet.

FRAME: Pressed steel channel section.

PILOT: Wrought iron and steel securely attached to frame.

EQUIPMENT: Electric head-light, brackets on front and rear for markers and classification Lamps.

BODY: Substantially constructed of steel by experienced body builders, electric lighted, handsome interior finish

SEATING CAPACITY: Can build these bodies to seat from 25 to 43 people. Seats arranged the same as in regular railway coaches.

UPHOLSTERY: Seat covering to suit purchaser.

ELECTRIC STARTING: Standard Motor truck type Westinghouse electric starter is provided for starting the engine from the driver's seat.

HEATING: Cars are heated by the exhaust from the motor or by hot water heat as desired.

SANDERS: Sand Boxes are provided to supply sand to driving wheels when needed.

WEIGHT: Model K-35 car weighs 9,000 lbs. Model K-50 car weighs 12,000 lbs. Trailer seating 32 people weighs 8,300 lbs.

SPEED: These cars can be geared to make any speed up to 45 miles per hour. This, however, would have to be regulated according to the prevailing grades over which the car is operated.

DETAIL SPECIFICATIONS AND PRICES

We would appreciate the opportunity to send an engineer to study your operating conditions which will enable us to present a detailed specification and proposal on the type of equipment that would be best suited to your particular conditions. Prices on application.

Edwards Railway Motor Car Company, Sanford NC

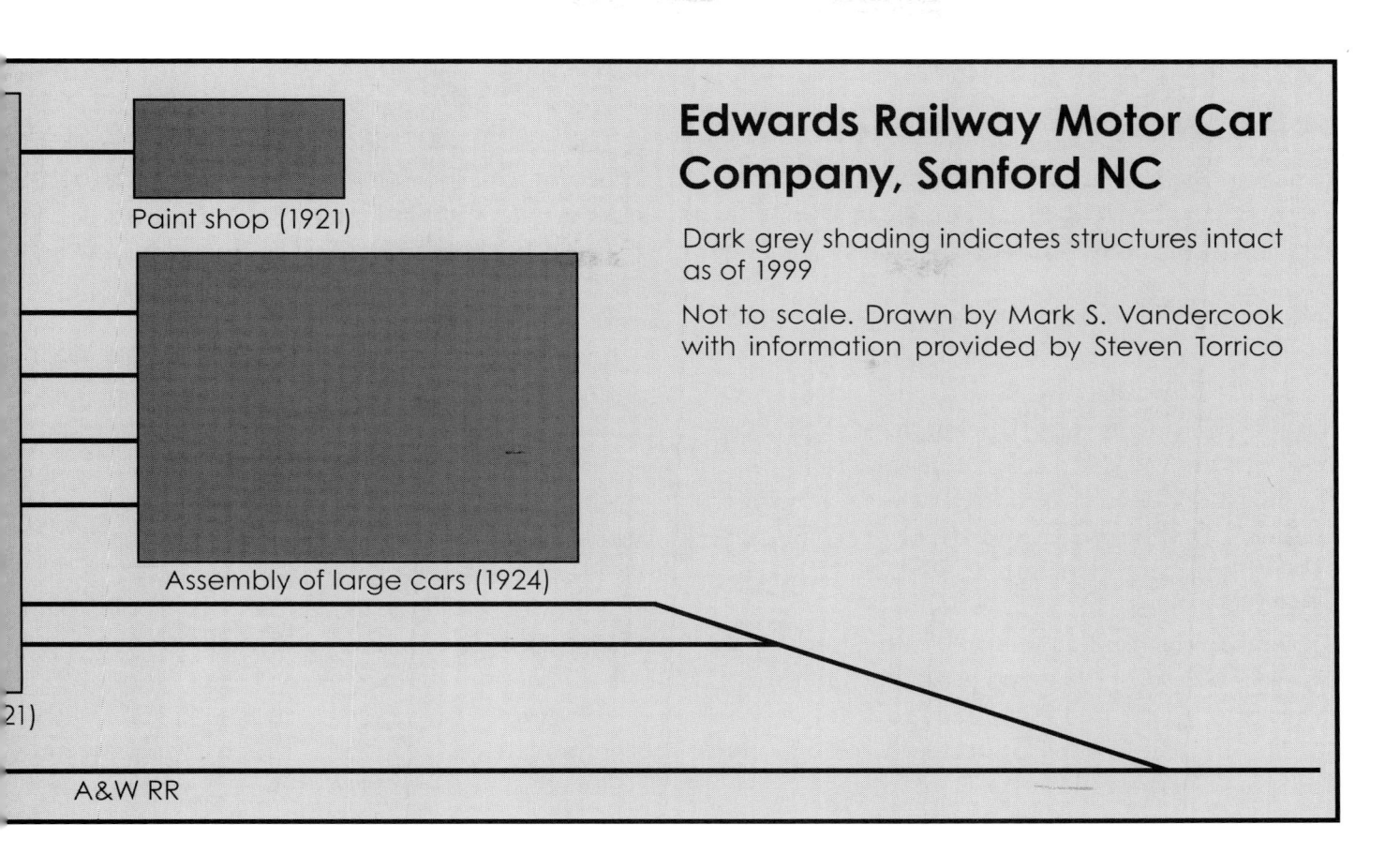

Dark grey shading indicates structures intact as of 1999

Not to scale. Drawn by Mark S. Vandercook with information provided by Steven Torrico

Paint shop (1921)

Assembly of large cars (1924)

A&W RR

The ERwyMCC plant as it appeared in the early 1940s. The photo was taken from the top of the Sapono Mills plant, a manufacturer of fertilizer and animal feeds. **Collection of Bill Parrish.**

1921 Incorporation

By 1921 the Edwards motor car had started capturing the attention of other railroads and their officials. Edwards finally created a company that was incorporated on August 20, 1921. The official name was the Edwards Railway Motor Car Company. The officers for the new venture were as follows:

H.P. Edwards, president; L.P. Wilkins, first vice president; T.B. Upchurch, second vice president; W.A. Crabtree, secretary and treasurer. The board of directors consisted of the following: J.R. Jones, Jr.; Harry P. Edwards; W.A. Crabtree; L.P. Wilkins; T.B. Upchurch; F.W. McCracken; O.P. Makepeace.

The initial capital was $200,000, of which $185,000 was subscribed and paid. The unbridled enthusiasm for the motor car had brought interest from around the United States, and the officers determined that construction of a facility to fabricate the cars was needed.

This property was located just outside the corporate limits of Sanford adjacent to the tracks of the A&W. Prior to the construction of this new facility, most of the work on the rail cars had taken place at the shops of the A&W. Until the plant ceased production of rail cars in 1942 with the onset of World War II not only was the A&W a customer of the ERwyMCC but its tracks also served as a test track for demonstration purposes.

The new Edwards factory was located on six acres of land and consisted of the following five buildings:

A 28' x 30' brick building which contained the dry kiln and boiler room producing heat and steam for the entire facility.

A 50' x 150' wood frame building with galvanized siding and a brick and concrete foundation. Part of the flooring was wood and the other part brick. This building had four bays with tracks running inside. The woodworking department facilitating the coach body assembly of the small cars used this building.

A 50' x 150' wood frame building with galvanized siding and a concrete foundation and floor. This building was used for the iron working machinery and for assembly of trucks for the rail cars. It was equipped with the necessary lathes and other metal working machines for rail car construction. This building also had four bays with tracks running inside. Sometime in the mid 1930s, this building received a new siding of brick.

A 25' x 50' wood frame building with galvanized siding and a concrete foundation. The paint department used this building, which had one track running inside.

A 45' x 10' transfer table of steel and wood construction. This sliding table allowed cars to be moved, with the least amount of space used, from one building and bay to another. Typically, the transfer table was used to pose trucks and chassis for construction photos.

In 1924 the factory was expanded to accommodate larger cars which were being developed, marketed, and sold. Additions to the physical plant were as follows:

A 40' x 90' steel frame building of fireproof construction with a concrete foundation and floor. This building was used for storing material and supplies and one end was used for office and drafting space.

An 80' x 100' all steel building of complete fireproof construction. This building contained four laid tracks for assembly of the larger cars and had a capacity for assembling eight large cars at a time.

On site were also two five-room cottages available for rent to company employees.

Yard facilities included two yard tracks coming off the A&W line, loading inclines, and the transfer table. When the facility was completed and at its fullest capacity, in 1925, the transfer table serviced a total of twelve tracks running inside four different buildings and two tracks leading to the yard and inclines for loading onto railway flatcars.

Most of the year 1921 was spent in the construction and outfitting of the new plant as well as designing and testing new equipment.

With the new plant up and running Edwards then started to assemble his own

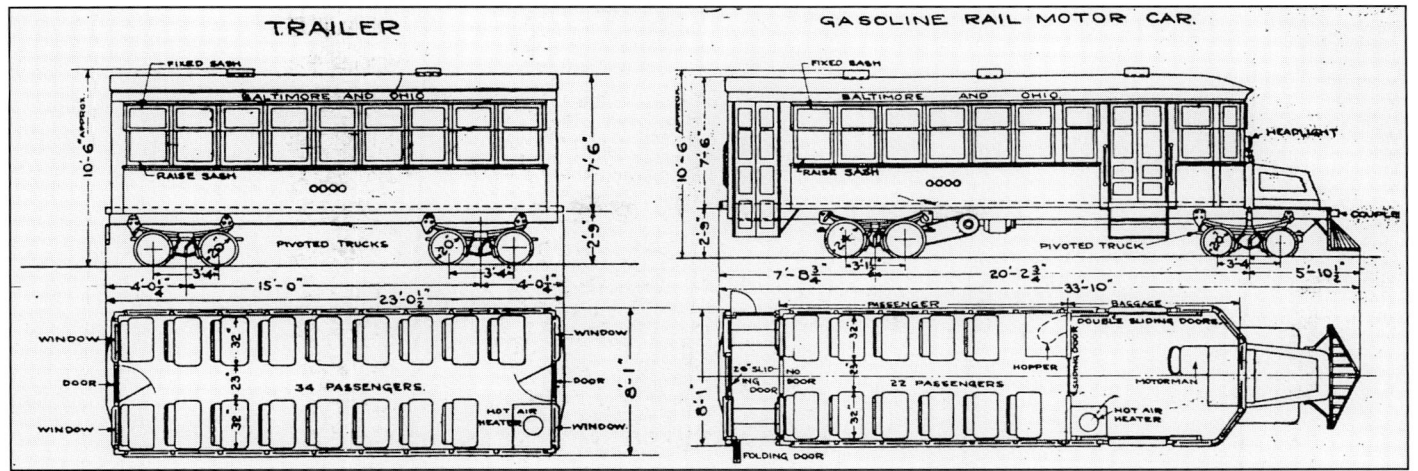

Diagram of the first B&O no. 6000 showing the Kelly-Springfield inspired front end. **Collection of Jim Mischke.**

group of machinists, carpenters, draftsmen and engineers especially hired for the purpose of building Edwards self propelled rail cars. Many of these people stayed with the ERwyMCC and the factory until the end of production in 1942. His workforce consisted of: Zimmerman, general sales manager; R.D. Deadrick, salesman; C.E. McIllreevy, salesman at Chicago, Illinois; D.B. Worth, engineer; Baker, engineer; Barber, engineer; M.H. Newland, sales engineer; Foster, Kelly-Springfield engineer; J.G. Huff, head draftsman; Miss. Pattie Cross, draftsman; Mathews & Hflin, stock salesman; O.T. Brown, shop foreman; Lewis Oliver, shop foreman; Margie Matthews, stenographer; J.M. Edwards, bookkeeper; Argus Wilks, production manager; Busbee, foreman wood working shop; Joe Busbee, storekeeper; Lewis Yow, painter; Harman, night watchman; Turner Hight, helper; Gilliam Glisson, truck driver & helper. Mechanics and machinists consisted of: Neil Harrington, John Cashion, Reid Moffitt, E.H. Harmon, C.K. Dowd, McRay, Phil Cross, Worth Moffitt, Joe Brown, J.M. Yoder. Carpenters consisted of: Bernice Cox, Edgar McNeil, E.H. Caviness.

1922 Transition

The year 1922 was a period of transition for Edwards as he sought to perfect the prototype and define a production line of cars. The early units were built largely of components from Kelly-Springfield Motor Truck Company. In 1922, however, Edwards began to rely less on Kelly-Springfield and started searching for other suppliers.

That same year also found the new factory in full operation and the ERwyMCC no longer needed to use the shop facility of the Atlantic & Western.

The third car built was for the Maxton, Alma & Southbound Railroad in North Carolina. This car was very similar, if not identical, to the A&W M-2, with the addition of a rear closed-style vestibule and folding side doors for entrance to the motor car, since no trailer was sold with this motor car. This unit was the first product to be produced in the new facilities.

The Maxton motor car and the A&W units were proving to be very reliable, and early in 1922 the little cars built in Sanford caught the eye of two much larger Class 1 railroads, the Baltimore & Ohio Railroad (B&O) and the Chicago, Burlington & Quincy Railroad (CB&Q).

The fourth unit built consisted of a motor car and trailer manufactured for the most prestigious of all rail lines, the Baltimore & Ohio. The B&O order was interesting in that it offered a glimmer of hope that multiple orders might be forthcoming from Class 1 railroads. This order consisted of a motor car seating twenty-two passengers and a trailer car seating thirty-four passengers.

The July 22, 1922, *Railway Age* magazine included these items:

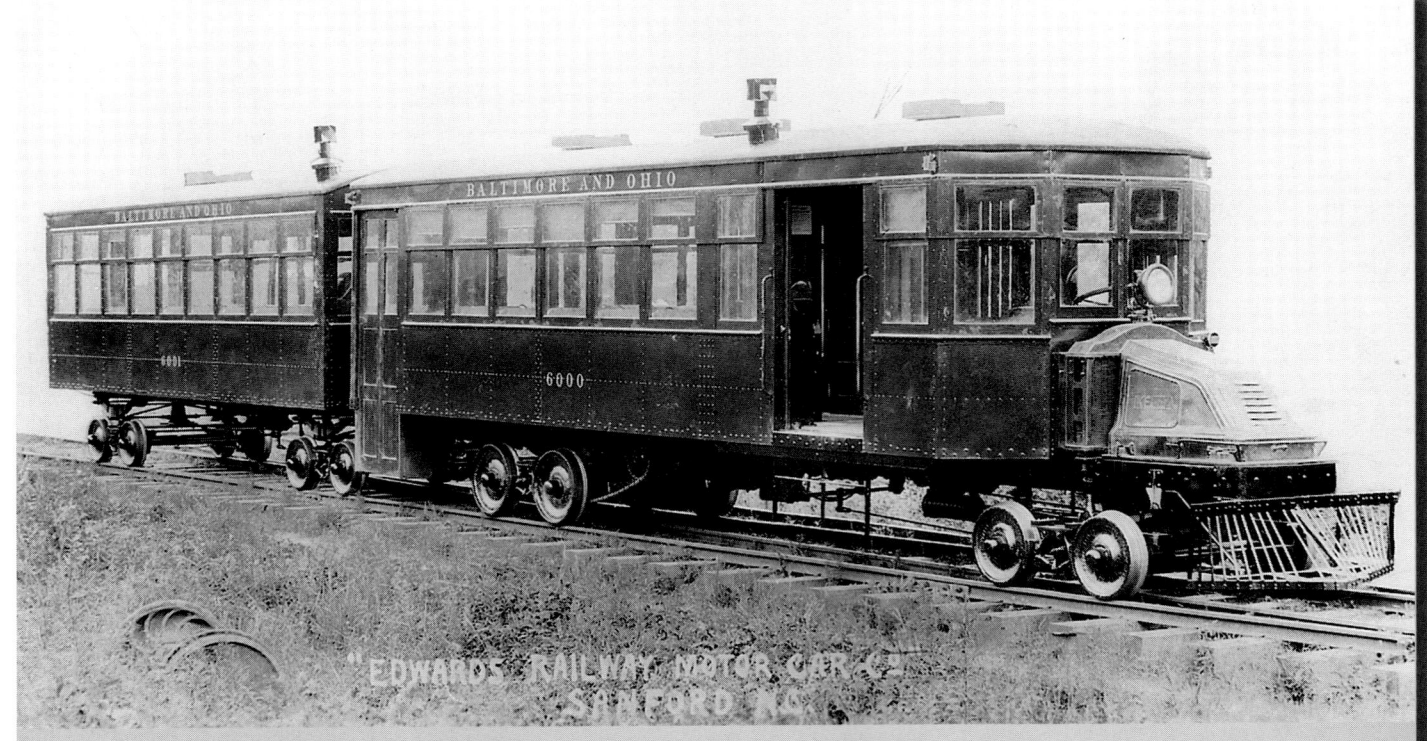

Gasoline Motor Car and Trailer for the Baltimore & Ohio

The Baltimore & Ohio has recently received from the Edwards Motor Car Company, Sanford, N.C., a gasoline motor car and trailer for use in passenger service on branch lines out of Green Springs, W. Va.

The motor car has a baggage compartment 9 ft. 3 in. long by 7 ft. 8 in. wide just behind the operator's compartment, the rear of the car being fitted with seats for 22 persons. In addition, the trailer has capacity for seating 34 passengers. The cars are equipped with water coolers and toilets. The total weight of the motor car empty is 17,200 lb., and weight of the trailer empty is 9,350 lb., or a total of 26,550 lb. It is stated that this equipment is lighter per seated passenger than any other or similar type due to the use of heat treated chrome nickel steel and aluminum castings in the construction. On a recent test trip from Baltimore to Philadelphia over the Baltimore & Ohio, these cars made an average speed of 30 miles per hour, the maximum speed being 40 miles per hour. Both the motor car and trailer are carried on two four-wheel trucks. The rear truck of the motor car has fixed axles and drives through three chains, two of the chains transmitting the power from the differential shaft, the third chain carrying the drive from the front to the rear axle. It is stated that driving on all four wheels gives unusually good traction and enables the car to run when snow or frost is on the rails. The power to propel the car is furnished by a Kelly-Springfield motor with four cylinders, 4 ½ in. x 6 ½ in., which develops 60 hp. at 1,600 r.p.m.

The equipment of the cars includes Westinghouse air brakes, an air alarm whistle, a hot air heating system and 12 volt lighting system. The hot air heaters are of special design with aluminum castings made by the Peter Smith Heater Company, Detroit, Mich. An electric fan is mounted on each heater which drives the hot air through the cars and distributes the heat uniformly.

The air brake system is a standard Westinghouse traction brake except the compressors are of special design made by the Edwards Railway Motor Car Company. There are two compressors, one driven from the line shaft and one from the axle of the rear truck. The compressor driven from the line shaft is used before the car is in motion. It is then cut out and the compressor driven from the axle is used thereafter. Both compressors weigh only 140 lb. and furnish 10 cubic feet of air per minute. An automatic cut-out device stops the compressor when the required pressure is obtained and reduction starts them again.

For the B&O order Edwards used the same design as the motor car built one year earlier for the Maxton, Alma & Southbound, a twenty-two seat motor car with a baggage compartment and a closed style rear vestibule with folding doors on each side. The trailer car for this order was almost the same design as that used on the Atlantic & Western two car unit, except that the trailer had no platforms, only train doors on the rear end bulkhead. Unlike the A&W two car unit, which required the trailer car to be attached in order for passengers to enter the motor car, the B&O two car unit could have the trailer car detached when necessary and the motor car operated on its own. This Edwards undoubtedly found to be a vast improvement over the A&W units, which had to remain coupled together at all times.

With the B&O order the ERwyMCC was off to a high profile start. The hopeful satisfaction of this major Class 1 railroad would set the tone for the fledgling motor car builder. No expense was spared to ensure the best possible equipment and reliability, which came to be an Edwards standard in the industry.

The July, 1922 issue of the B&O house organ, the *Baltimore & Ohio Magazine* included the following report from W. B. Whitsitt, the "chief draughtsman, office of mechanical engineer."

The drive assembly of B&O no. 6000 can be viewed **above**. The chain and sprocket assembly became the weak link in the entire car and was later replaced by Edwards's patented motor that was dropped directly onto the front truck. No. 6000 poses for a photograph **(opposite page)**. Kelly-Springfield supplied the truck chassis used to make the first handful of Edwards cars. This first no. 6000 was quickly traded in for a new Model 10 also numbered 6000. ***Above, courtesy of the Railroad House Collection, collection of Calvin Harward. Opposite page, collection of Jim Mischke.***

The first test trip of the first Gasoline Motor Car of the Baltimore & Ohio on its own rails, was made on June 26 (1922).

The car left Camden Station at 8:15 a.m., stopped for a minute at Mt. Royal Station, and again on the division to watch the operation of the new automatic ballast cleaners for a few minutes and after being turned on the wye at Elsmere Junction, arrived at Landenberg at the end of the Landenberg Branch at 12:10 p.m. Leaving there at 12:22 p.m., and retracing the morning route with other brief stops, the car arrived at Camden Station at 4:41 p.m.

The average running time on the main line was 29 miles per hour, the maximum, 39 miles per hour. The maximum speed allowed on the Landenberg Branch is 15 miles per hour, and the power of the car was such that it was necessary to run at second speed to keep inside the limit. The maximum grade on the branch was 1.44% and the car could have made this comfortably on high gear had the speed limit permitted.

The car carried what was perhaps an average load. There was, however, no baggage or milk or other heavy commodities, as it is expected the car will have to carry when it is placed in operation on the railroad.

The mechanical performance was good, several minor repairs only being necessary any those such as might be expected with a new car on one of its first trips.

Everybody who made the trip was impressed with the generally satisfactory performance. There was much more comfort than is obtained in any interurban electric car that the writer has ever ridden on. At first this was attributed to the splendid roadbed of the main line, but also apparent on the Landenberg Branch, where the track is admittedly not a first class one. The explanation of this is not alone that the car seems to be well balanced from a mechanical standpoint but also that is has been built up to the ridged specifications of the Interstate Commerce Commission, with frame, parts, etc., that are considerably over strong for a unit of this type.

The advantage of having no smoke from soft coal is apparent. It will not only cost less to keep the car clean but will also contribute to the comfort of the passengers. The windows are high and wide, and afford an unobstructed range of vision for the passenger, something that will undoubtedly be greatly appreciated by those who have the opportunity to travel the beautiful county through which many of the branch lines of the Baltimore & Ohio run. The electric lights are well placed for reading and afford plenty of light for that purpose.

The principal reason for building the unit in two sections, the car with its trailer, instead of a single car with the same capacity, is because of the fact that the trailer can easily be disconnected from the motor car when the lightness of traffic warrants it., with consequent considerable saving in the cost of gasoline and oil for operation.

On the test trip the actual cost of operation, including gasoline, oil and wages of engineer and conductor was 16 cents a mile. This does not include interest on investment, depreciation, overhead, etc., which, when taken into consideration, will probably bring the cost of operation up to about 23 cents a mile. The cost of operating an average typical branch line steam train is about a dollar a mile. It is seen therefore that a considerable economy will probably be effected by the use of the Gasoline rail car where is practicable.

One of the most apparent economies in the use of this car comes from the fact that when it is going down grade the gasoline consumption can be reduced to practically nothing, while steam pressure in the locomotive has to be kept high by constant application of coal to the fire, even when running down hill. The most interesting feature of the car from a mechanical standpoint (and this will surprise most owners of automobiles) is the fact that gears can be shifted from high to neutral and vice versa, without disengaging the clutch.

The general plan of the car is shown by accompanying picture. It will be noted that the motor car is arranged for a baggage space in front and a rear passenger section, with capacity of 22 passengers, and the trailer is arranged for 34 passengers.

Interior woodwork finish of the car and trailer is mahogany color with roof in white. The seats are covered with rattan. Both car and trailer are equipped with specially designed hot air heaters, manufactured principally of aluminum, in order to save weight. Both car and trailer are lighted by electricity.

The motor car is driven by a four cylinder gasoline engine, having a four and one half inch bore by six-and-one-half-inch stroke, and will develop at 1600 revolutions, 60 horse power. The car is geared to operate at 35 miles per hour on straight level track, and at this speed the speed of the engine is 1330 revolutions per minute. The transmission has three speeds forward, and with a separate reverse gear, three speeds in reverse, so that the car can travel as fast in one direction as in the other. The car is controlled the same as an ordinary motor truck.

The front and back trucks are both four wheel, also the trucks on the trailer. All wheels on the motor car rear truck are driving wheels, and the front truck on the motor car and both trucks of the trailer are provided for easy curving.

Both car and trailer are equipped with semiautomatic air brakes controlled from the motor car. The air brake system has the emergency feature, so that if the cars break apart the brakes will automatically set on both cars. The trailer has an independent conductor's valve for setting the brakes, if necessary, and both car and trailer have hand brakes.

In designing this equipment special attention has been given to keep everything as light weight as possible, consistent with strength, in order to keep within the power that can be delivered by a truck type gasoline engine.

All wearing parts on both cars are of high grade alloy steel, carefully designed, in order to get maximum strength with the minimum weight. The sides, roof and floor of the bodies are insulated.

The weight of the motor car without passengers is 17,200 pounds and trailer 9,350 pounds.

The designs and specifications for the car were prepared in this office and built by the Edwards Railway Motor Car Company at Sanford, N.C. The chassis of the motor car was furnished by the Kelly-Springfield Motor Truck Company.

On runs at Sanford before the car was delivered, it averaged seven and half miles per gallon of gasoline, without the trailer, and six and half miles per gallon with the trailer. Approximately one quart of bearing oil is used per 1,000 car-trailer miles. The engine will use about one quart of oil for each 150 miles, and the transmission gear and differential on the motor car will each require about five pounds of grease per 10,000 miles.

It is expected that this car will be put into operation on the Romney Branch, running between Green Spring and Petersburg.

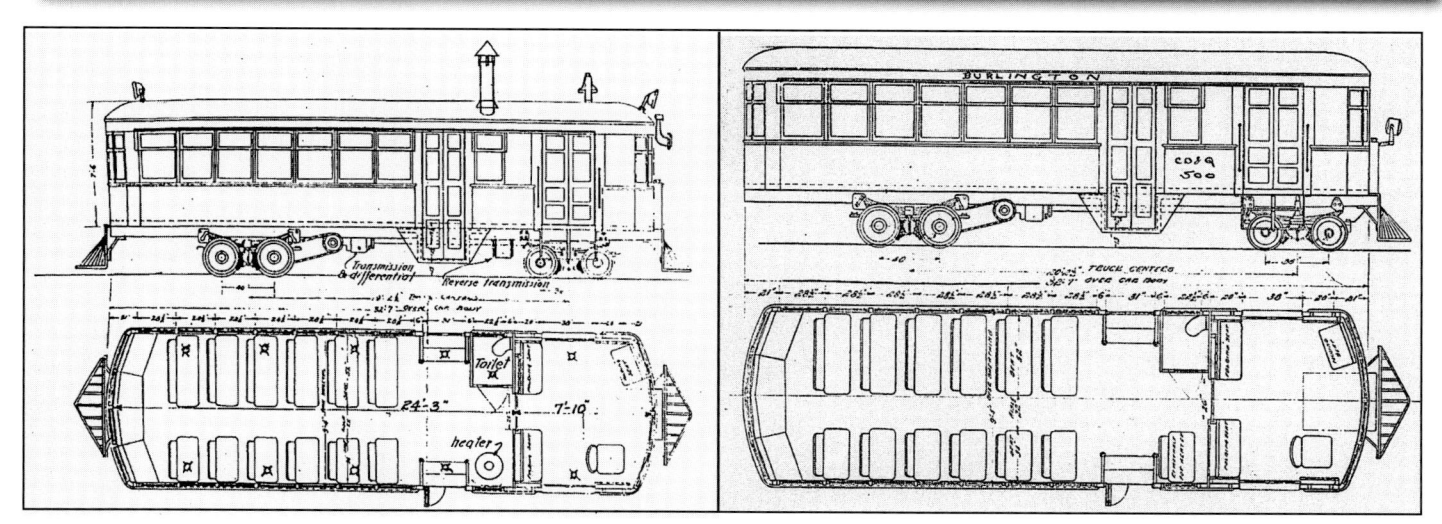

No. 500 was the first of eight units going to the CB&Q **(above left)**. The chain-driven rear axles proved to be the weak link with this particular model and major modifications were soon employed in future units. As the ERwyMCC began to ramp up for production of the Model 10, Edwards shopped for subcontractors to help with the construction. In the drawing by Perley A. Thomas **(above right)**, the car is nearly identical to the car on the left manufactured in-house by the ERwyMCC. *Above left, collection of the Edwards Rail Car Co. Above, right collection of John D. Porter.*

Indeed, the Edwards two car unit ran on the Green Spring, West Virginia branch to Petersburg, West Virginia, a distance of 51.9 miles, and it did so daily. Interest in the car was enormous, with railroad men traveling great distances to observe the car in action. One visitor traveled three thousand miles from Winnipeg, Canada to make observations of the car on the B&O.

During 1922, Edwards had made bids totaling two million dollars on projects scattered across the country, though only a small percentage of the bids was awarded to the company. However, the interest was so intense, two separate set of capitalists offered to fund the construction of a manufacturing facility if Edwards would choose between Columbus, Ohio, or Baltimore, Maryland, to relocate his factory. Edwards remained loyal to Sanford and hoped local capital could be raised to facilitate the growth of the plant in his hometown.

The fifth car built by Edwards was for the Chicago, Burlington & Quincy Railroad. An additional nine units were to go to this railroad over the next few years.

The first was numbered 500, later renumbered 9500. The car was assembled at St. Joseph, Missouri, in July of 1922 and was placed in service on January 2, 1923 as train nos. 14, 24, 111, 41, 21, 20 operating between Atchison, Missouri and Armour, Missouri. Total distance per day was forty-eight miles, seven days a week.

The car was removed from active service by September 17, 1934. The purchase price of the car was $11,550 with an additional amount of $144 for freight of car from Sanford to St Joseph. Surviving CB&Q records indicate that the final disposition of the car was recorded on September 17, 1934 as A.F.E. no. 28055, with "Value of Salvage or Scrap" listed at $105.

The car was the last Edwards car to employ the Kelly-Springfield truck chassis and was known as the Edwards Model K-50. As with the first four cars built, this car also employed the use of an external chain-and-sprocket drive. This type of drive set up was thought at the time to be the most rugged and reliable, and for the next few cars Edwards would employ this method of providing power transmission to the driving wheels.

With so much time being spent on marketing, research, development, and setting up the new facility, Harry Edwards tried to out shop the construction of this unit and openly solicited the Perley A. Thomas Car Works of High Point, North Carolina to supply at least the building diagrams. On April 12, 1922, the Perley A. Thomas Company delivered a quote of $3,897 to produce CB&Q no. 500. Ultimately Edwards built the car. However, the design submitted by the Thomas Company was the final design chosen as the first car to be delivered to the CB&Q.

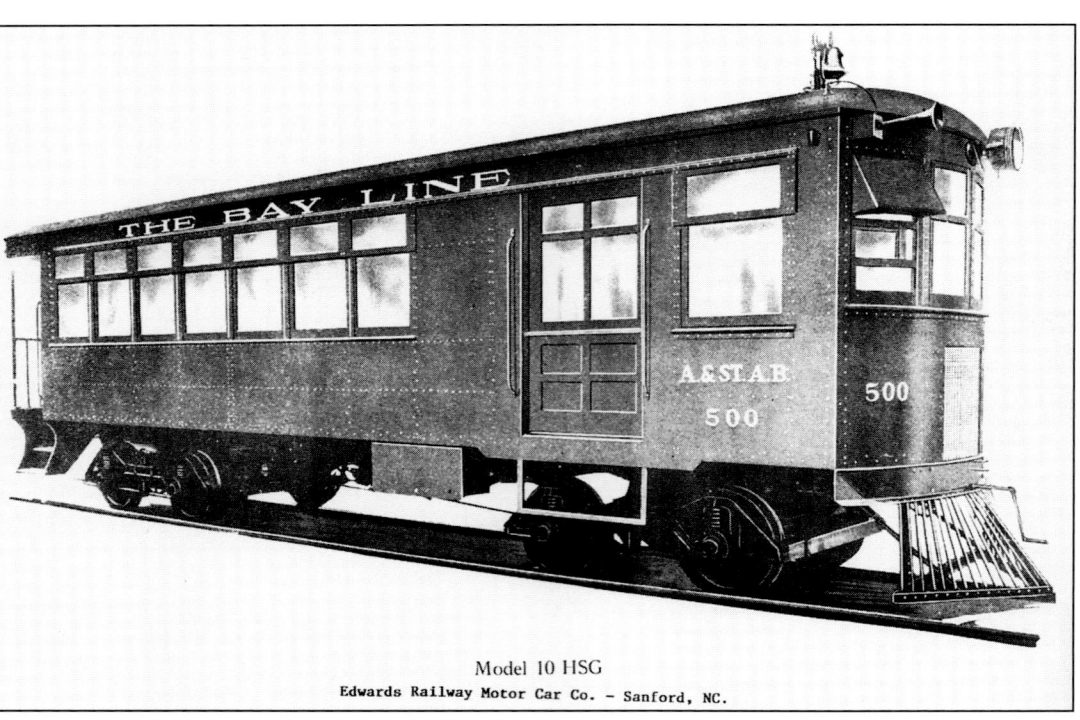

Atlanta & St. Andrews Bay (Bay Line) no. 500 was a standard gauge Model 10. Edwards would later become manager of the Bay Line due to contacts made while at the ERwyMCC. **Collection of the Edwards Rail Car Co.**

Model 10 HSG
Edwards Railway Motor Car Co. - Sanford, NC.

This car design, Number 199, was promoted for a number of potential orders over the next few years, but early on this design was eliminated by Edwards and ultimately just a few of these type cars were built. Compared to the previous cars built, this car was much larger: 32' 7" long, 9' 4" wide, 10' 5" high from top of the rails to the top of car. The weight of the car was twenty-one thousand pounds with a capacity of eight thousand pounds, seating for forty-two, and equipped with one water closet. Entrance to the car was from either side through a pair of folding doors. This feature was more in keeping with design of the typical trolley car, of which at the time the Perley A. Thomas Co. was a leading manufacturer. It later become the preeminent manufacturer of the familiar highway school bus.

With this car order Edwards made the transition from the Kelly-Springfield truck chassis, and thus the CB&Q car became a hybrid leading to what the standard Edwards Model 10 became with the very next order.

As was typical for all Edwards cars up to this time, the chassis was built separately from the coach body, which was ultimately lowered onto the chassis

Cape Fear no. 504 **(left)**, a Model 10, is on the infamous Hay Street in Fayetteville, North Carolina, on its way to Ft. Bragg. Sumter & Choctaw no. 500 **(below)**, a Model 10, was photographed at Bellamy, Alabama, in September, 1959. ***Left, collection of John D. Porter. Below, collection of Harold K. Vollrath.***

Georgia Northern no. 12 **(above)**, a Model 10, was photographed in Moultrie, Georgia. Atlantic & Western no. M-6 **(left)**, a Model 10, is seen at the A&W shops in Sanford. The car is parked on the coal chute tracks. The second B&O no. 6000 **(below)** represented a Model 10. There is some speculation that the ERwyMCC traded this unit for the first no. 6000 in exchange for a chance to sell additional units to the prosperous railroad. *Above, C.W. Witbeck photograph, collection of Louis Saillard. Left, Photo John D. Porter. Below, collection of Jim Mischke.*

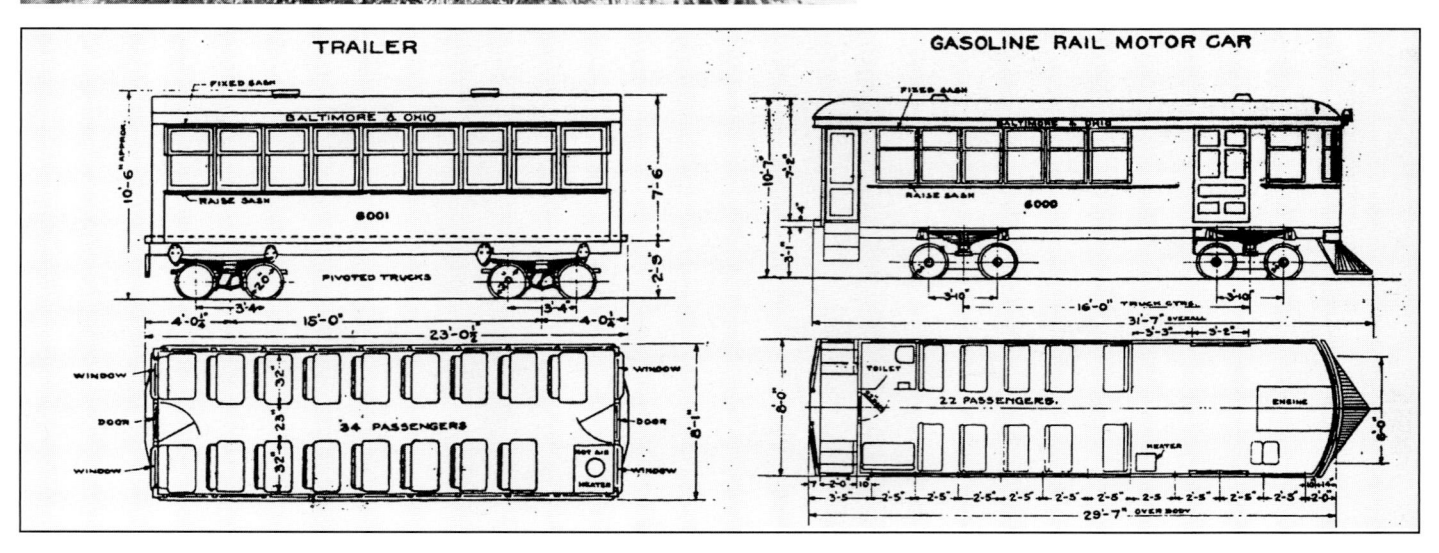

32

and bolted on. It is this basic construction technique which Edwards employed on all Model 10s until 1928, at which time the chassis and body were built integral to one another.

In the rail car building industry there were two basic ideas of method of construction. One method practiced by the J.G. Brill Company was to manufacture all components in house. This followed the mass production method developed by Henry Ford for the burgeoning automobile industry.

The other method, which is the way Edwards eventually followed, was to purchase as many standard components as possible from outside manufacturers, such as engines, transmissions, engine accessories, lighting fixtures, seats and window hardware. Edwards favored this method because costs and inventory stock could be controlled. The Edwards factory would build the chassis and coach bodies and manufacture trucks, wheel sets, and journal boxes. All materials would be purchased as needed for the construction of cars.

Birth of the Standard Model 10

As 1923 began Edwards had units at two of the biggest Class 1 railroads in America, the CB&Q and the B&O, as well as units operating on the shortline Atlantic & Western and the Maxton, Alma & Southbound railroads.

As was to become an Edwards trait, exact records of performance on all the cars were kept by the Company in order to relate problem areas as well as performance data, to be used in research, development, and marketing of future cars.

During this period, Edwards strove to develop new production models and also worked to develop new markets. One such market was in the rebuilding and refurbishing side of the rail car business. An example of this was the refurbishing of a Birney streetcar into a self propelled rail car for the Virginia & Carolina Southern Railroad. This car resembled a cross between the earliest Edwards car and the not yet developed Model 10. The car had an ungainly "homemade" hood added over an extended chassis frame. The motor used was a Buda, which may represent one of the first applications of the Buda gasoline engine by the ERwyMCC.

The year 1923 was a major turning point for Edwards and the fledgling company. Not only did Edwards finally develop and design a standard production model, to be known as the Model 10, but the firm was most prosperous in selling and building seventeen motor cars and five trailer cars for the year.

The standard Model 10 car was marketed to seat anywhere from fifteen to thirty, depending on the length of the chassis and coach body. Unlike the other major car builders whose models came as-is, a hallmark of the Edwards firm was the ability of the

Yadkin Railroad, no. 100, an early Model 10, is shown with a load of passengers. **Collection of Bob Drake.**

customers to have the car size somewhat customized to suit their traffic needs, the thought being that customers should not have to pay for a bigger car than they really needed.

The very first Model 10 to be built was not for a new customer but for the Baltimore & Ohio. Since the B&O was the most prestigious of clients, Edwards spared no expense in order to make them happy. As they received their second Edwards car, they turned in their original car for the more updated version. Photographic evidence demonstrates the K-50 was constructed and delivered, yet mechanical records from the B&O demonstrate a second unit was clearly a Model 10. It is speculated that Edwards took the K-50 unit back in trade and utilized it for parts, since there was a transition period between that model and the fully developed Model 10. Both units ended up being numbered 6000, also allowing for speculation that the B&O accountants did not see a difference between the two models as long as revenue was being produced by the unit in service.

The Model 10 emerged as Edwards's standard production model in 1925. It was, in its largest form, a thirty-two foot long by eight foot wide car with seating for thirty. Cars smaller in length would be built to seat as few as fifteen. Both front and rear trucks were of the "inside" frame and journal bearing type. The front truck was a swiveling truck, and the rear was fixed. The typical mechanical setup was as follows: Engine mounted on the chassis frame in the most forward portion, drive shaft running back to a four speed transmission mounted amidships, drive shaft going to a reversing unit equipped with one or two sprockets mounted on each side. One or two chains were connected to a sprocket on the front axle of the rear truck. An additional chain was connected to the rear axle of the rear truck in order to transmit power to both axles of the rear truck. This method of power transmission would be standard on all Model 10s manufactured for the next few years.

The typical weight of the standard Model 10 at this time was sixteen thousand to nineteen thousand pounds. All frames and chassis were now produced at the Edwards factory and tested on the tracks of the A&W before shipment. It was during 1925 that the ERwyMCC made quite a name for its rugged and reliable cars, much like Henry Ford's durable Model T automobile.

A typical 1923 catalog description for the standard Model 10 is as follows:

Atlantic & Western Model 10, no. M-6 at the A&W depot in Sanford. The unit made two round trips per day from Sanford to Lillington, which was the end of the line. No. 6 lasted until 1939, when it was replaced with a Brill unit which came from the Long Island Railroad. **Collection of John D. Porter.**

MODEL-10

The Model-10 car was designed for branch line service for traffic within its capacity. The coach is of steel construction, very substantial and well built. The car is easily made for either standard or narrow gauge tracks, and is built for either double or single end control. The interior arrangements are made in accordance with specifications of the purchaser viz; arranged for all passengers, all baggage or combination of passengers and baggage.

The car is completely equipped with electric lights, air brakes, air whistle, air sanders, self-starter for motor, water cooler, toilet, ventilators and heating system. The car employ's two four wheel trucks with the power applied to all four wheels of the rear truck.

POWER PLANT

The power plant typically consist of a six cylinder, 80 horse-power, gasoline motor, a ten plate multiple dry plate clutch, a four speed transmission, and a final drive which also acted as the reversing unit. The entire power plant is mounted in the chassis frame. The driving connection from the final drive unit to the rear truck is made with a double roller chain.

TRUCKS

The wheels are typically 24 inches in diameter, made of cast iron or steel and are pressed on the axles. Cast iron brake shoes apply the brake pressure to all eight wheels of the car. Axles are chrome nickel steel.

The non powered truck for the new Model 10 which was used with many of the Edwards models. The box between the two left wheels was the sand box, the long rectangular box to the left of the right wheels was the chain housing, and the tube running from the axle to near the king pin mount was the lubrication line. *Courtesy of the Edwards Rail Car Co., collection of Robert Richardson.*

THE CAR BODY

The body or coach of the model-10 is substantially constructed of steel. The side sills, two in number, run the entire length of the body are 5-16" x3x3 steel angles, and this frame is stiffened with cross members made of 3" 5lb. steel channel spaced 40" centers, between these steel cross members are placed additional cross members of ash. The body is attached to the chassis frame, which forms the center sill construction of the car.

The side posts are steel tees, these tees also form the car lines (rafters) and are one continuous piece running from side sill to side sill. The corner posts are formed from 12 gauge steel sheets and run from side sill to letter panel. The side sheeting is 14 gauge patent leveled sheet steel. The letter panel extends back 6" on top of the roof and is flanged down to form a stiffer for the roof.

The roof is of the turtle back type, extending full length of the car. The roof is covered with tongue and grooved poplar boards dressed to a smooth surface, painted and covered with eight pound canvas, bedded in white lead. Roof is then painted with two coats of roof preservative in brown color.

INTERIOR FINISH

The interior of the car is very attractively finished in a hardwood of natural birch. The ceiling is covered with Agasote, securely attached to the carlines (rafters) and painted with ivory gloss enamel. Along the center of the ceiling are placed attractive electric light fixtures. The partitions and toilet are made of neatly paneled birch stained and varnished in natural color. Inside walls from floor to bottom of the windows are covered with Agasote.

All sash and doors are well and substantially made of hardwood and fitted with regular heavy pattern coach hardware.

The walls of the baggage compartment are covered with tongue and grooved poplar painted a buff color. Floors are double the entire length of the car and have insulating material between the two floors.

Each window in the passenger compartment is fitted with a curtain of lace design fabrikoid.

The rear end of the car has a regular platform with steps on each side and a neat railing around the end.

BRAKES

A complete set of standard Westinghouse Air Brakes are installed on this car, which is the straight air type with emergency feature. The air compressor is a six cubic foot capacity, Westinghouse automotive type and is driven direct from the transmission, and

Catalog photo showing the interior of an Edwards car. *Collection of the Edwards Rail Car Co.*

so arrange that it will operate by momentum of the car when coasting down long grades with the motor cut off. The compressor is equipped with a governor which cuts the compressor out when the required pressure is attained and starts up again when the pressure drops below 60 pounds. The car is equipped with hand brakes.

ELECTRICAL EQUIPMENT

Electric current for lighting the car and starting the motor is furnished by a Leece-Neville 12 volt 150 watt generator directly driven from the motor. In event of any mechanical failure to the generator the car has storage batteries sufficient to supply all electrical requirements for four hours without the generator in operation.

OTHER EQUIPMENT

The car is equipped with one toilet, water cooler, spring cushion seats upholstered in rattan or fabrikoid; Westinghouse Air Brakes; Exhaust heating System; Half size automatic couplers at rear end; tow bar coupler at front end; Electric lights; Self starter for motor; storage battery. All necessary grab handles, steps, etc., to comply with I.C.C. requirements.

ECONOMY OF OPERATION

As this car only weighs 19,000 pounds consequently its operating cost is low. Car of this type now in service are making from eight to ten miles on a gallon of gasoline and the total operating cost on an average is about as follows:

Gasoline at 25 cents per gallon	.027
Oil at 30 cents per gallon	.005
Maintenance	.03
Depreciation	.02
Interest on investment	.01

Making a total of 9.2 cents per mile. To this figure must be added the salaries of the crew which of course varies according to the wages paid. Two men are generally used as a crew. With the use of these cars all roundhouse expense is saved such as cleaning fires, cinder removal, water tank and coal chute expense. Gasoline rail cars eliminate entirely the hazard of right of way fires.

STANDARD EQUIPMENT USED ON THESE CARS

All equipment used on this car is the standard design of old and responsible manufacturers; such as Zenith Carburetors, Bosch magnetos, Cotta Transmission, Waukesha Motors, Leece-Neville Electrical equipment; Gurney Ball Bearings; Hyatt Roller Bearings; Westinghouse Air Brakes; Excite Storage Batteries, and the like. Therefore service can be conveniently obtained on any of these parts throughout the country.

TRAILER CARS

This car has ample power to handle one of our light weight trailer cars which weighs 13,000 pounds and seats 30 passengers. We also make a light weight box car for use with this motor car for handling merchandise, freight, express, etc., this car has a capacity of 15,000 pounds.

OTHER MODELS

We manufacture several different sizes of cars to meet the varying traffic requirements of railroads.
MODEL 5—Eight feet wide by twenty-five feet long.
MODEL 10—Eight feet wide by thirty-two feet long.
MODEL 20—Eight feet four inches wide by forty-three feet long.
MODEL 25—This is the same car as the Model 20 except it has two motors.
MODEL 45—Nine feet six inches wide by 55 feet long. This car has two motors.
MODEL 65—Sixty-five feet long, built by H. K. Porter Locomotive Works.

Detailed specifications of any of these cars will be furnished promptly on application.

COMPARISON OF OPERATING COST AND SAVINGS EFFECTED WITH
SINGLE ENGINE MODEL 10-LMG MOTOR CAR
OPERATING WITHOUT TRAILER
AS COMPARED WITH PASSENGER STEAM TRAIN OPERATION
ON AN AVERAGE RUN OF 200 MILES PER DAY.

STEAM TRAIN COSTS: Cost per train mile.
  Locomotive engineer - - - - - - - - - - -   .05.90 cents
       "   fireman - - - - - - - - - - -   04.42 "
  Conductor - - - - - - - - - - - - - - - -   04.32 "
  Flagman or Baggage-master - - - - - - - -   03.28 "
  Engine house expense - - - - - - - - - -   03.50 "
  Fuel - - - - - - - - - - - - - - - - - -   13.00 "
  Water - - - - - - - - - - - - - - - - -   01.08 "
  Lubrication - - - - - - - - - - - - - -   00.43 "
  Other locomotive supplies - - - - - - -   00.35 "
  Locomotive repairs - - - - - - - - - - -   13.25 "
  Train supplies and expenses - - - - - -   02.15 "
  Passenger car repairs (2 cars) - - - -   06.24 "
                                                   57.92 "

EDWARS MOTOR CAR TRAIN COSTS:
  *Fuel, 5 mi. per gal. @ .15 - - - - - -   03.00 "
  Lubrication - - - - - - - - - - - - - -   00.15 "
  Round house and terminal expense - - -   01.75 "
  Other motor car expenses - - - - - - -   00.50 "
  Repairs to motor car - - - - - - - - -   01.26 "
  Depreciation and retirements - - - - -   01.00 "
  Interest on investment - - - - - - - -   00.56 "
         Motor car cost per mile   08.22 cents

If standard union wage scale is used, add
the following for crew cost:

  Motorman - - - - - - - - - - - - - - - -   05.90 cents
  Conductor - - - - - - - - - - - - - - -   04.42 "
         Total crew cost   10.32 cents
                                                           18.54 "
NET SAVINGS PER TRAIN MILE - - - - - -   39.38 "
NET SAVINGS PER DAY - - - - - - - - - - $ 78.76
NET SAVINGS PER YEAR - - - - - - - - -   28,747.40

NOTE: In the steam train cost figures above, standard union
       wage scale was used. No charge was made for depreciation,
retirements and interest on investment, as it is assumed that the
railroad would retain this equipment in the capital account.

       In the Edwards motor car cost figures above, standard
union wage scale was used. Fuel and other costs effected by
weight were based on our standard all steel construction. Motor
cars and trailers built with aluminum, alloys or duralumin substituted for steel where practical will show an added saving.

I-434   *Gasoline.

Harry P. Edwards was one of the first railroaders to understand the cost savings of the gasoline powered railcar over that of a steam-powered passenger train. The above notes are some of his calculations, which he distributed to prospective customers. *Collection of the author.*

EDWARDS RAILWAY MOTOR CAR CO.
SANFORD, N. C.
U. S. A.

KUSHEQUA ROUTE

MT. JEWETT, KINZUA & RITERVILLE R.R. AND LEASED LINES

OFFICE OF THE PRESIDENT

Telephone and Telegraph Address
MT. JEWETT, PA.

ELISHA K. KANE, President

KUSHEQUA, PA.,

March 24, 1924.

Edwards Railway Motor Car Co.,
Sanford, N. C.

Gentlemen:
    The railway motor car which we purchased from you has proven very satisfactory. It was put into scheduled service November 12, making four round trips, 90 miles, daily, except Sunday, with the exception of 3 days when we substituted other service on account of very heavy snow storms or to make repairs. All our passenger and mail service, and most of our express has been handled by this car, and we have never missed a connection. For 84 of the 90 miles it is run by one man acting as motorman and conductor and keeping it clean and in repair, at a cost of $6.00 per day for wages and $3.00 for oil and gas. On every trip the car climbs a continuous grade of $3\frac{1}{2}\%$ equalized for curvature on its second highest speed. Although seated for 24 passengers, last court week we made a 9 mile trip to the county-seat with 53 passengers, no one of whom expressed the slightest dissatisfaction.

    Yours respectfully,

    MT. JEWETT, KINZUA & RITERVILLE R. R. CO.

    by *Elisha K. Kane*
    President

EKK:C

The Mt. Jewett, Kinzua & Riterville Railroad was one of the few railroads to request ERwyMCC cars fitted with center doors rather than the standard rear entrance. From a 1924 marketing brochure. *Collection of Billy Page.*

THE EDWARDS SPECIAL

A New Edwards Model Gasoline Car with Twin Engine Developing from 140 to 150 Horse Power, Especially Adapted for Heavy Duty Work.

CAPACITY 100 PASSENGERS AND 10,000 POUNDS OF BAGGAGE.

This car will pull load of from fifty to three hundred tons, according to conditions and speed desired. It is designed to pull one standard 25-ton, wooden passenger coach, with capacity load, at speed forty miles per hour, or will pull two specially-constructed, Edwards Trailers of fifty passenger capacity each, at same speed. Can be used efficiently and economically for switching purposes.

COMBINATION BAGGAGE CAR AND LOCOMOTIVE

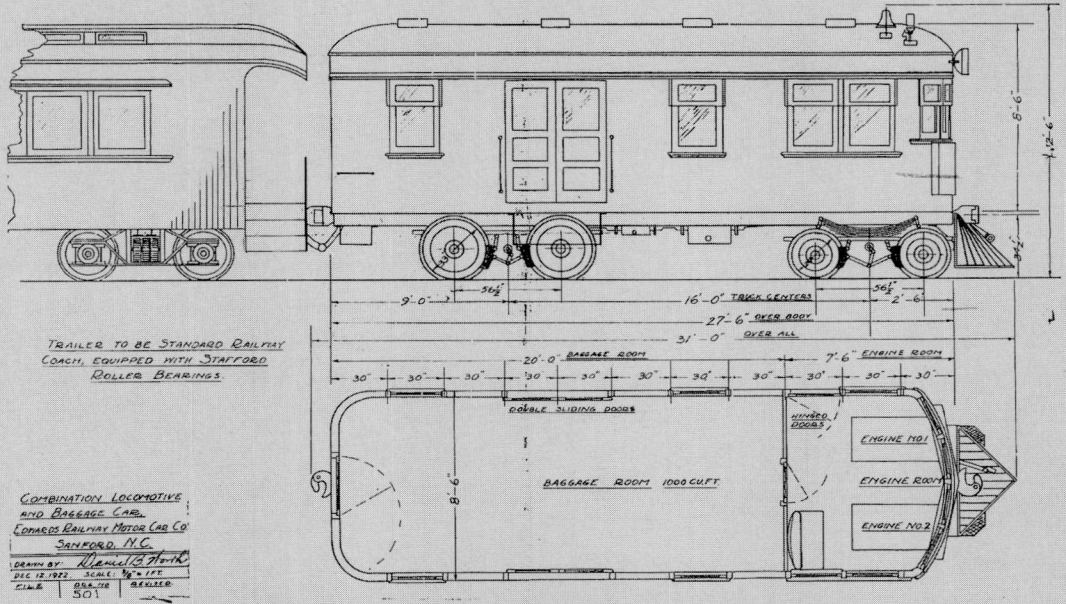

SUMMARY OF SPECIFICATIONS ON COMBINATION GASOLINE LOCOMOTIVE AND BAGGAGE CAR.

1. This car is designed so that the entire power unit constitutes the driver's, the baggage, mail and express compartment. All passengers are carried in a trailer, which is to be a regular standard wooden railway passenger coach. The railroad company can, therefore, utilize equipment it already has in service.

2. Power. The power plant consists of two seventy-one horse power motors, one motor driving each truck and so arranged that both can be used together or separately. In starting, and ascending grades both motors can be used, but after the train develops a maximum speed, or ascends the grade, one motor can be cut off, thus producing economy in operation.

3. Speed. The car is designed to produce a maximum speed of 40 miles per hour, with full load. When the motor is turning over at its maximum speed of 1600 r.p.m the car will make 52 miles per hour.

4. Construction. The car will be of substantial steel construction throughout. The motor, clutch, transmissions, radiators, magneto, carburetor, electric system, etc., are manufactured by old established motor truck concerns, which will insure the obtaining of repair parts at all times regardless of the existence of the car builder. All the vital parts that enter into the construction of this car will be of standard motor truck design now being manufactured in production quantities, such as Midwest Motors, Stromberg Carburetors, Eisemann Magneto, Cotta Transmissions, Westinghouse Electric System, etc.

5. This car will be equipped with standard M. C. B. automatic couplers, and air hose connection at both ends and will couple with any standard railway equipment.

6. This car can be made to drive from both ends if desired by purchaser. This standard design, however, is made for driving at one end only.

7. For further details of its construction send for drawings and detail specifications.

As the ERwyMCC moved away from the Kelly-Springfield prototype, the Model 10 began to emerge as a viable and reliable mode of transportation. In an early advertisement dated 1922, it was claimed the unit could carry one hundred passengers (while pulling two Edwards trailers) and ten thousand pounds of luggage. *Rare Book, Manuscript, and Special Collections Library, Duke University.*

Until the end of 1924 trucks for the Model 10 are most simple in design. They are inside frame trucks. Inside journal bearings are used, and the journals are equipped with Hyatt Roller bearings. It is very important to note that from the very beginning Harry P. Edwards viewed the use of roller bearing, as opposed to the common "friction" journal bearing, to be the most cost effective feature of the operation and maintenance of his cars. From the very beginning all Edwards cars are equipped with roller bearings and can mainly account for there tremendously low operating cost.

As the Edwards company continued to evolve, so did its line of product. During the latter half of the 1920s, the company produced the following items:

Model 10 — LMG/HSG

The smallest of the three models, the Model 10 was designed primarily to operate alone, but in level situations it could tow a trailer. It was ideally suited for branch line work where speeds of 50 MPH were not exceeded and seating ranged from fifteen to thirty. The Model 10 was actively marketed to overseas customers in a variety of gauges. Tucson, Cornelia & Gila Bend, number 401, which is preserved at the Nevada State Railroad Museum in Carson City, Nevada is an example of a thirty seat car. In the late 1920s, a typical Model 10 was sold by the Edwards Motor Car Company for eight thousand dollars.

The LMG and HSG designations were used more for overseas sales than domestic sales. Prospective customers could order from a variety of gauges and the LMG stood for "lower (than) meter gauge" or for gauges smaller than a meter (narrow gauge). The HSG stood for "higher (than) standard gauge" and meant a customer could order a gauge larger than a meter (known as standard or broad). Both models were available with 12'5" or 19' between truck centers and in 7' or 8' widths. The shorter 24'5" body carried eighteen passengers and the 32' body was designed for thirty-two passengers. The narrow gauge cars tended to be 4" shorter and 5" lower, but carried the same number of very crowded passengers.

Overall frame dimensions were 32'5" long and 8'4" wide for domestic units. The power plant was generally a Model GF-638 gasoline powered Buda engine. The engine had a bore of 4¾" x 6" and delivered one hundred horsepower.

A long time identifying characteristic of the Model 10 was the four front windows. In addition to the windows, the

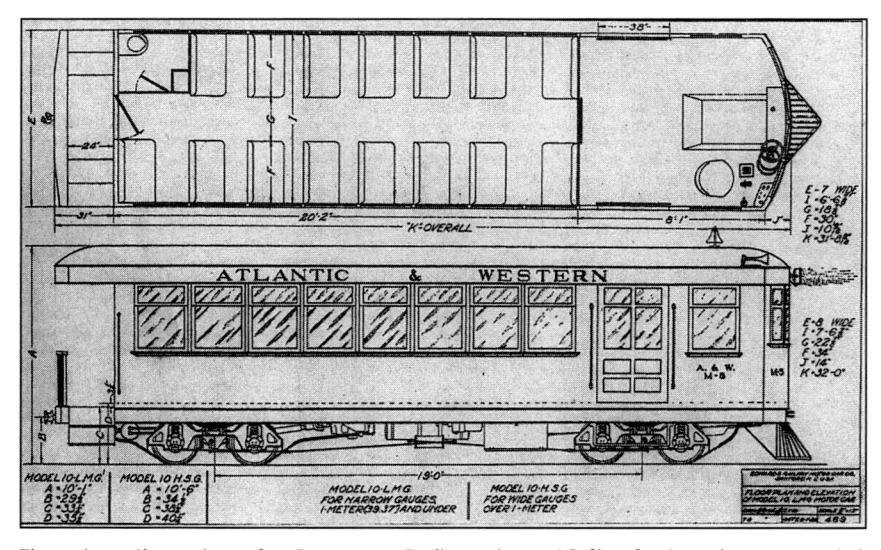

The elevation plans for Panama Railroad no. 10 **(top)**, showing a Model 10 "LMG." The elevation plans **(above)** for a Model 10 "LMG," depicting Atlantic & Western no. M-5. Compare this model at 32' with the above Panama Railroad model at just over 24'5" and the model on the previous page at 27'6." **Both, collection of the Edwards Rail Car Co.**

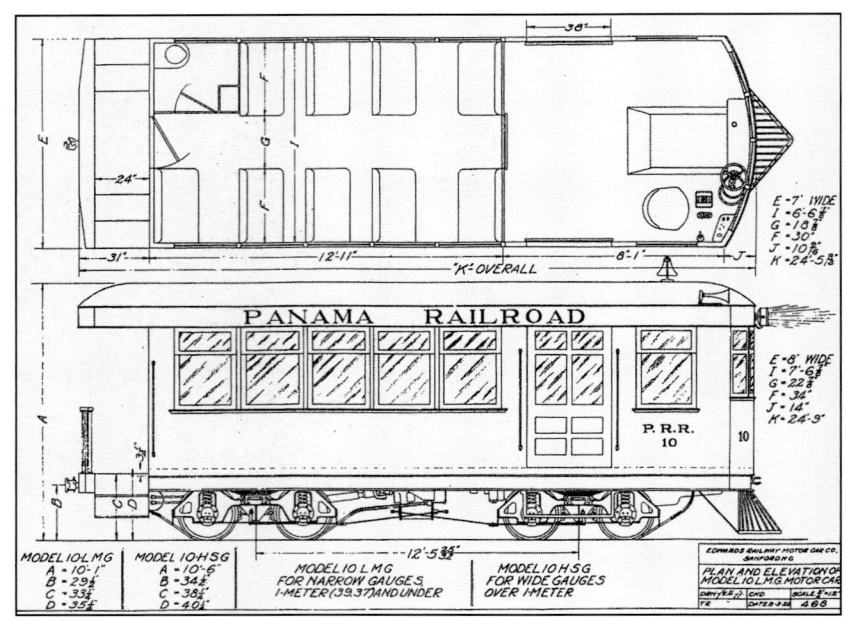

No. 102, a dual engine Model 10 with a center entrance **(left)**, was built in 1927 for the Ferrocarril Nacional de Chiriqui (the National Railway of Panama). No. 102 was later de-motorized and used as a trailer through the 1950s. There is some evidence the hulk may still exist. ***Collection of John D. Porter.***

Ferrocarril de Caldas no. 1 **(above)** was an early Model 10 with a crankshaft for starting the engine. Estimated seating capacity was twenty or fewer. In 1924, Nacionales de Mexico placed an order for five Edwards cars, three Model 10's and two freight motors. Model 10 no. G-4 posed for its builder's photo **(left)** outside the shops before shipment to Mexico. ***Above, collection of Stella B. Mashburn, courtesy of the Edwards Rail Car Co. Left, collection of the Edwards Rail Car Co.***

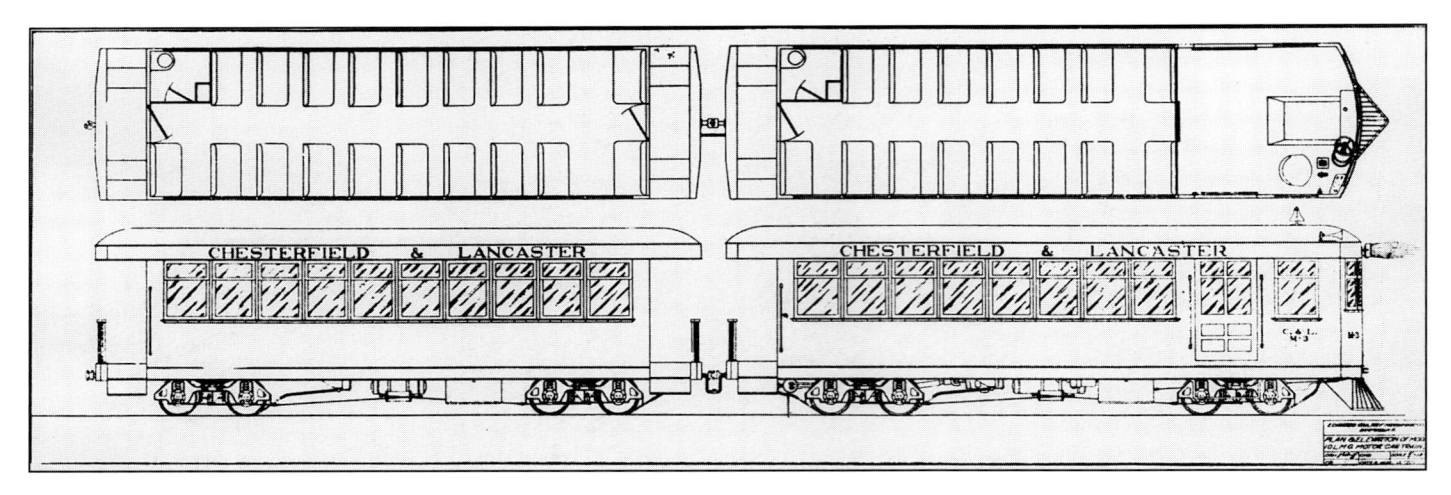

Model 10 was also noted for having a radiator mounted on the front grill; early models came complete with a crank handle.

Model 20

The Model 20 was the car that revolutionized the self propelled car industry. Edwards had developed a means by which the gasoline motor was dropped below the floorboards and mounted on the front truck. Edwards applied for and received a patent for the design of the power plant and drive mechanism on the Model 20. Dropping the engine below the floor allowed uninhibited access to the baggage compartment. The unit contained a single engine, but could be ordered with a second engine as an option. A dual set of controls was located in the operator's compartment. An identifying characteristic of the Model 20 was the single roof-mounted radiator which could circulate air throughout the moving car.

The propulsion unit was a 4½" x 6" stroke Model 14-H gasoline Buda engine which produced 100 horsepower. As with all Edwards models, he favored the Buda gasoline engine, and as Buda increased the horsepower rating, there was an overall increase in power from the early models through to the last of the production.

The car was 43' in length and 8'4" wide. The baggage compartment was 16'3" long and 8' wide. The compartment was accessed by two 48" doors, one on each side. The seating capacity was set at thirty-four, though it could be increased or decreased depending on the final baggage compartment configuration. The unit came standard with one restroom. The sales tag for a Model 20 in the late 1920s was $16,500.

The ERwyMCC designed specifications for several models of railcars and sent various catalogs to companies hoping for sales. The above diagram **(top)** shows a Model 10 with matching trailer capable of hauling sixty-eight passengers. Birmingham & Southeastern, Model 10 no. 500 **(above)**, photographed at the Milstead wye in June, 1963. The unit survives today and has been restored by the new Edwards Rail Car Company. *Top, collection of the Edwards Rail Car Co. Above, photo by Michael Dunn, collection of John D. Porter*

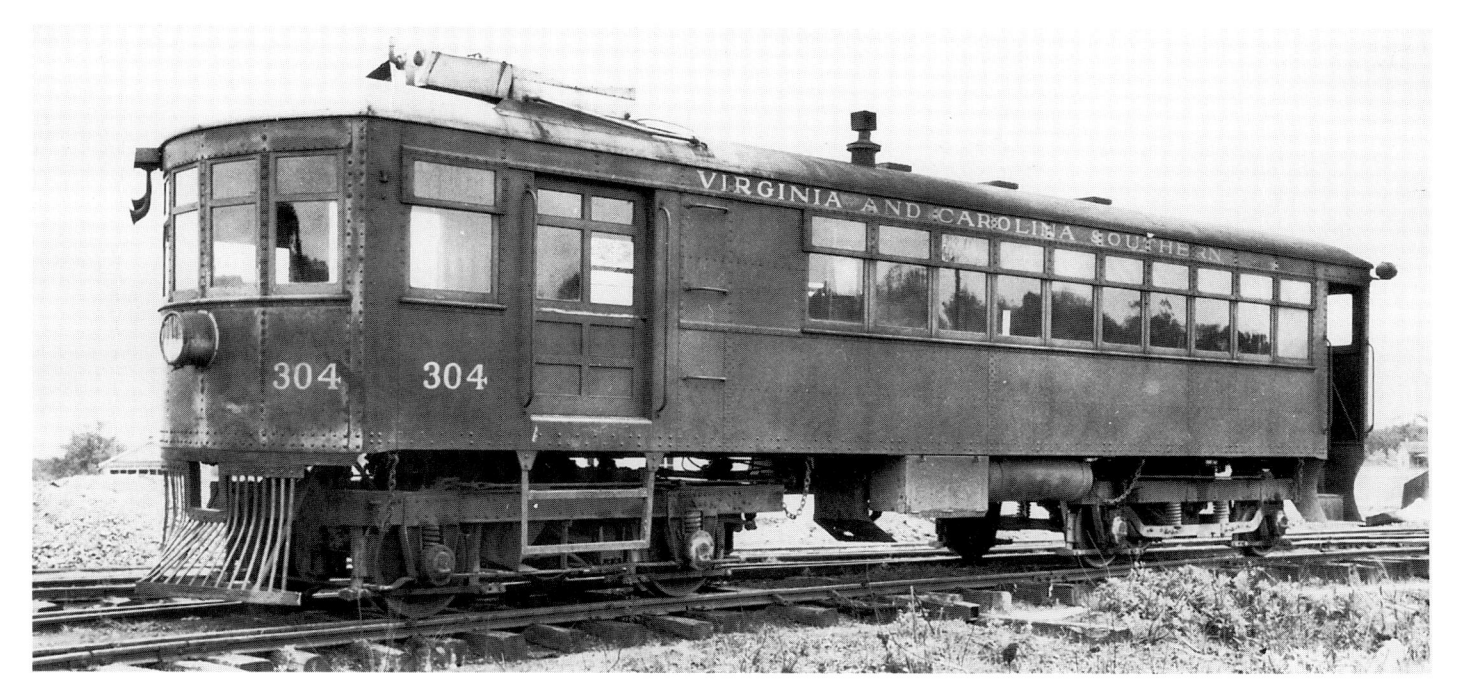

Virginia & Carolina Southern no. 304 **(above)** was photographed on April 12, 1938 in St. Pauls, North Carolina. Birmingham & Southeastern no. 502 **(right)** was a Model 20 which was usually coupled with a matching thirty-six passenger trailer. The floor plans for a Model 20, **below**, contained dual motors with a matching trailer. It could hold seventy-six passengers and the two car combination could make 2 1/2 to 3 miles per gallon of gasoline. *Above, photograph by John Allen, collection of John Porter. Right, Courtesy of the Railroad House Collection. Below, collection of the Edwards Rail Car Co.*

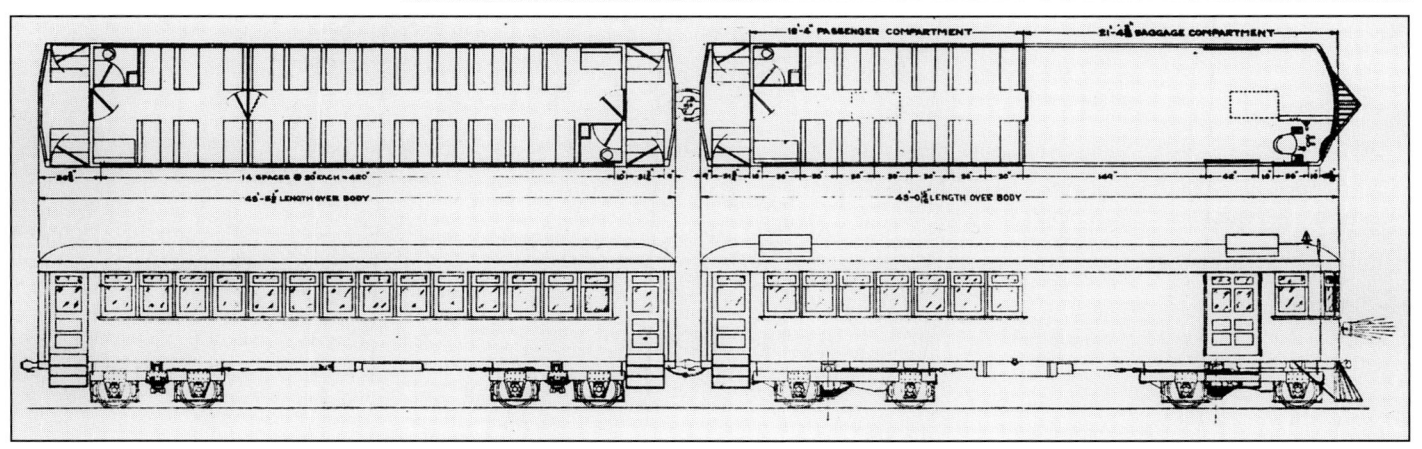

Patented Aug. 25, 1925.

1,551,092

UNITED STATES PATENT OFFICE.

Aug. 25, 1925.

HARRY POWELL EDWARDS, OF SANFORD, NORTH CAROLINA.

SELF-PROPELLED VEHICLE.

Application filed September 27, 1924. Serial No. 740,354.

To all whom it may concern:

Be it known that I, HARRY P. EDWARDS, a citizen of the United States, and a resident of Sanford, in the county of Lee and State of North Carolina, have invented certain new and useful Improvements in Self-Propelled Vehicles, of which the following is a specification.

My present invention relates to a gasoline-driven locomotive or railway car.

The principal object of the invention is the provision of means whereby the power plant will be included in a truck containing the wheels of the car, so that in case of break-down or repair, the body of the car may be jacked up, the truck removed therefrom, and another power plant substituted.

Another important object is an arrangement of parts whereby the engine comprising the power plant is mounted within the main frame carrying the bolsters which support the car body in such a manner that no shocks are transmitted to the engine, but said shocks are absorbed by springs or resilient members between the wheels and the engine or the engine frame.

Still another important object of the invention is the provision in a railway car of two sets of trucks, as above described, each containing a power plant, the controls therefor extending to the driver's seat, by manipulation of which controls the driver may operate both or either of the power plants at will.

To this end my invention consists in providing a truck of the usual type, including wheels having axles, and a frame supported thereon adapted to receive the car body. Within the frame is yieldingly mounted a second frame, herein referred to as the engine frame, to which the engine and transmission assemblies are bolted. The engine frame is so supported from the body supporting frame that it is capable of up and down movement and also a horizontal movement. The driving connection between the transmission and the wheel axles consists of a chain, so that there is no rigid connection between the wheels and the body supporting frame and the second frame supporting the engine and the transmission assembly.

The invention also comprises a novel arrangement of hydraulic controls, whereby the driver may have selective control of either or both of the power units, and also in the particular arrangement of a reversing unit, whereby the motion of the truck may be in either a forward or a reverse direction, as desired.

The invention further consists of the particular arrangement, structure, and combination of parts herein shown and described.

In the accompanying drawings I have illustrated the invention in its most preferred form, although obviously I do not wish to be limited thereto, as the embodiment illustrated is merely selected to show the principle involved.

In these drawings:—

Fig. 1 is a general plan view of a truck and assembly with parts broken away.

Fig. 2 is a side elevation of the device of Fig. 1 partly in section.

Fig. 3 is an enlarged sectional elevation of the transmission assembly.

Fig. 4 is an end elevation partly in section of the assembly of Fig. 3.

Fig. 5 is a side elevation partly in section of the clutch control mechanism.

Fig. 6 is a partial plan view of the mechanism of Fig. 5.

Fig. 7 is a front view of the clutch shaft control partly in section.

Fig. 8 is a plan view of Fig. 7.

Fig. 9 is a fragmental side view of the engine showing the clutch shaft control mechanism mounted thereon.

I have illustrated at 1 the truck frame, which is the car body supporting frame, and is of substantially ordinary construction, using preferably structural channel sections to form sides and ends suitably braced. Hangers 2 are bolted to the frame 1 and support journal boxes 3 adapted to receive the axles 4 connecting the wheels 5, which in this instance are flanged, as the invention is particularly adapted to replace the steam or electric propelled railway stock.

Upon the truck or body supporting frame 1 I provide a bolster 6 upon which the car body is to rest. The car body may be mounted for pivotal movement in the ordinary manner, where desired. Springs 7 are provided to take the direct shock from the wheels 5 and the spring 8 is associated with the bolster 6 to aid in absorbing shocks

Edwards was awarded patent no. 1,551,092 by the U.S. patent office. The patent involved the placement of the motor directly on the front truck. This allowed for more space in the baggage area and ease of maintenance, since the entire front truck could be removed for servicing. **Collection of the Edwards Rail Car Co.**

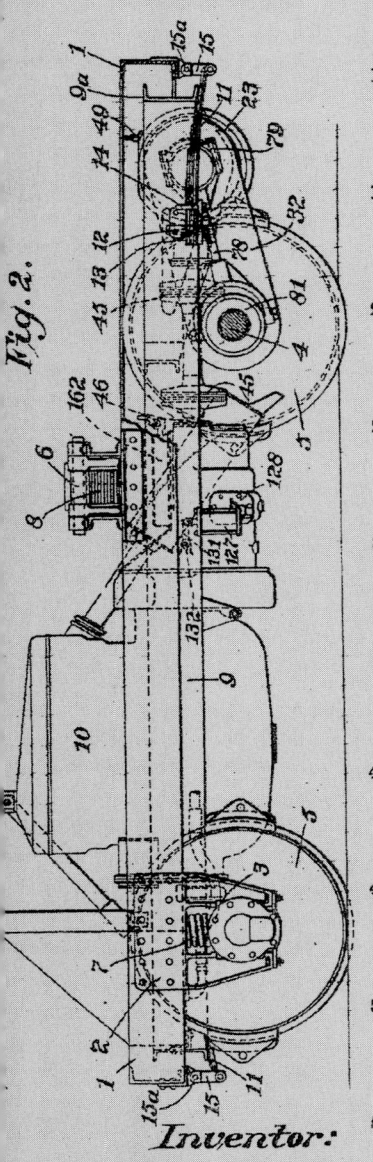

which would otherwise be transmitted to the body, and thus serves to resiliently support the body.

A supplemental or engine frame is shown at 9, also consisting of U-beams suitably braced, which supports the engine 10. The engine is preferably bolted as at 18 to the beam 17, which is in turn bolted to the spacing element 16 secured to the frame 9.

The transmission assembly is shown generally at 23 which is secured to intermediate beams 21 which are connected as by corner brackets 22 with stringer 19 between the long sides of the supplemental frame 9 and the end 9ª of said frame.

In mounting the engine frame 9 within the main frame 1 I make use of the leaf springs 11 secured to a bracket or hanger 12, which is attached to the frame 9. The bolts 13 and shackle 14 assist in securing the inner end of the spring 11 to the hanger 12. The spring 11 is attached at its outer end to a link 15 which is in turn pivoted to the frame 1 as at 15ª. It will be seen that the springs 11 extend longitudinally of the structure and are the sole support of the frame 9. In this way any shocks transmitted through the wheels and to the frame 1 are absorbed by the springs 11, thus freeing the engine and the transmission from undue vibration.

The engine 10 is of any standard construction and provided with the usual gearing structure, so that there are preferably four speeds forward. The gear shifting assembly may be ordinary or designed to suit special circumstances.

I have found a convenient transmission to consist of a jack shaft 24 contained within the housing 23 which is mounted in bearings 25 held in the journal box 26 secured to the frame 9. A second bearing 27 also supports the jack shaft 24 and is carried within the housing 23. Oil ring assemblies 28 prevent the escape of oil or lubricant from the bearings, as it is desirable that these parts float in oil. A sprocket 29 is keyed or otherwise secured to the jack shaft 24 and is engaged by a chain 30 passing around the same. Said chain also engages a similar sprocket 31 secured to the axle 4 and thus rotation of the jack shaft causes a similar rotation of the axle. It is desirable to provide a housing 32 for said chain 30 in order that the sprocket may run in oil or other lubricant. Obviously a plurality of such sprockets and chains may be provided. As a matter of fact, I find it desirable to provide two such assemblies.

A radius rod 78 attached to journal assembly 79, which lies in the channel 80 of the bearing housing 26 on the jack shaft, terminates at its other end in a similar bearing 81 on the wheel axle 4 for the purpose of keeping the driving chains tight.

The bearing parts 79 and 81 are so constructed that the shafts passing within them may rotate freely. The radius rod 78 may be adjusted as is usual in these cases. A similar radius rod is provided in proximity to the other driving chain on the other side of the transmission assembly.

Mounted for the free rotation on the jack shaft 24 is a ring gear 33. A similar ring gear 34 is also similarly mounted on the jack shaft 24 opposite to the gear 33 and between the two a splined dog 35 mounted for a limited longitudinal movement on the jack shaft, but held against rotative movement thereon. The splined dog 35 is provided with teeth 36 adapted to mesh with either teeth 37 on the ring gear 34 or teeth 38 on the ring gear 33, as the dog 35 is moved to either the left or the right. A beveled gear 39 mounted on the stub shaft 40 and housed within the casing 41 is adapted to engage the teeth 42 of ring gear 34 and 43 of ring gear 33. The shaft 40 is connected by universal flexible joints 45 to the drive or propeller shaft 46 of the engine 10. It will be apparent that as the beveled gear 39 rotates ring gears 33 and 34 will rotate freely on the jack shaft 24 in opposite directions. When, therefore, the splined dog 35 is moved either to the right or the left to engage with either the ring gear 33 or the ring gear 34, the jack shaft 24 will be caused to rotate in the same direction as the ring gear with which the splined dog is meshed. Any suitable or specially designed controlling device may be used to cause longitudinal movement of the splined dog 35 into selected engagement with either of the ring gears.

The instrumentalities whereby the splined dog 35 may be moved either to the right or to the left on the jack shaft 24 may consist of a yoke 47 terminating in a cylindrical portion 48 adapted to surround the actuating shaft 49. A pin 50 passing through both the elements 48 and 49 causes integral movement between the two. The yoke 47 is adapted to engage the splined dog 35 in a circumferential channel 51. Any desired means may be utilized to actuate the shaft 49.

I contemplate placing the driver's seat at some distance from the clutch mechanism of the engine, and I have therefore designed certain instrumentalities whereby the control of said clutch assembly may be positive, and where two power plants are to be used in the same vehicle said control may be used either selectively or together. Such mechanism may consist of a bracket 115 secured to the floor of the car beneath the driver's seat. This bracket carries a cylinder 116 within which operates a piston 117 having packing 118, said piston being connected by means of connecting rod 119 to a clutch foot pedal 120. Said pedal is pivoted to the bracket 115 as at 121 and is provided with an extension 122 to which a spring 123 is attached. The other end of the spring is secured to an eye 124 in the cylinder assembly, so that when pressure on the clutch pedal 120 is released the spring 123 will retract the parts to their normal position. The lower end of the cylinder 116 is provided with a port 125 which connects with the pipe line attached to a port 126 which connects with a clutch cylinder 127 secured by a bracket 128 to the side of the crank case of the engine. Within the cylinder 127 is provided a piston 129 to which is attached a connecting rod 130 which is connected at its upper end with a link 131 which encircles the clutch shaft 132. This clutch shaft projects through the wall of the crank case and operates in the usual manner to engage and disengage the clutch mechanism within the engine proper.

The cylinders 116 and 127 and the pipe line connecting the two are adapted to be filled with a non-compressible fluid, such as oil, so that when the lever is compressed the displacement of the oil beneath the piston 117 will cause a like displacement in reverse direction of the piston 129 and a partial rotation of the clutch shaft 132. When spring 123 is allowed to act, this will retract the piston 117, which will cause a similar but reverse movement of the piston 117, and the parts will then occupy their normal position.

I contemplate the use of two such clutch assemblies, the clutch pedals being located in the same bracket, but each power plant having its own clutch cylinder at the take-off end of the hydraulic line. These clutch pedals are to be located sufficiently close together so that the operator may, by placing his foot over both, depress them together or selectively, as he desires.

Various mechanisms may be used to control the shifting of the gears.

It will now be apparent that I have devised desirable instrumentalities whereby a vehicle may be driven by a series of power plants or a selective plant, and the other plant or plants cut in as necessity may dictate. It is not necessary that the two motors be accurately synchronized together, as it is common practice to provide two power plants for the same train, such as steam locomotives which are in no way synchronized together.

I have not illustrated the braking system nor the gasoline and spark control nor the details of the engine, as these are ordinary and may be readily designed to suit various circumstances.

I claim:

1. A motor car including a plurality of trucks, each having its own power plant, independent control means for each power plant, including a manually operable lever, the said levers being mounted adjacent each other, whereby the operator may manipulate them simultaneously.

2. A motor car including a plurality of trucks, each having its own power plant, independent and selective control means for each power plant including a foot pedal, said pedals being disposed adjacent each other whereby the operator may manipulate them simultaneously.

3. A motor car including a plurality of trucks, each having its own power plant, and independent and selective control means for each power plant, a car body mounted on said trucks, said control means being located at one end of said car body.

4. A motor car including a truck frame, road engaging wheels carried thereby, a secondary frame resiliently hung from the truck frame, a power plant and transmission mechanism mounted on said secondary frame, and a driving connection between the transmission mechanism and the road engaging wheels.

5. A motor car including a truck frame, road engaging wheels carried thereby, a secondary frame resiliently hung from the truck frame, a power plant and transmission mechanism mounted on said secondary frame, and a driving connection between the transmission mechanism and the road engaging wheels, said resilient connection including leaf springs swung from the under portion of said truck frame.

6. A motor car including a truck frame, road engaging wheels carried thereby, a secondary frame resiliently hung from the truck frame, a power plant and transmission mechanism mounted on said secondary frame, and a driving connection between the transmission mechanism and the road engaging wheels, said secondary frame being capable of vertical and longitudinal movement.

7. A motor car including a truck frame, road engaging wheels carried thereby, a secondary frame resiliently hung from the truck frame, a power plant and transmission mechanism mounted on said secondary frame, and a driving connection between the transmission mechanism and the road engaging wheels, said resilient connection including a leaf spring secured to said secondary frame, the free end of said spring being mounted for pivotal movement.

8. A motor car including a truck frame, road engaging wheels carried thereby, a secondary frame resiliently hung from the truck frame, a power plant and transmission mechanism mounted on said secondary frame, and a driving connection between the transmission mechanism and the road engaging wheels, said resilient connection in-

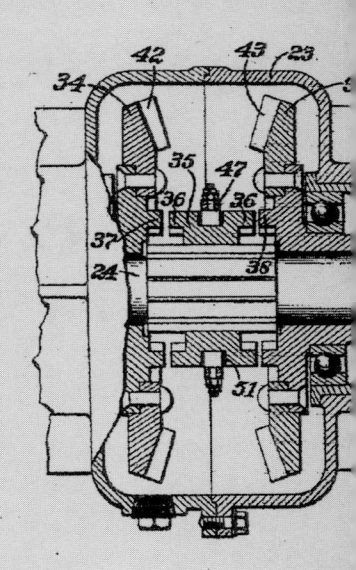

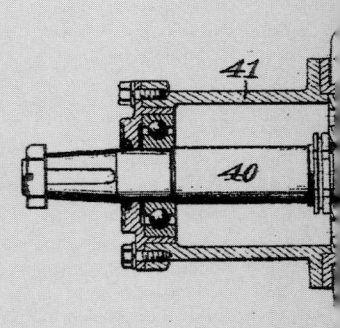

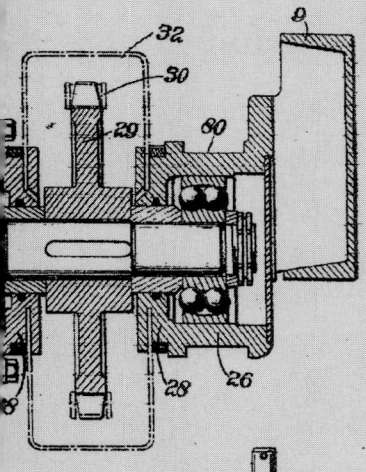

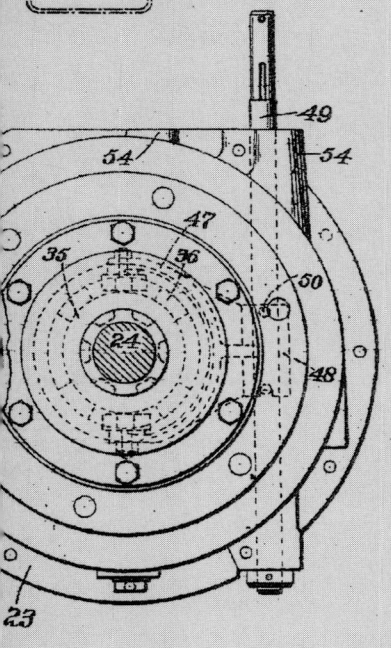

cluding a leaf spring secured to the secondary frame, the free end of said spring pivotally engaging a link, said link being pivotally hung from the truck frame.

9. A motor car including a truck having a frame, road engaging wheels carried thereby, a secondary frame resiliently hung from the truck frame, a power plant mounted on said secondary frame, a transmission mechanism for said truck, and a driving connection between the transmission mechanism and the road engaging wheels.

10. A motor car including a truck having a frame, road engaging wheels carried thereby, a secondary frame resiliently carried by the truck frame, a power plant and a transmission mechanism mounted on said secondary frame, and a driving connection between said transmission mechanism and said road engaging wheels.

11. A motor car including a truck having a frame, road engaging wheels carried thereby, a secondary frame resiliently carried by the truck frame, said resilient means including a leaf spring, a power plant mounted on said secondary frame, a transmission mechanism for said truck, and a driving connection between said transmission mechanism and said road engaging wheels.

12. A motor car including a truck having a frame, road engaging wheels carried thereby, a secondary frame resiliently carried by said truck frame, and mounted for longitudinal and vertical movement, a power plant carried by said secondary frame, a transmission mechanism for said truck, and a driving connection between said transmission mechanism and said road engaging wheels.

In testimony whereof, I affix my signature.

HARRY POWELL EDWARDS.

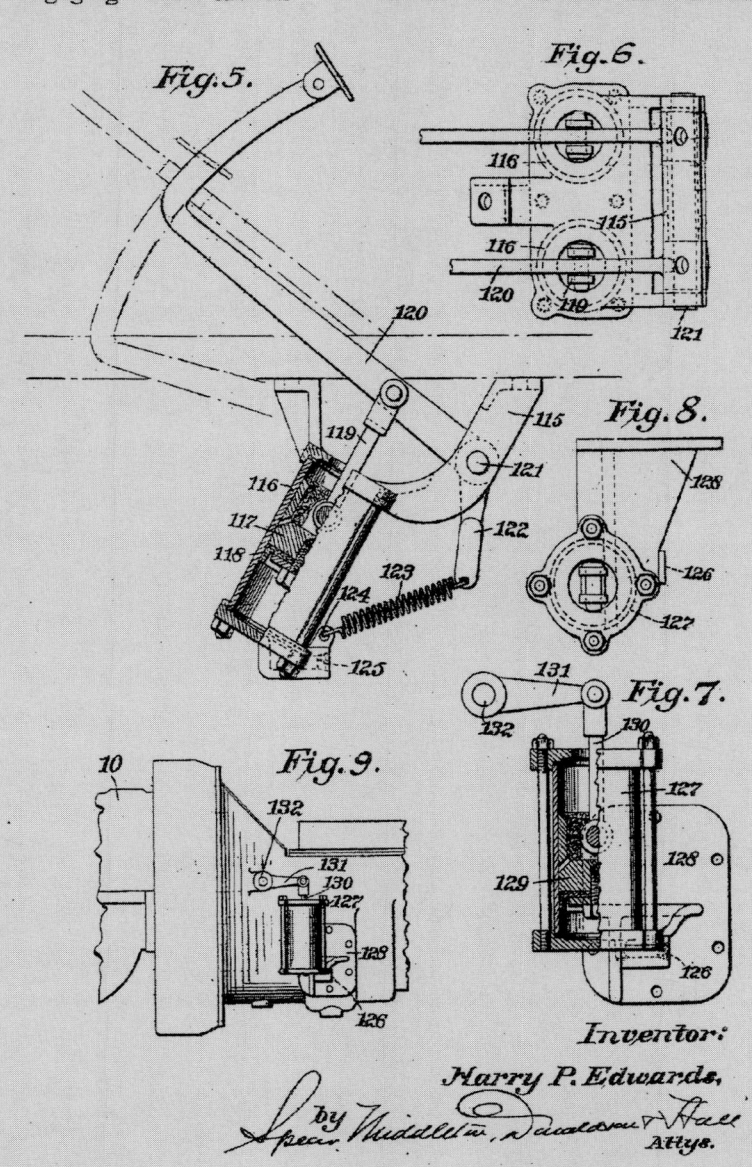

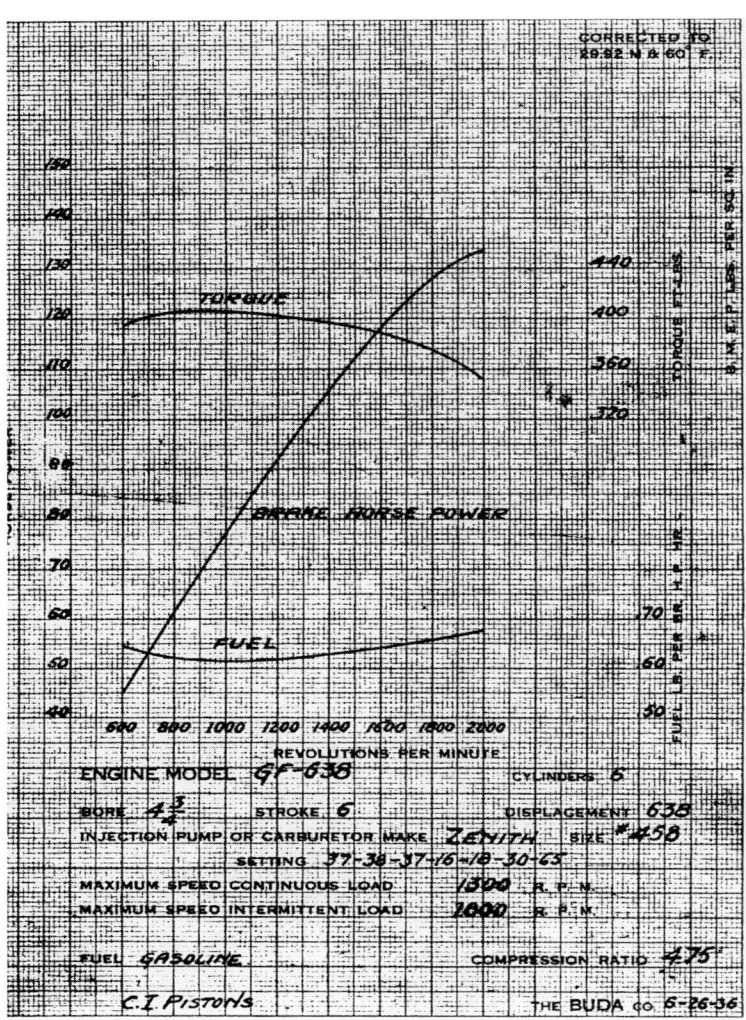

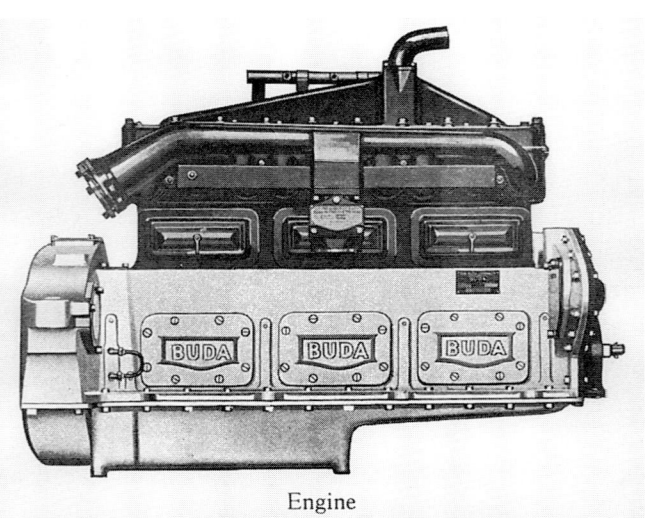

Engine
Edwards Railway Motor Car Co. - Sanford, NC.

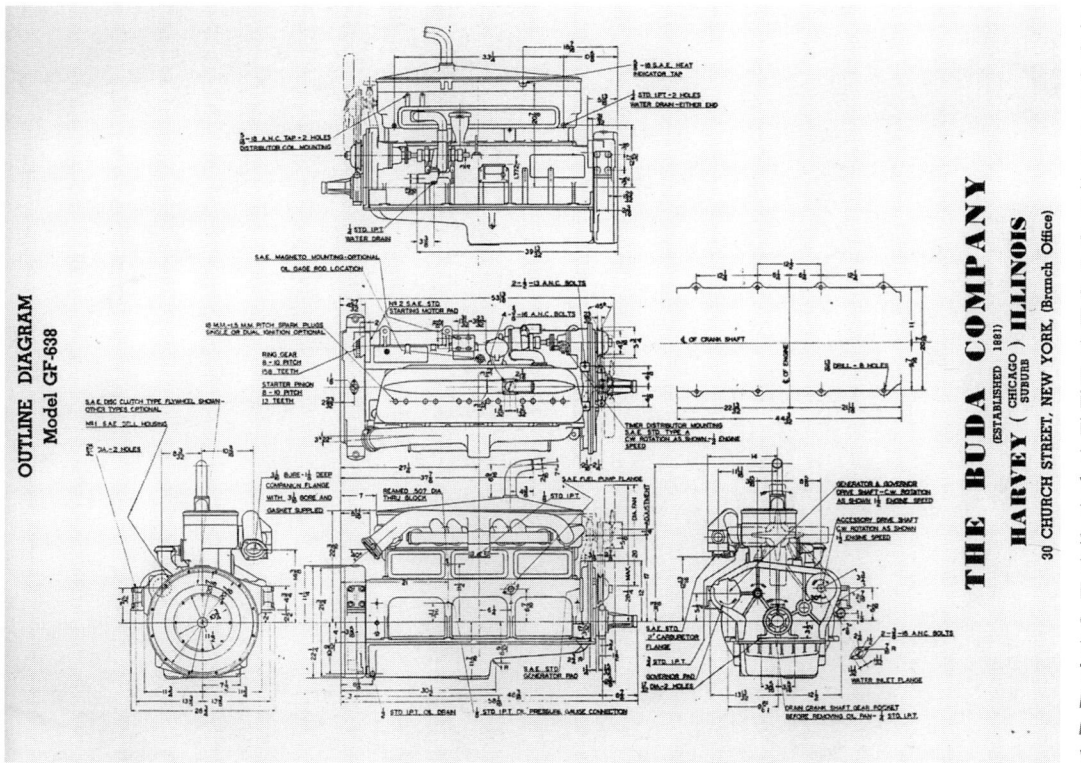

All, the Buda GF-638 six cylinder engine was used on most ERwyMCC cars. Buda had a long running relationship with the ERwyMCC, and produced several lines of engines. During World War I, many of the smaller U.S. tanks used in Europe were powered by Buda engines; and later, many domestic farm tractors had Buda power plants. Buda even entered into the motor car business in 1928 when it produced three versions of a lightweight motor car aimed at three specific markets: to serve as an inspection car, to haul LCL freight, and to haul men around railroad classification yards and timber harvesting areas. *Top left & left, author's collection. Top right & middle right, collection of the Edwards Rail Car Co.*

The standard construction for a Model 20 was:

Engine

The favored gasoline engine was the Buda built six cylinder GF-638 power plant. Over the entire production time frame, the horsepower rating ranged from 60 to 130, depending upon improvements being implemented as the engine developed. As with the Edwards product, if the customer desired a different power plant, he would readily quote the requested motive power (in some cases, the high price of gasoline in certain countries forced perspective owners to request diesel power). The ignition was supplied by a Bosch high-tension magneto equipped with company designed and built automatic spark advance mechanism. The bore size was 4¾" and stroke was 6" with a piston displacement of 638 cubic inches.

Carburetor

The carburetor was designed and built by Zenith. The sizes of the jets and venturi were adjusted to give best possible performance to the customer's specific conditions of the car's home tracks and schedule. Special fuel pumps were available if conditions—high altitudes, hot climates or extreme gasoline mixtures—would require.

Voltage Regulator

A twelve volt Leece-Neville voltage regulator generator, which was driven by the engine, supplied electrical current for all electrical requirements. The unit was also equipped with a twelve volt Leece-Neville electric self starter. Choking the engine was done by means of an electrically operated choke. The prospective owner was also instructed on how to calculate a rough estimate of the weight of the engine, which translated into approximately ten pounds per horsepower rating.

Clutch

The clutch was the multiple disc type and was designed for extremely heavy duty use. The clutch's efficiency was well proven over time, and the pressure per square inch of friction surface was very low.

Transmission

The transmission was the amid ship type with all moving parts mounted on anti friction bearings were supplied with the transmission. The gears were designed to have an extra wide face and to remain in constant mesh, which eliminated the danger of stripping. The speed changes were accomplished by shifting jaw clutches that interconnected the various gears.

The transmission had four speeds, and the gear ratios were worked out to customers' specifications to provide the most economical and efficient operation. However, Edwards had worked out a "standard" combination ratio as follows:

1st speed	5.18 to 1
2nd speed	3.70 to 1
3rd speed	2.20 to 1
4th speed	1.00 to 1

A Model 20 powered truck as patented by Harry P. Edwards. The Buda 6 cylinder engine was mounted in the front of the truck with the drive shaft extending to the differential case located in the rear of the truck. **Collection of the Edwards Rail Car Co.**

Reversing Unit

The unit as designed was unusually massive and substantial in construction. The reversing unit was designed to change the direction of the rotation of the drive shaft between the transmission and the final drive to provide the same speed and same gear changes in either direction. The gears were hardened and had ground teeth, lapped in pairs to insure quiet operation. The shafts were mounted on ball bearings and the gear ratio is one to one in either direction.

Compressor Drive

The air compressor was driven by means of a power takeoff built into the reverse unit, by helical cut gears. The drive was arranged so that the main engine, regardless of whether or not the car was in motion, could operate the air compressor. This would ensure ample air for brake and signal operations before the car started moving. An advantage of the compressor drive was that by putting the main transmission in neutral and leaving the reverse unit in gear, the compressor was driven through the wheels and final drive to provide ample air for brake work on a long roll downgrade without the necessity and expense of operating the main engine.

Double Reduction Final Drive—Figure No. 2
Edwards Railway Motor Car Co. - Sanford, NC.

Final Drive

The final drive was mounted in the rear truck and, like the reversing unit, was quite substantial in construction. The drive was of the double reduction type driven from the reverse unit by a large hollow cylindrical drive shaft. The ring gear and pinion, comprising the first reduction, were of the spiral bevel type, hardened, ground and lapped in pairs to ensure quiet operation. The spur gear and pinion comprised the second and final reduction and were of the helical type.

A high pressure oil pump was built into the unit to maintain "a flood" of oil passing through all bearings. The oil pump was arranged for easy access and for cleaning purposes.

The drive or helical gear end was mounted on the main driver axle with large Hyatt bearings for the radial load and SKF thrust bearings on the thrust load. The drive shaft end was supported on a torque spring by means of a high pressure lubricated nose end collar and spring shackles to ensure free movement.

Torque Spring—Figure No. 3
Edwards Railway Motor Car Co. - Sanford, NC.

Gear box of a new Model 20 **(top)** transmitted power from the gasoline engine to the car axles. **Above**, Torque Spring suspension arrangement for the drive shaft and universal joint for the new Model 20. **Both, collection of the Edwards Rail Car Co.**

Power was transmitted from the main drive by means of a triple width roller chain, which was encased in an oil tight steel case. The chain drive applied power to all four wheels of the rear truck. Adjustable journal box wearing shoes were provided to compensate for wear of the chain.

Journal Bearings

The journal bearings were located on the outside of the wheels to provide easy accessibility for inspection, oiling, and general maintenance. The journals were provided by SKF self aligning roller journal bearings

Trucks

The trucks were of the four wheel type with the wheels pressed on the axles, with outside roller bearing journals. The one piece cast steel side frames were cast out of the finest electric furnace steel castings. The journal boxes were equipped with dust tight, oil retainers and had fully machined pedestal guides. The standard truck carried 24" chilled cast iron solid (non spoked) wheels on a 42" wheel base.

Air Compressor

The air compressor was driven directly from the reversing unit. Its capacity was twelve cubic feet at 1200 rpm. The compressor was equipped with an automatic unloader, which allowed the air in the tanks to be maintained automatically between certain predetermined minimum and maximum pressure levels. In most cases, the pressure was kept at seventy to seventy-five pounds per inch. Moving parts were automatically lubricated from the oil in the crankcase, requiring only an occasional replenishing of the oil reservoir.

Air Brakes

The brakes were supplied by the Westinghouse Corporation and were of the self lapping type. The term self lapping describes a class of brake valve which automatically laps off the flow of air when the brake cylinder pressure builds up to a pressure corresponding to the position of the brake valve handle. If lower cylinder pressure is desired, the handle is moved to the left; if greater pressure is needed, the handle is moved to the right. In an emergency, the brakes could be applied by pulling the emergency cord on the platform of the motor car or trailer. This would open the conductor's valve and stop the car.

Piping and Seamless Copper Tubing

Very little commonly used black iron pipe was employed in an Edwards car. The majority of the air lines were constructed of continuous seamless

The patented front truck assembly with the motor sticking up just behind the front axle. *Stella Brown Mashburn collection, courtesy of the Edwards Rail Car Co.*

copper tubing running between terminating points. Edwards believed the additional costs of copper tubing over black iron pipe was overall a good investment because it minimized air leaks which could produce wear and tear on the compressor and regulator.

Couplers

A standard Edwards motor car was outfitted with a yoke and pin connection in order to facilitate emergency towing or yard switching. For an additional charge, half size automatic couplers with spring draft gear could be supplied.

Roof

The roof was built of ⁷⁄₁₆" x 2½" poplar or pine tongue and groove boards. The roof boards were properly scraped and smoothed after they were in place and then covered with several coats of heavy lead and oil. Before the last coating, heavy cotton duck covering was stretched and tacked in place to the drip moulding with galvanized tacks. The finished roof was then painted with a special canvas preservative paint and then finished with several coats of finely ground aluminum paint.

Ceiling

The ceiling was constructed of ³⁄₁₆" Agasote (a fiberboard, now known as Homasote, manufactured by the Agasote Millboard Company) or 18 gauge aluminum sheets, which were securely attached by screws to the rafters. The ceiling then had paneled moulding applied to the roof and finished with Satinamel enamel (an interior/exterior enamel that has a soft satin finish).

Floor

The coach had a double floor running the entire interior length of the car. The sub floor was constructed of ½"x 2½" poplar, which was tongue and groove and laid diagonally. Three plies of insulating paper were applied on top of the diagonal sub floor, over which the top floor of ¹³⁄₁₆" x 2 ½" pine or oak planking was laid lengthwise throughout the interior of the coach. Several coats of brown floor paint were applied; for a small additional charge, the purchaser could specify their choice of floor covering.

Bulkhead, Partitions and Doors

The bulkheads, partitions and doors were designed and constructed to Edwards's specifications. The center was a hardwood core of skeleton construction, which served as a dead air space for insulation. Fastened to both sides of the core was a three ply ¼" wood veneer panel. To the veneered panels, twin steel sheets were attached by a bonding process. The steel sheets extended around the exposed edges of the partitions, bulkheads and doors and sealed the wood against moisture, mildew and dry rot.

View from an Edwards catalog, showing the body construction of a Model 20 built for the Panama Railroad in 1926. Seen before being installed over the chassis, the two openings on the first crossbar on the floor support allowed the body to be "clipped" onto the chassis. **Collection of the Edwards Rail Car Co.**

Restroom

One restroom was provided in the rear of the passenger compartment on the left hand side of the coach-end door. The toilet was of the dry hopper type with mahogany woodwork on the vanity and baked enamel finish for the sink. Additional restrooms could be installed for an additional charge. (It should be noted that at least one Edwards car was outfitted with two restrooms due to Jim Crow segregation laws in the South.)

Water Cooler

Each Edwards car was furnished with a water cooler, which was placed in the restroom, complete with faucet and drain base running to the passenger compartment. The cooler was a two compartment type, which allowed ice to be stored in one compartment and water in the second compartment. The cooler was designed to be easily steamed for cleaning and met all U.S. Public Health Service requirements.

Windows and Window Frames

The window frames were constructed of aluminum and painted to match the finish of the car. The windows were fitted with double strength A Grade glass.

An early characteristic of an Edwards car was the four windows in the front of the unit. The characteristic evolved once the company departed from the Kelly-Springfield truck bodies and before it started to market the shovel nose cars of the mid to late 1930s. Other manufacturers were also known by their window arrangements; McKeen had the famous porthole windows, and most Brill products had three large windows in the front of the unit.

Doors

The side or passenger door and the partition between passenger compartments were of the single swing type, the upper section fitted with wire inserted glass. The baggage doors were of the single sliding type and were equipped with the roller sheaves. The baggage door opening was fitted with steel threshold covers to withstand the handling of heavy baggage and express. Slatted door recesses were provided to receive the baggage doors when in the open position so as to protect the doors and prevent the baggage, mail, or express from interfering with their easy operation.

Curtains

Each window in the passenger compartment was fitted with a curtain of lace fabrikoid (a DuPont product marketed as artificial leather) mounted on a metal roller and fitted with improved metal fixtures and pinch handles.

Seats

The passenger compartment was fitted with stationary type, spring back and cushion bottom seats. The upholstery was the best grade of imitation leather or rattan fabric. For an additional charge, customers could choose from any fabric they wished.

Hardware and Fixtures

All door locks, hinges, window locks and light fixtures were of the heavy duty railroad type, made of aluminum with satin aluminum finish. The sliding door sheaves, baggage doorstops and other heavy duty hardware were either of brass, bronze or malleable iron, all of which were finished to correspond with the interior finish. Door locks could be furnished to operate by the customer's standard key if a key was supplied in advanced so the locks could be made to match it.

Lighting

The lighting fixtures were finished to correspond with the body hardware and were fitted with shades. A fixture was located between each window and located high enough to prevent interference with headroom. Each fixture in the passenger compartment was equipped with one twelve volt, 32 candle power (CP) bulb. The restroom and vestibule areas were equipped with 21 CP bulbs. The headlight was equipped with a 50 CP bulb, and all lighting bulbs were twelve volt, with automotive type bases.

Wiring

All wiring, where possible, was concealed and protected in conduit. The wiring was installed in accordance with the National Code of Standard Rules for car wiring.

Heating

This feature was specified by the customer and accrued an additional charge. Depending upon the climate where the car was headed, any of three options could be chosen. In tropical climates, no heating was suggested. In milder weather, heat from the water of the engine's radiating system could be forced through a small hot water heater and distributed through the car via electric fans. For a colder climate, a separate hot water heating system would need to be installed.

Interior Painting

The interior was finished throughout, except for the floor, with Satinamel, which gave the finished product a satin finish. A typical paint scheme was for the ceiling to be painted ivory, the window sections to be buff, and the sidewalls from the belt rail to the baseboard to be brown. Color cards could be furnished by the Edwards Company if customers wished to choose other color schemes.

The floor was machine surfaced to a smooth finish and was then given a coat of lead and oil wood primer. The undercoat of floor enamel was then applied, followed by a finishing coat of enamel. A customer could also have linoleum or carpet installed for a small additional charge.

Exterior Painting

The side sheets used for the siding were selected with extreme care, so as to eliminate the need for sanding and filling. The coach was thoroughly washed down with special preparations prior to receiving the lacquer primer coat. After the primer dried, a thin coat of surfacing material was sprayed over the entire surface of the coach. Next, six to eight very thin coats of lacquer color were applied.

The under frame and all steel, with the exception of the side sheets, was sand blasted and given a through coat of pure lead and oil before being hot riveted in place. This practice reduced to a minimum the possibility of rust. After all parts of the coach were riveted in place, the scale was removed from the rivet heads, and the entire structure, with the exception of the surfaces to be lacquer finished, were given another coat of pure lead and oil. When this application dried, the under frame was given a finishing coat of durable black Satinamel.

Interior view of a newly completed motor car looking toward the rear from the baggage compartment. *Courtesy of the Edwards Rail Car Co., collection of Robert Richardson,*

Controls

The operator controls were installed on the forward right hand side of the coach. The controls consisted of the gear shift lever, reverse lever, clutch pedal, throttle, duplex air gauge, instrument board with instruments, toggle switch for controlling all lighting circuits, air brake valve, emergency hand brake lever, air sander control, and whistle valve. A spring loaded cushioned operator's chair was supplied in either imitation leather or rattan finish and was centrally located as to reach all the above mentioned controls.

Instruments

The instrument board was arranged in front of the operator's seat and contained an oil pressure gauge, ammeter, speedometer (which operated either in forward or reverse), and duplex air gauge. Convenient to the operator was the electric starter button and a toggle switch for controlling instrument board illuminating lights.

Whistle

A Westinghouse two tone pneuphonic horn was supplied with the whistle valve handle located near the operator's seat.

Sanders

The sanders forced sand in front of the rear trucks, where the traction effort was supplied. The sanding system was controlled by the operator by means of a conveniently located hand valve for ordinary use near the operator's chair. For an additional charge, the sanding system could be arranged to work fully automatically and set in operation when the brake valve was placed in the emergency position or if the conductor's valve was opened.

Marker Brackets

Marker brackets were attached to each of the four corners of the coach. The brackets were designed to hold any standard marker or classification lamp. The brackets could also hold signal flags if the customer chose to use this form of classification.

Signal System

An electrically operated single stroke bell was located near the operator's station and could be operated by the conductor from convenient locations in the coach. In this manner, the conductor could signal the operator to stop or proceed without walking the length of the coach. If a trailer was employed, the signal cable was contained in a waterproofed socket at the rear end of the coach and carried on to the trailer.

Radiator

The radiator was constructed of the tubular type and was constructed entirely of copper and brass.

Gasoline Tank

The gasoline tank was installed under the coach floor and came in thirty, fifty, or sixty gallon capacities.

Tools

Each coach was equipped with a full set of tools for making adjustments and minor repairs. An oil can and high pressure grease compressor were also furnished with each car.

Fire Extinguisher

A one quart fire extinguisher was installed convenient to the operator's seat.

Windshield Wiper

The wiper operated in a horizontal movement and was powered by air pressure from the main air reservoir. The wiper was located in the forward window directly in front of the operator. A valve located near the operator's instrument panel controlled the mechanism.

Numbering and Lettering

The car was numbered and lettered in gold leaf according to the customer's specifications. This final process completed the construction of an Edwards Motor car.

Edwards's other models shared most of the same features and attention to quality and detail as the Model 20s. The rest of the ERwyMCC line of products are listed below:

Model 21

This model was developed later on in the production history, and many of the units were shipped overseas. It was characterized by the streamlined, or shovelnose front end. The Model 21 was essentially a Model 20 car with one power truck and a streamlined front end. The car could be configured for all passenger, mail, or express service. The Model 21 could also be equipped as an office, observation, or private car.

The standard engine supplied was a six cylinder gasoline Buda engine. The 4¾" by 6" stroke engine produced 133 horsepower at 2000 rpm. Diesel engines and other gasoline engines could be substituted if required by the purchaser. The engine was mated with a four speed manual transmission.

The dimension of the car body was 46' 4" in length, making it the longest of the three models. The standard baggage compartment was 13" long by 8' 4" wide, accessed by two 34" doors, one on each side of the car.

Each Edwards car was made to order and with few exceptions they were custom built, hand finished objects of fine craftsmanship. The following descriptions have been taken from surviving Edwards catalogues and represent a sampling of the workmanship details of the finished motor cars.

Model 25

The Model 25 was the basic configuration of the Model 20, but had two power trucks. While some Model 20s were sold with two power trucks, the company later adapted the designation "Model 25" to distinguish the difference between the models. An identifying characteristic of a Model 25 was the dual roof mounted radiators.

Interior photograph of a newly completed Model 25 showing the operator's compartment. The engine is contained in the center mounted housing to the left of the operator's controls. *Courtesy of the Edwards Rail Car Co., collection of Robert Richardson.*

Model 45

The Model 45 was designed to be an "expandable" unit by which the customer could specify a specific length for the car body. While a concrete example of this model was never produced, two units that were delivered for customers would fit the basic description. The Atlanta & St. Andrews Bay no. 503 (later Tallulah Falls) was over 55' in length and would certainly fall into the category of longer than ordinary Edwards cars. The Porter built CB&Q no. 552 was 65' in length and would also be included in this specific category. Incidentally, the CB&Q referred to no. 552 as a Model 65, probably referring to the length of the car body. The 1923 Edwards catalog lists the Model 65 as well. Thereafter the designation seems to have been dropped in favor of the catchall Model 45.

Trailers

A variety of trailers could be constructed to match or complement the above listed powered units. Trailers generally were pulled by the power unit and were connected via communications with the emergency brake cord running the length of both the powered and the non powered units. Trailers were also generally equipped with a restroom and baggage compartment if desired.

Interior close up **(above)** showing the dual controls of a Model 25, belonging to the Ferocarril Nacional de Chiriquie's no. 102. The operator would have to gear shift each set of controls in order to increase the speed of the unit. Tallulah Falls no. 201 **(right)**, a Model 25, seen in Cornelia, Georgia, on August 17, 1955. No. 201 was the former A&SAB no. 501. The unit was later shortened and used as a post office and express car. The car survives today after being used as a private residence, and awaits restoration. *Above, Collection of John D. Porter. Right, photograph by Tom King, collection of the Edwards Rail Car Co.*

Tallulah Falls no. 201, seen on Queen's Trestle south of Mountain City, Georgia in 1953. ***Photograph by R. D. Sharpless, collection of Frank Ardrey, Jr.***

Freight Motors

Although not actively marketed as a separate model, the ERwyMCC built a version of a flat bottomed open platform freight hauler. The units were referred to as "Special Fast Freight and Express Models." These units could be used in less than car load (LCL) freight service or for moving supplies on a railroad. The flat storage area allowed for 19' x 7' of cargo storage. The favored motor was the Buda GL-6, which produced 109 horsepower, though a larger Buda GH-6 could be substituted which delivered 123 horsepower.

Apparently the units did not find favor in the U.S., as no orders were placed with domestic lines, but three Central and South American railroads did place orders. The orders were concentrated in the later part of the 1920s when an

At an unknown American port, an ERwyMCC trailer car is being prepared for loading aboard a transport for overseas shipment **(top)**. It is surmised that the car is destined for the FC Panama Nacional, where seven open-platform narrow gauge trailers were ordered. A Model 10 LMG "Special Fast Freight and Express" unit is leaving Medellin, Columbia **(above)** with four tons of supplies for the construction of the Tranvia de Oriente. The unit was later converted into a traditional motor car capable of hauling passengers once the line was constructed. *Top, courtesy of The Railroad House Collection, Calvin Harward collection. Above, John D. Porter collection.*

Model 10 LMG—Special Fast Freight and Express

Edwards Railway Motor Car Co. - Sanford, NC.

Floor Plan and Elevation of Fast Freight or Express Motor Car, Capacity 6 Tons. 12' 5 25-32" Truck Center with 19' 0⅝" Loading Space. Also Furnished with 19' Truck Centers and 26' 0⅝" Loading Space.

Edwards Railway Motor Car Co. - Sanford, NC.

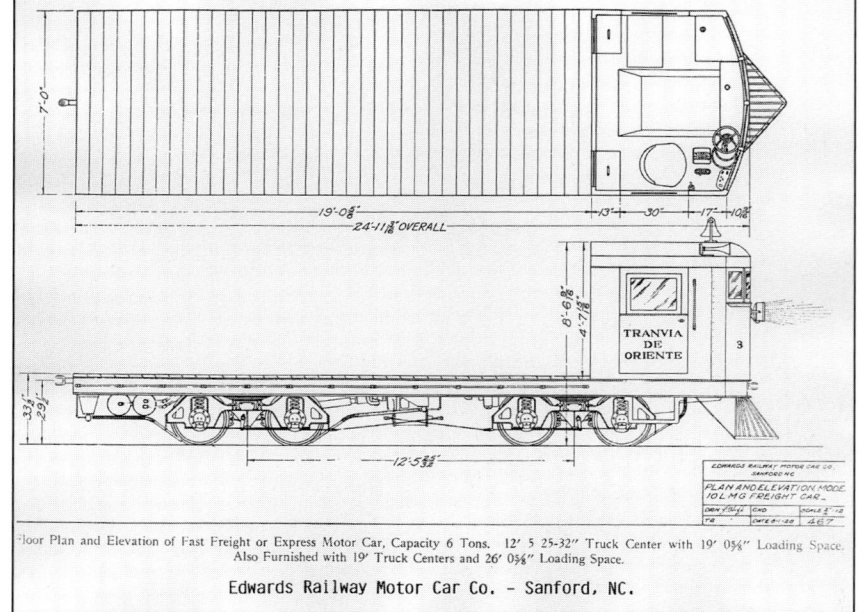

The Model 10 LMG Special Fast Freight and Express motor car as it appeared in a 1926 catalog **(top)**, sparked sales to a handful of overseas railroads, but none in the U.S. The elevation plans for the same car **(above)**. Butte, Anaconda & Pacific, no. M-10 **(right)** was a one of a kind unit. Most likely, the ERwyMCC provided the chassis and the body with the elevation basket being added by the BA&P shops. The purpose of the basket was to lift men to work on the overhead electrified lines, which powered the rest of the motive fleet. *Top & Middle, collection of the Edwards Rail Car Co. Bottom right, collection of Harold K. Vollrath.*

Edwards catalog featured the unique units in 1926. Production peaked by 1929 and no orders were placed after that time.

Line Inspection Car

In 1925, the Butte, Anaconda & Pacific Railway of Butte, Montana, needed a gasoline motorized car to service the electric catenaries, which powered the other locomotives the railroad used for regular service. At the time, Edwards was actively promoting a "locomotive" type car, which could pull two standard weight coaches or four Edwards built trailers. The car ended up being used as a line inspection car and no other orders were placed for this "locomotive."

ERwyMCC and the CB&Q

The total production of Edwards Railway Motor Cars for the CB&Q was ten cars of varying configurations. While the CB&Q represented a repeat order for the Edwards plant, it probably represented a disappointment as well for the company. The first unit, no. 500, was re-powered fairly quickly with a Continental 103 hp engine. The last unit, no. 552, was sent to the Electro-Motive Corporation and virtually stripped down

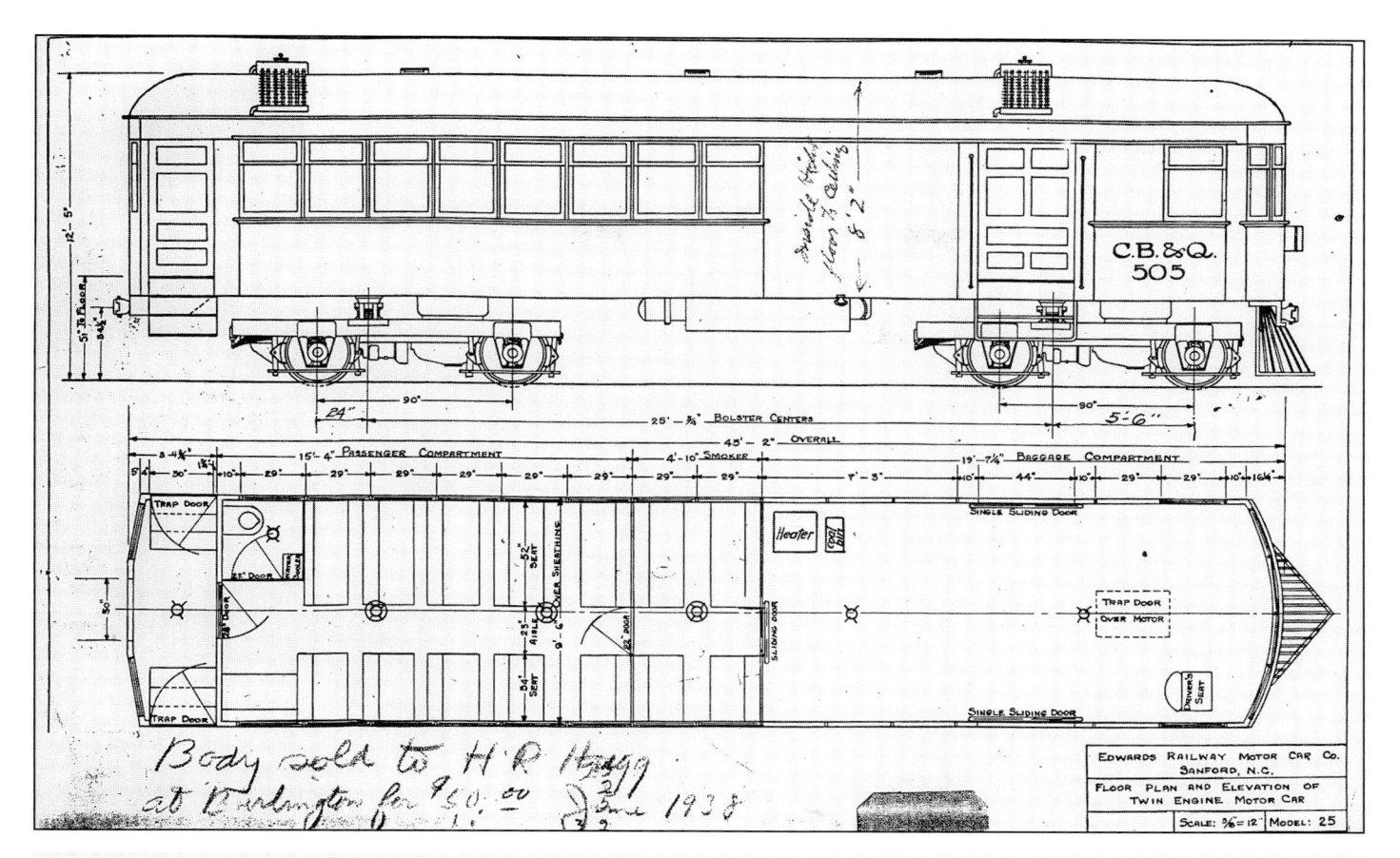

The sale of eight units of three different models to the CB&Q represented the single largest order for the ERwyMCC. No. 505 **(top)** was a Model 25 with dual motors. CB&Q no. 503 **(above)** was a model 25 dual Buda powered car. The car was dismantled in 1934 and the body was sold to a railroad employee for forty dollars. Colorado & Southern no. 500 **(left)**, began its career as CB&Q no. 504. Sold to the C&S in 1926, the unit was then sold to the Graysonia, Nashville & Ashdown in 1929 as its no. 600. It survived as a diner in Hope, Arkansas, for many years. It now travels around the south as a mobile trailer used as an antique shop. *Top, collection of Dave Miner. Middle, courtesy of the Edwards Rail Car Co., collection of Stella Brown Mashburn. Bottom, collection of Edwards Rail Car Co.*

to the frame and rebuilt with new power plants, trucks and controls. The initial order in which no. 552 was placed could have been a gold mine for the ERwyMCC. With an individual price tag of $27,169.70, it could have gone a long way to solving the company's financial problems. The remaining eight units were the dual engine Model 25 and differed among themselves only through the number of seats and the length of the baggage compartment.

If no. 552 had performed well, an additional five units were to follow. The problem with no. 552 is that it was not built under the direct control of the ERwyMCC; rather, it was constructed by the H. K. Porter Co. of Pittsburgh, Pennsylvania. The specifications called for the car to be 65' in length, which exceeded the length of the building shop in Sanford. This forced Edwards to subcontract the work to Porter. Not only was it constructed by another company, but also the time tested Buda engines were substituted with Porter's own gasoline engines. These engines seemed to be the undoing of the car, as the unit was underpowered and the subsequent orders were not placed.

The CB&Q had compiled a cost analysis of the various Edwards cars and found them to cost from a low of .3228 cents a mile to a high of .4279 cents a mile. Ironically, no. 500, the first unit, was the most expensive to operate. As stipulated in correspondence to Harry Edwards, if no. 552 performed satisfactorily, additional units would be purchased. The same cost analysis also included days in service/days out of service data and the no. 552 was listed as having been fit for duty ninety-three days and out of service for ninety-one days.

This model was not manufactured again by the ERwyMCC, but the CB&Q referred to the unit as a Model 65. The unit was rebuilt by EMC in 1929 with a new motor, trucks, and controls, but was eventually retired by March 2, 1939. Although no. 552 originally cost the CB&Q $27,169.70, the refitting by the EMC cost an additional $12,519.64, for a grand total of $39,689.34 for the unit, explaining why the CB&Q scrapped the idea of additional Edwards units.

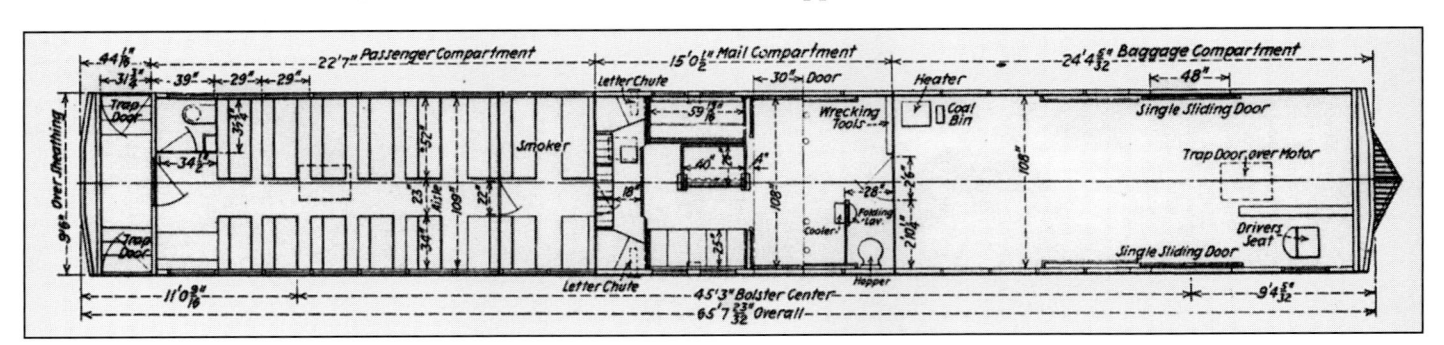

The second of two ex-CB&Q Model 25s to end up on the Laramie, North Park & Western is still sporting its last CB&Q roster number, 9508, in this photograph **(top)** taken in Laramie, Wyoming in the 1930s. The units were sold to the LNP&W for four thousand dollars apiece. Original purchase price for each unit was just over eighteen thousand dollars. The largest ERwyMCC car built was the Model 65 built for the CB&Q **(middle & above)**. The unit was subcontracted out to the H.K. Porter locomotive works, which supplied the unit with its own production gasoline engine. The 100 hp gasoline engine proved ineffective, and the unit was later rebuilt by EMC with a 220 hp gasoline-electric drive power plant. *Top, photograph by William Moneypeny. Middle, collection of the author. Bottom, collection of the Edwards Rail Car Co.*

62

The chain and sprocket driven no. 500 was purchased for $11,550. Numbers 501–509 were the dual motor Model 25s. The price tag for this group of cars ranged from $16,500 to $18,295, depending on the outfitting of each individual car. The CB&Q used this group of cars as complete passenger units in some cases, or with large baggage compartments with a minimum of seating. This difference in configuration is what caused the price to vary from unit to unit.

The gasoline-electric car was rapidly developing, and the CB&Q purchased a Brill car in 1925, at the same time it was accepting delivery of the Edwards cars. The gasoline-electric had proved its worth in less than a year, and the CB&Q cancelled the remaining order with the Edwards firm. Instead, it placed an order for sixteen additional cars, this time from EMC. By 1928, the railroad placed an additional order for thirty more cars from EMC and one from Mack International.

The CB&Q found the EMC cars much easier to operate than the Edwards cars. With the EMC cars, the operator simply applied throttle and the prime mover generated electricity, which was then applied to the electric traction motors on the trucks. To operate an Edwards car with dual engines took a bit of agility on behalf of the motorman. The following description is a generalized account of how a motorman would shift between the two engines of the typical ERwyMCC car ordered by the CB&Q:

The motorman would start the car by engaging each clutch in first gear on both engines using both feet. Each hand would be on one throttle and eyes on the tachometer. If the motorman was pulling a trailer, much slipping of the clutch and manipulating of the throttles would be required to keep from spinning the single drive axle per engine or from killing the engines. Once both engines were engaged in first gear and throttled up to 1600 RPM, one engine's clutch was disengaged and at the same time the throttle closed. The shift stick was placed in neutral, clutch engaged, engine revved slightly, clutch then disengaged, shifted to second gear and the clutch engaged while opening the throttle to match the car speed. The transmissions were not synchromesh, so the above double clutching was necessary most of the time. This procedure was repeated with the second power plant; then the whole process started again for both the third and then fourth gears. It could only be imagined that a motorman was very happy when he got the unit into high gear and didn't have to stop for several miles. It should be noted that on wet or otherwise slick rail, one power plant still engaged when the other was being shifted and this might cause the unit to lose traction immediately upon disengaging of the other clutch. If the motorman missed a shift, which occurred very often in dealing with non synchromesh transmissions, he might have to come to a complete stop and start all over with the process of getting the unit moving.

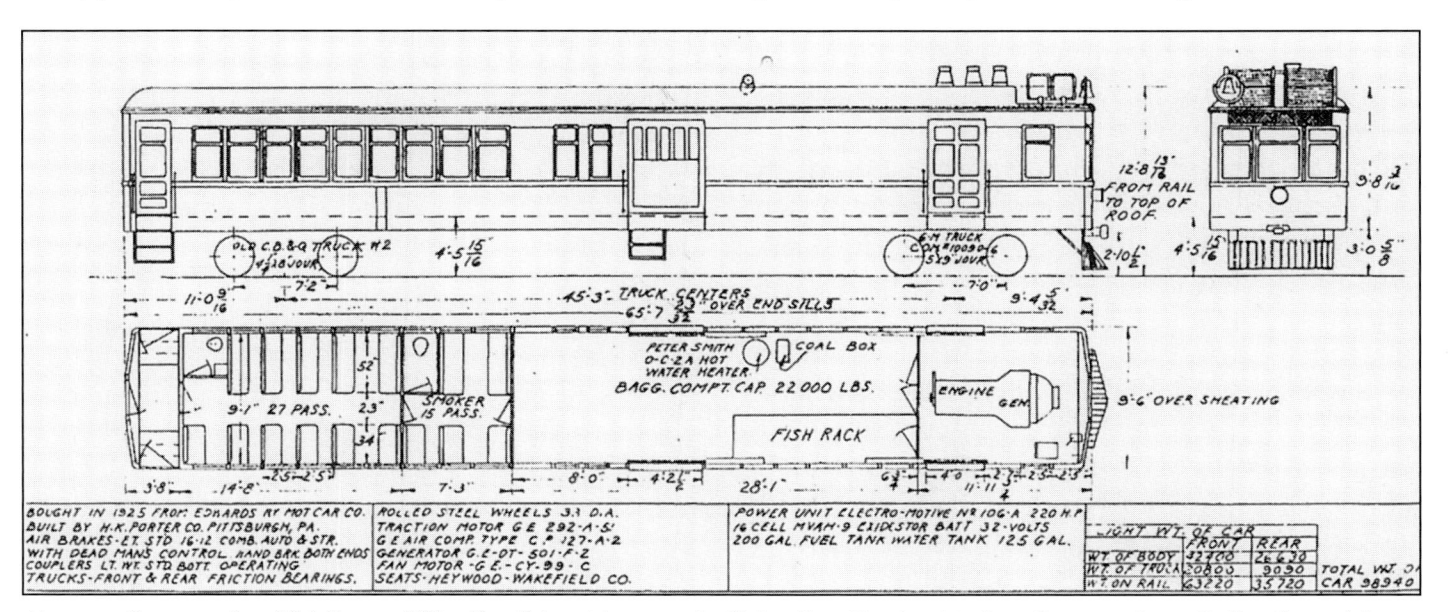

Above, diagram for CB&Q no. 552 after it had been rebuilt by the Electro-Motive Corporation. **Collection of Dave Miner**

The sale of the Edwards cars to the CB&Q was not a typical sale, as most sales were in the nature of one unit and a possibility of a second car. Such was the case with the Morehead & North Fork Railroad (M&NF) of Clearfield, Kentucky.

The Morehead and North Fork purchased a Model 20 car in 1925, and it was placed in service on July 22, 1926. As with Edwards's original plan to supplant steam with a gasoline powered, self propelled coach on the A&W, the M&NF was experiencing the same problem with spiraling steam operation costs. After placing the Edwards car in service, the auditing department conducted a cost analysis between steam operations and the gasoline motor car. The steam locomotive was costing 59 cents a mile to operate as compared to 25.8 cents a mile for the gasoline motor car, saving the shortline an estimated $6,424 yearly. Harry P. Edwards secured this information with permission from M. C. Crosley, the M&NF Auditor and Superintendent, and used the information in various advertisements and fliers. Even with the free publicity generated from the fliers, the M&NF failed to place a subsequent order. As with many shortlines, they were very satisfied with the product, but they simply didn't need another unit for the limited amount of passenger traffic the railroad carried.

The purchase cost for the M&NF unit was a testimony to Harry P. Edwards in that he would go as far as financing a sale in order to land the deal. The original cost for the M&NF unit was $15,033, and an initial down payment of $3,759 was made on the unit. The railroad then paid thirty-six monthly notes of $315.15 until the balance was paid off.

Interestingly, this very car survives today on the Sierra Railroad operated "Skunk Train" (the former California Western) now a tourist line out of Ft. Bragg, California. Purchased from the Morehead & North Fork in 1936, the car is now numbered M-100 and has been extensively modified from its original appearance and has been lengthened to carry a total of fifty-six passengers on excursion trips.

Morehead & North Fork no. 200, a Model 20. In order to facilitate sales, Edwards often allowed the purchasing railroad to pay in installments. The M&NF paid $315.15 a month until the note was paid off. No. 200 was later sold to the California Western. **Collection of the author.**

Expanding Latin American market

While the CB&Q represented a railroad which placed multiple orders, but eventually went elsewhere for additional units, the Morehead & North Fork placed one order, but was satisfied with the product; the Panama Railroad represented a third type of customer for the ERwyMCC: a customer who placed multiple orders over an extended period of time.

The Panama Railroad began construction in 1849 and completed in 1855 after battling several serious obstacles, including the diseases that brought death to large numbers of construction workers. Malaria and yellow fever were thought to have killed thousands of people in the area. The Panama Railroad was one of the rare jewels in the investment area of railroads when, between 1855 and 1898, it showed a net profit of five times the original cost of its construction.

In 1904, the United States Government purchased the entire capital stock of the railroad for seven million dollars. An additional nine million dollars was spent in relocating the roadbed and making overall improvements on the line. Within ten years, the line had achieved such profitability that the entire sixteen million dollar amount used to purchase the line and finance the rehabilitation was repaid.

The railroad had forty-seven miles of main line track running east to west through the Isthmus of Panama and ninety-five miles of branch-line track. The line was as thoroughly modern as its American cousins, was well ballasted, and was controlled by electric block signals.

The Panama Railroad placed its first order for ERwyMCC cars in 1927 and made additional purchases in 1928, 1936, and 1938. This allowed the Panama Railroad to become an all Edwards fleet in respect to its passenger service. The railroad management conducted extensive trails on no. 5, an Edwards Model 20 motor car. On one particular test conducted on August 6, 1936, the car carried forty-two passengers and averaged seven miles per gallon of gasoline over a 92.52 mile run, averaging forty-two miles per hour.

The repeat orders from the Panama Railroad were received over Harry P. Edwards's two periods of tenure: the first during the 1920s, the second during late 1930s. Connections with Central American countries helped Harry Edwards during other times over his railroad career. It was directly through his contacts with Minor C. Keith of the United Fruit Company, that he became vice president and general manager of the Atlanta & St. Andrews Bay Railway of Panama City, Florida, which Keith owned. During Edwards's second tenure at the ERwyMCC, he renewed his Central and South American ties and sold the majority of his products to foreign countries. It is known that the Panama Railroad, though a loyal Edwards customer, did shop elsewhere at times. At the time of the 1938 order, which produced the streamlined no. 6 and matching no. 6A trailer,

One can almost hear "all aboard" in Spanish as the conductor rounds up riders in this Model 21 Edwards car **(top left)**. The location is the depot at Panama City, Panama. The Panama Railroad was an all Edwards line. The railway ordered its Edwards cars in two batches, the first in 1928 and the second in 1938. The line preferred ordering the cars with the open vestibule, as seen with no. 10 **(top right)**, a Model 10 from 1928. A Model 21 with a matching trailer **(middle right)** dates from the 1938 order. Later in its service the railroad installed a much larger grill on the front of the unit. Rapid City, Black Hills & Western no. 5, a Model 10, is shown with matching trailer (right). The car was destroyed by fire in 1947 and the line shut down one year later. *Top left, collection of the Edwards Rail Car Co. Top right, collection of John D. Porter. Middle right & right, author's collection.*

Budd was also competing for the order. Budd's proposal was to build a "Zephyr" looking motor car, but the Panama Railroad remained loyal and stayed an "all Edwards" fleet.

As for domestic sales, many shortlines pinned their hopes of survival on cutting costs, which amounted to finding alternatives to steam propulsion. One hard scrabble railroad, the Rapid City, Black Hills & Western, better known as the Rapid Canyon Line, bet its survival on two Edwards cars. The addition of the Edwards cars allowed the railroad to focus the use of the steam locomotives for freight service, which primarily served the mining and timber industries. The railroad operated over thirty-four miles of track, but traversed only nineteen and one-half miles as the crow flew. The curvature of the track was so severe, it is said that, if relaid it could have made fourteen complete circles.

The two units purchased were both Model 10s, but quite different from each other. No. 5 was a typical unit, which seated twenty-eight passengers, but no. 6 had a large baggage compartment, which was used to haul in prospecting supplies for the local gold miners. The line struggled, being largely unprofitable until its demise in 1948. Both units were

The Argentine Railways Ferrocarriles del Estado purchased a Model 10 in 1925 **(top)** and later purchased two Model 20s in 1928. The units served for years as a shuttle between the cities of Cordoba and Cruz del Eje and Cosquin. No. 2700 of the Ferrocarriles Nacionales de Colombia **(middle)** was originally built as a Fast Freight unit for the Tranvia de Oriente de Medellin and then sold to the Ferrocarril de Girardot in 1931. There the unit was numbered 705, later it became no. 700 and even later no. 2700 when it served as a special car for the general manager. Two Tranvia de Oriente de Medellin freight motor cars were rebuilt into standard passenger carrying units **(left)** by the Ferrocarril de Girandot in 1931. *Top, collection of the Edwards Rail Car Co. Middle & left, collection of Gustavo Arias.*

semi permanently coupled to a coach in order to maximize passenger service. No. 5 burned in 1947, a harbinger of the shutdown of the line which occurred less than a year later.

While the Edwards motor car had proven the cost efficiencies of gasoline internal combustion engines over steam, it appeared to be losing out to other rapidly developing forms of self propelled motor cars. Correspondence during the early 1920s showed a tremendous amount of interest in the Edwards product, but many potential deals were never completed. A few examples would include the prospect of a one hundred thousand dollar order from the government of Brazil. The Southern Railway negotiated in the early 1920s for the prospect of building six cars for a total order of ninety thousand dollars.

Interest from foreign governments continued to filter in from Cuba and Canada and as far away as France and Australia. Our neighbor to the south, Mexico, eventually ordered a few cars for the National Railway of Mexico, although there were initial discussions of building sixty to one hundred cars.

After building no. 500 for the CB&Q, Harry P. Edwards realized the exposed mechanical chain and sprocket drive was the weakest link in the drive mechanism. In the early 1920s, he hired a young engineer located in Washington, D.C., who had visited the plant looking for employment. This hiring would have a monumental impact on both the young man and the ERwyMCC.

The young man hired was John "Gates" Huff, who had grown up near Winston-Salem, North Carolina and attended North Carolina State College. Huff would contribute immensely to perfect the Edwards car design. One of the first tasks for Huff was to redesign the chain and sprocket drive of the cars and allow for a more solid, dependable mechanical drive. His initial power train replacement was similar to that of a modern automotive transmission in which power was transmitted from a drive shaft to a set of beveled gears, which turned the axles. Huff had previously helped design a Perley

The Chilean State Railway placed two orders for ERwyMCC cars, the first was delivered in 1926 and the second in 1936. C.M.-1 was a Model 10 which was delivered with the first batch in 1926. **Collection of the Edwards Rail Car Co.**

A. Thomas trolley car as well as a trackless trolley that Perley A. Thomas had built for Duke Power Company (serving the Piedmont Carolinas).

After a few years of perfecting the drive mechanism, Edwards applied for a U. S. patent on September 27, 1924, and it was granted as U. S. Patent no. 1,5541,092 on August 25, 1925. The issuance of the patent allowed Edwards to include the mention of the patent in subsequent advertisements to prospective customers. The official application was referred as New and Useful Improvements in Self-Propelled Vehicles, and in it he described in great detail the advantages of his power truck design. His first two paragraphs summarized the entire patent:

> The principal objective of the invention is the provision of means whereby the power plant will be included in a truck containing the wheels of the car, so that in case of break-down, or repair, the body of the car may be jacked up, the truck removed there from, and another power plant substituted.
>
> Another important object is an arrangement of parts whereby the engine comprising the power plant is mounted within the main frame carrying the bolsters which support the car body in such a manner that no shocks are transmitted to the engine, but said shocks are absorbed by springs or resilient members between the wheels and the engine or the engine frame.

Receivership & Depression

The A&W Railway, which was tied closely with the ERwyMCC, was placed in receivership on December 8, 1926. On this shortline, Edwards was able to carry out demonstrations and field test his motor cars, and since the railroad was founded by his father, he naturally had very close feelings for the railroad. Harry P. Edwards was listed as the receiver for a short time, but the company was sold at public auction and Edwards resigned that position. A year later, the ERwyMCC was placed in receivership, though Edwards remained in place as its manager. On June 30, 1927, Edwards concluded his first tenure with the company by announcing his resignation. It would appear that lightning had struck again in the same place, although Edwards used his ERwyMCC contacts to immediately establish gainful employment. In his resignation letter, he noted the company had 252 stockholders and that the company had produced only one dividend in the previous four years.

He further mentioned in his resignation letter that his cars were competing directly against 570 similar cars made by the competition, which included at least fifteen different manufacturers. He elaborated on just how stiff some of the competition had become. Despite this, the ERwyMCC was second only to the J. G. Brill Company of Philadelphia in the volume of cars produced. He mentioned in his correspondence that Brill had thirteen million in capital and was owned by the American Car & Foundry Company, which had capital in excess of fifty million dollars. He made the point, however, that one of the company's cars had completed twenty-seven thousand miles of service without the expenditure of a single cent for maintenance.

Hampton & Branchville no. 200 was a Model 20 built in 1926, which ran in regular passenger service until suffering a catastrophic engine failure on November 6, 1951. The car is preserved at the North Carolina Transportation Museum and represents one of the best preserved ERwyMCC cars in its original configuration. **Collection of John D. Porter**

The Edwards crew poses for a group photograph. Two of the most notable people are: Gates Huff the chief draftsman, who designed much of the Edwards equipment, on the far left; and Mike Newlin, chief salesman, with the white hat in hand. Newlin was responsible for promoting the ERwyMCC product both domestically and worldwide. **Collection of John D. Porter**

In his later years, Edwards remembered the men and women who made such an impact on the American railroad industry:

Mr. Zimmerman, general sales manager
R. D. Deadrick, salesman
C. E. McIllreevy, salesman; Chicago
D. B. Worth, engineer
Mr. Baker, engineer
Mr. Barber, engineer
M. H. Newland, sales engineer
Mr. Foster, Kelly-Springfield engineer
John Gates Huff, draftsman
Miss Pattie Cross, draftsman
Mathews Heflin, stock salesman
O. T. Brown, shop foreman
Lewis Oliver, shop foreman
J. M. Edwards, bookkeeper
Argus Wilks, production manager
Mr. Busbee, foreman woodworking shop
Joe Busbee, storekeeper
Neil Harrington, mechanic
John Caswin, mechanic
Reid Moffitt, mechanic
E. H. Harmon, mechanic
C. K. Down, mechanic
Mr. McRay, mechanic
Phil Cross, mechanic
Worth Moffitt, mechanic
Joe Brown, mechanic
Bernice Cox, carpenter
Edgar McNeil, carpenter
E. H. Caviness, carpenter
Lewis Yow, painter
Mr. Harman, night watchman
Turner Hight, helper
Gilliam Glisson, truck driver & helper
J.M. Yoder, Mechanic

In concluding the resignation letter, Edwards sounded part preacher and part cheerleader while he touted the good fight and the reliability for which his product had become known. He made mention of the fact that the International Motor Truck Company had expended a half million dollars in experimental work on their version of a motor car, while the ERwyMCC had spent only a few thousand for research and development, yet produced a far superior product. Harry P. Edwards left to become vice president and general manager of the Atlanta & St. Andrews Bay Railway, based out of Panama City, Florida. His departure also spelled a major slow down of production for the ERwyMCC, from 1927 through 1935.

With his departure, production dwindled even before the Depression hit. Prior to his departure, however, Edwards had put in place a very loyal and skilled workforce that struggled on for the next few years. Gates Huff, who would have a long time association with the ERwyMCC, helped chronicle the plant after Edwards's departure. During an interview in 1970, he recalled that a skeleton staff was kept on during the Depression, when normal staffing levels would have been approximately thirty employees. Sometimes Huff found himself the only person to report to work for several days at a stretch. Often the plant was so low on cash that heating had to be curtailed and Huff often had to wear his overcoat in the office. As a long time bachelor, Huff remained with the company and eventually retired in 1966 from Saco-Lowell, a company which had taken over the manufacturing facility of the ERwyMCC. Huff had also worked as a consultant for Harry P. Edwards when Edwards was general manager of the Atlantic & East Carolina Railway (A&EC). Huff's job was to draw up the blueprints for a transfer table to be used with the newly purchased diesel locomotives that would soon appear on the railroad.

Huff was well known for his mechanical ability and was also a skilled metal worker. During the Depression a local moonshine maker hired Huff to construct a still. After the still was finished and put to use, it was discovered by the Local (Lee) County sheriff's department. The sheriff so admired how well built the still was that he brought it back to the courthouse and put it on display. Huff heard the story and went down to the courthouse to see if it was the one he had designed. While he was in the courthouse admiring his own handiwork, he overheard the sheriff say to another visitor, "Whoever made that still did some good work."

Among currently available information on the Edwards Railway Motor Car Company, blueprints seemed to be conspicuously absent. During the Depression, the white linen cloth they were printed on was bleached and turned into tablecloths, curtains and napkins; this was the only means by which the families of Sanford could afford these luxuries.

The company entered into receivership again in 1930 and once more in 1934. During 1935, the ERwyMCC slowly emerged from the Depression and began to receive a limited number of orders, primarily from Central and South America. In reviewing the production roster, it should be noted that only ten motor cars were produced. However, the distinctive shovelnose or streamlined look which would be a characteristic of future Edwards motor cars was developed at this time. There is some thought that this distinctive look was developed by Gates Huff.

Ferrocarril de Girardot no. 709, a Model 25, makes a scheduled stop at the la Esperanza Hotel in Colombia. The car is traveling in reverse as it navigates through the only switchback located in Colombia. **Collection of Gustavo Arias.**

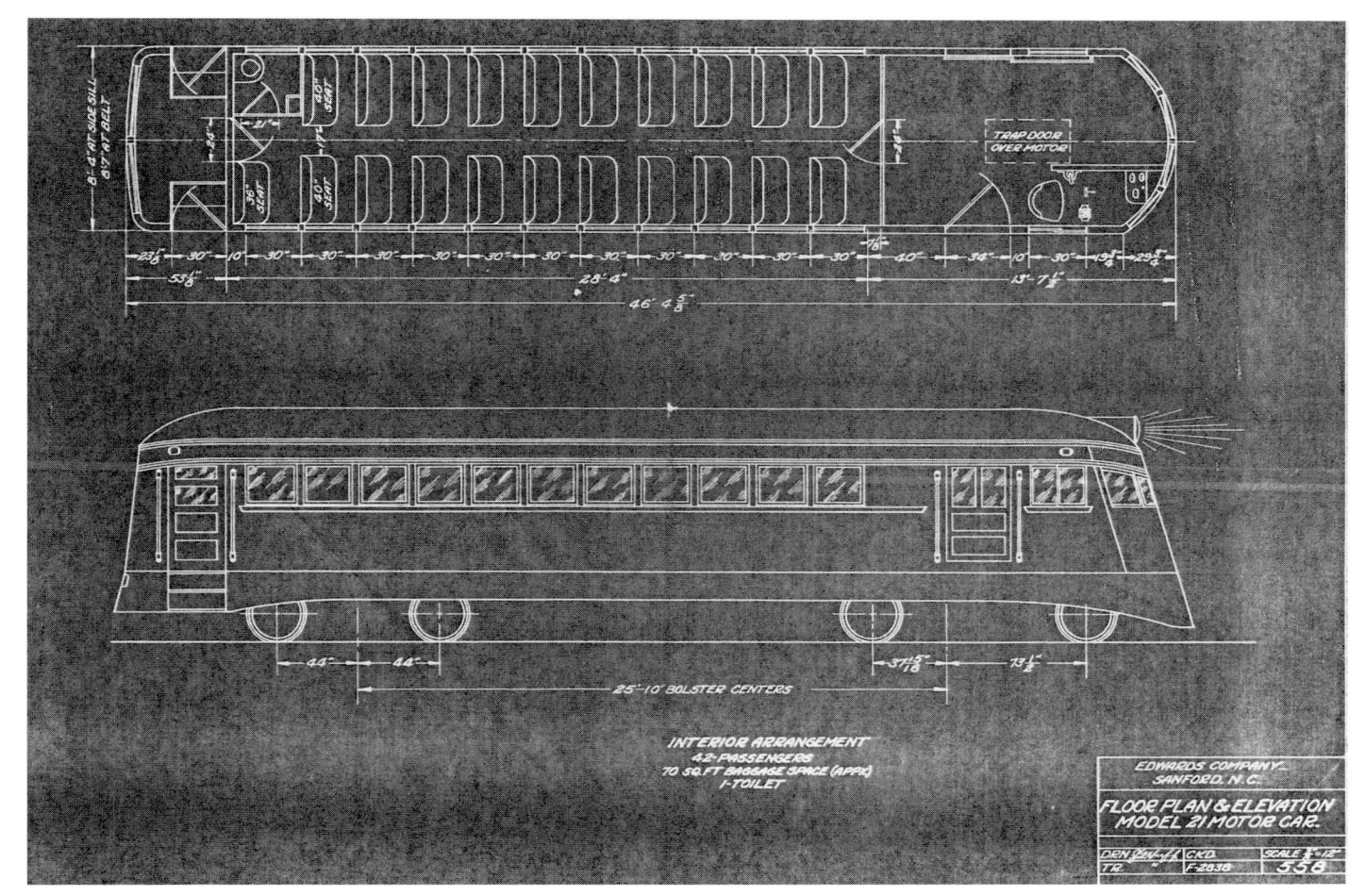

Edwards Returns

Harry P. Edwards rejoined the company in 1937 as vice president for sales, and again became its biggest proponent and salesman. Unlike during his first tenure with the ERwyMCC when most cars were sold domestically, upon his return, Edwards built upon the trend his company had taken and focused his attention south of the boarder. Edwards had developed and cultivated markets in Central and South America during his time at the Atlanta & St. Andrews Bay Railway, and had many contacts through the United Fruit Company and Minor C. Keith (see chapter four). Developing countries in these areas were behind the U.S. in their highway infrastructure and naturally turned to railroads to provide mass transportation for their citizens. Edwards also felt these regions were less

Floor plans for a Model 21 **(top)** capable of hauling forty-two passengers. The Model 21 began the shovelnosed appearance, which was characteristic of the units constructed during Edwards's second tenure with what was now becoming known as the "Edwards Company." Ferrocarriles Nacionales de Pacifico no. 707 **(above)**, a Model 10, poses for its builder's photo at the Edwards shops in 1938. The unit was owned by Ferrocarril de Girardot which operated a 36" (914 mm) line in Colombia. *Top, collection of the Author. Above, collection of John D. Porter.*

Overleaf - Ferrocarriles Nacionales de Colombia's no. 704 **(top)**, a Model 10 poses at Bucaramanga depot. This postcard suggests that no. 704 ran until at least 1965. Panama Railroad no. 5 **(bottom)**, a streamlined Model 20, was the first for the railroad and was built in 1935. It was constructed with an open platform on the rear end. The unit survived until 1967 when it was scrapped. *Top, collection of Gustavo Arias. Bottom, collection of Robert Richardson.*

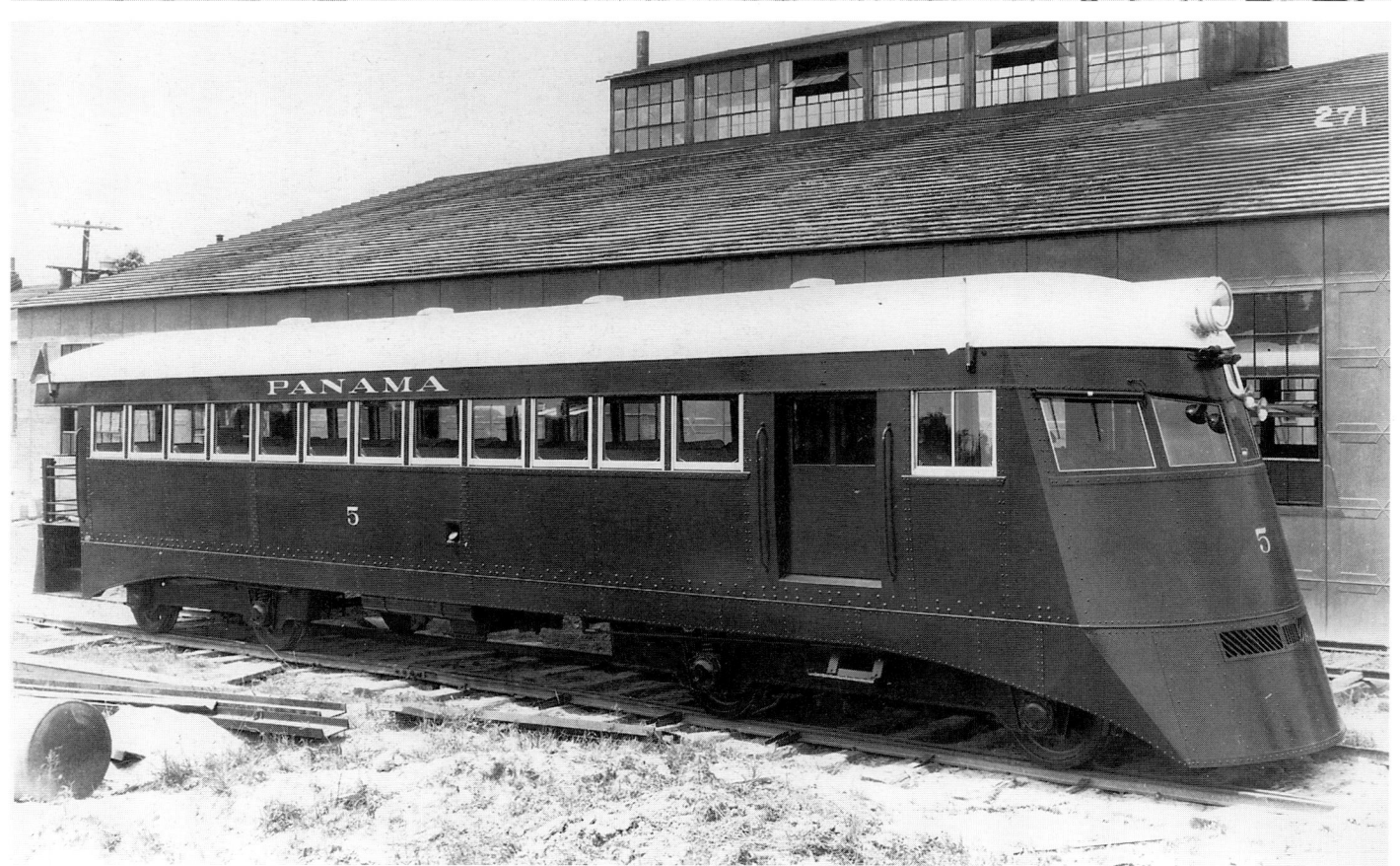

Bucaramanga - Barranca 1965

WARDS RAI
MOTOR CA
200

FERROCARRILES DEL ESTADO
214

FERROCARRILES NACIONALES
CENTRAL DEL NORTE-SECCION 1ª
704

impacted by the Great Depression and therefore could better afford his motor cars. During his first tenure with the ERwyMCC, Edwards had pressed his marketing abilities directly with railroad officers. With the bulk of the sales going overseas during his second tenure with the company, Edwards had to contend with governmental decrees; or at the very least, the sales had to meet with the approval of the host country. Undoubtedly, Edwards's contacts through Minor C. Keith cannot be underestimated in his navigation through foreign bureaucracies.

One problem which kept Edwards from cracking the American market was the lack of a hybrid motor car. EMC had lead the way with a gasoline-electric hybrid, which was finding a much more solid following than the direct mechanical drive that Edwards offered. The CB&Q had clearly demonstrated the superiority of the gasoline-electric car when it rebuilt at least one Edwards car into such a format. South and Central American countries, on the other hand, were much more capable of working on the mechanical drive of an Edwards car than a gasoline-electric drive. In many ways, other competitors had far outstripped the Edwards Company in keeping up with emerging technologies, but Edwards countered by finding available markets which needed less complicated mechanical drives, yet, at the same time, durable motor cars.

During Edward's second tenure at the ERwyMCC, approximately twenty-one cars were constructed, all streamlined in some fashion with the very distinguished shovelnose appearance of the front end of the units. Of the twenty-one, four went to the U.S. Navy and the rest were sold to countries

Panama Railroad no. 6, **(above)**, a Model 21, is shown uncoupled from its trailer. The photograph was taken circa 1955, approximately twenty years after entering service for the railroad. ***Collection of Louis A. Marre.***

Overleaf - The ERwyMCC built a demonstrator, no. 200 **(top)**, to show off to possible clients. The car was a streamlined Model 10, which sold mostly to Central and South American clients. Brand new Ferrocarriles del Estado (Chile), no. R-t1 **(middle)** poses for its builder's photograph in Sanford. R-t1 was a Model 10 LMG with dual Buda motors and weighed 30 1/2 tons. Ferrocarriles Nacionales Central del Norte (Colombia) no. 704 **(bottom)** poses for its builder's photograph in 1938 outside the Edwards plant. ***Top & bottom, collection of John D. Porter. Middle, collection of Robert Richardson.***

Edwards found a small amount of business with the U.S. military services during the late 1930s. The Model 25 demonstrator unit seen on the top of page 73 was sold to the Navy and was assigned to the Dahlgreen Proving Grounds. It can be seen sporting its new paint job on the ERwyMCC transfer table **(right)**. The building to the right of the unit is the old machine shop for constructing small cars. A different angle from the same photo session is seen **below**. U.S. Army no. P-40-1 **(bottom)**, a Model 10, was the first of four cars built for the Army for service on a military base in Newfoundland, Canada. Two of the four units were lost when a German U-boat sank the transport they were shipped on. *Right & below, collection of Marvin Black. Bottom, collection of John D. Porter.*

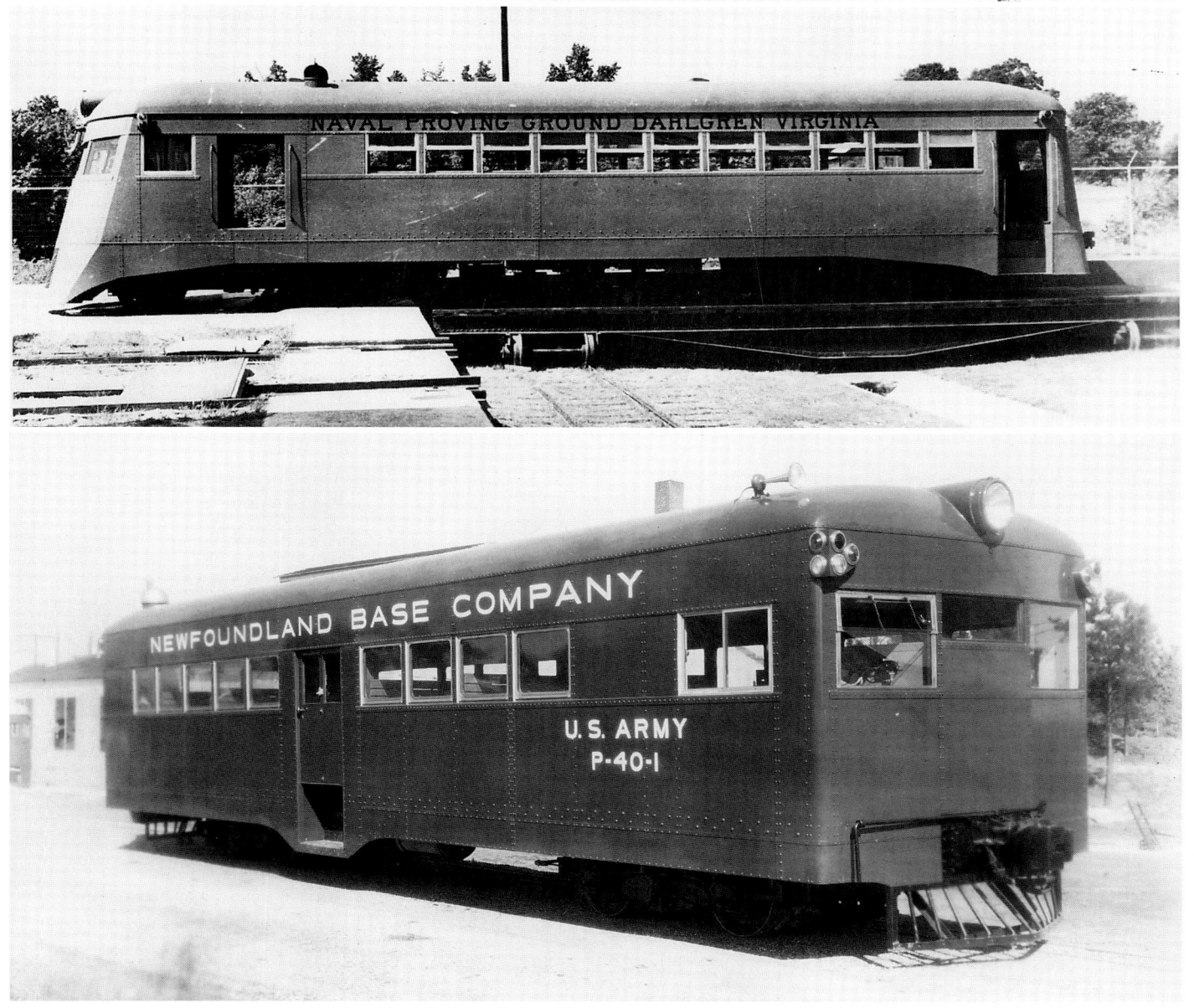

75

south of the border. There is a slight mystery surrounding some of the cars that went to the military. The Navy purchased the original demonstrator model and it went to the Dahlgren Proving Grounds, a Navy testing site in Virginia, and was largely out of sight of the public. Two of these streamlined, shovelnosed cars served for a time at Fort Pepperrell, a large U.S. military base at St. Johns, Newfoundland, Canada, before making their way to the Alaska Railroad. There is a strong belief that a total of four of these cars may have been ordered for the military (as well as the demonstrator model). It is thought that two never made their final destination as they went down with a cargo ship sunk by a German U-boat after the declaration of war. The construction of the last four cars fully depleted any left over materials used in car manufacturing (as raw materials were rationed for the war effort).

Unlike his previous business dealings, Edwards's relationship with the A&W Railway was now civil at best. Previously, when he controlled both the A&W and the ERwyMCC, there was a sense of cooperation between the two companies. During his second tenure, Edwards found himself as just another customer who needed to request permission to test new motor cars on the A&W tracks. At this time, the A&W went in search of a new motor car, but apparently could not arrive at a price satisfactory to both companies and ended up purchasing a Brill car, a direct competitor to the ERwyMCC.

Some believe the high tide of the ERwyMCC occurred from 1937 through 1939 under his direction. While the volume of production was not as great as in the mid 1920s, the product that came out of the plant in Sanford was a work of beauty and reliability. The majority of sales to South and Central American countries could be classified as group sales, usually in two-, three-, or four-car orders.

Edwards motor cars were viewed as extremely dependable pieces of railroad equipment. On more than one occasion, a railroad administrator would write to Edwards regarding the success of his equipment. For example, M. Allarino, general superintendent of the Ferrocarril Nacional de Chiriqui, wrote thus of his pleasure in the performance of one car:

It is with great pleasure I inform you that the first of the three which you are building for us has been received and a test was made on our Boqut run which as you know is our most difficult section, and has a grade of 5% for a distance of 25 kilometers. This test was carried out with astonishing success being the first motor car to go up that grade at a speed of 25 miles per hour and without over heating the engine. Let me congratulate you for this master piece, as I am sure no other car built can ever give such a performance.

Edwards units were highly regarded by the FNdeC. Though numbered 11 at the Sanford shops **(top)**, this unit was renumbered to either 100 or 101 when it arrived in Panama. The unit is unique in that it is a Model 10 with a Model 20 radiator mounted on the roof. The FNdeC purchased several coaches from the ERwyMCC, including this front and rear vestibule coach **(above)**. *Top, collection of John D. Porter. Above, collection of Billy Page.*

United Fruit Company no. 150 (renumbered 1150) was a Model 25 built in 1938. The car served as an inspection car and as a private car for management. It came complete with its own stateroom and galley **(middle left & right)**. The car survives today in Guatemala. The rear end of no. 150 can be seen peeking out from the ERwyMCC plant **(top left)**. The unit is narrow gauge; note various gauge of track on the plant floor. Still looking shiny and new **(top right)**, and by now renumbered 1150, the unit is seen at Guatemala City in April 1952. *Top left, collection of John D. Porter. Top right, collection of Louis A. Marre. Middle left & right, collection of the Edwards Rail Car Co. Above, collection of W.J. Edwards.*

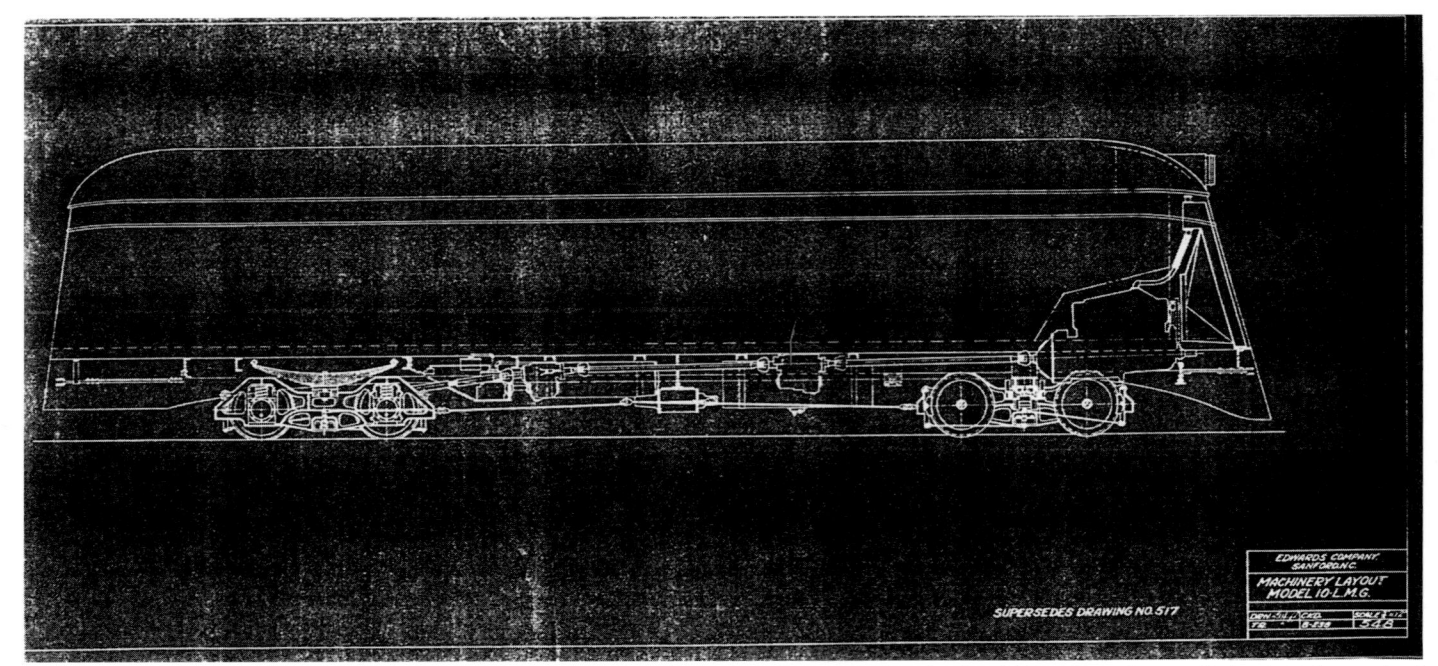

Mechanical drawing showing the layout of a Model 10 LMG unit. Most, if not all, of the shovelnosed Model 10s ended up in either Central America or South America. **Collection of the author.**

Harry P. Edwards left ERwyMCC in 1939, never to return to employment with the company. On September 1, 1939, North Carolina awarded him control of the Atlantic & North Carolina Railroad (A&NC), which he promptly renamed the Atlantic & East Carolina Railway. Many might question why Edwards went back to railroad management, but all speculation could be quelled with a simple statement: he was always a railroad man. Being in the close vicinity of the A&NC Railroad, he would surely have known that it was always operating in the red and the current operators were not willing to plow any capital back into the system. As he had done with other ventures, Edwards made the A&EC a family operation with his wife, sister-in-law, and both sons working for him. In addition to family, he also employed a number of former ERwyMCC employees, including Gates Huff at various times.

One of the last cars attributed to Harry P. Edwards's management was built for the United Fruit Company of Guatemala in 1939. The car was intended to be used as a private inspection car for the line. The car in many ways was well ahead of its time and represented the zenith of ERwyMCC construction. The car was equipped with air conditioning, which was quite a luxury, and seldom seen at the time even on American railroads. The car also carried a galley and stateroom. This sale was a direct result of Edwards's business contacts with the United Fruit Company. At this writing, the car survives and is awaiting preservation.

It is known that the plant in Sanford produced a limited number of boxcars. While no exact numbers are known, it is speculated that the cars were built for nearby shortlines and represented only a small percentage of the overall production from the facility. One surviving photograph shows what appears to be a narrow-gauge Sumter & Choctaw Railroad boxcar loaded onto a standard-gauge flatcar. A sign proudly proclaims: "Built By Edwards Motor Car Co. Sanford, NC."

Several railroad researchers have investigated the possibility that the Edwards Railway Motor Car Company produced a builder's number list or a comparable means of tracking the production. This writer could find no direct evidence of a list. There is, however, a reference by the Panama Railroad in which an extensive cost analysis was conducted on a particular Edwards car. In the cost analysis comparison, the Panama Railroad refers to this car as Edwards car number 185. Even though the car was built later in ERwyMCC production, the number is much higher than any total known number of Edwards motor cars to have been built.

What If?

Before Edwards returned to the ERwyMCC in 1937, he had developed a prospectus and business plan for starting a new rail car company using options he held on the Sanford plant and his own patents for ERwyMCC cars. He proposed moving the plant and manufacturing to Birmingham, Alabama. This prospectus was drafted and submitted on January 10, 1933, four years before he returned to employment with the ERwyMCC. As part of the prospectus, Edwards outlined why and how he thought the plan would work and become prosperous.

For the data in his prospectus, Edwards once again compared the operating cost of a motor car to a steam passenger train. He had crunched the numbers per mile for a light steam locomotive at $.55 cents to a high end of $1.50 for a larger locomotive. The cost of operating a gasoline railway passenger motor car varied from only $.12 to $.35 cents per train mile, depending on the size of the cars, whether or not trailers were used and the condition the of the roadbed.

Edwards further submitted to investors that:

[T]ravel in a motorcar is more comfortable, as they are quiet, clean, and smoke and cinders are eliminated. Motorcars will not require as much track maintenance as large heavy steam trains. They eliminate fire claims, expensive service at terminals such as cinder removal, making and banking fires in locomotives, boiler washing. The steam locomotive is an antiquated piece of machinery when it comes to efficiently competing with other modern methods of transportation such as the automobile, bus and aeroplane. The steam locomotive must be discarded if the railroads expect to effectively compete with highway transportation.

Edwards went on to compare his product to the Brill Company's product when he said "The design of their car however does not compare favorably with the Edwards car, and no difficulty has been encountered in making sales in competition with their cars. He pointed out that on two occasions the U.S. Government wanted gasoline railway passenger cars for operation on the Panama Canal Railway and his cars were selected in both of these purchases in competition with Brill cars.

The ERwyMCC was known to produce a limited number of box cars for regional railroads (**above**), as depicted in this undated photograph with a narrow gauge car en route to the Sumter & Choctaw. *Courtesy of the Railroad House Collection, collection of Calvin Harward.*

If the plan had succeeded, Edwards had hoped to build 100 motor cars a year with a gross value of $3,000,000 annually. In the Sales plan, Edwards outlined his proposal to lease the cars to railroads in exchange for a share of their savings over a steam passenger train. In the example given in the prospectus, Edwards used the Central of Georgia's Griffin, Georgia to Chattanooga, Tennessee route. Edwards estimated the savings at $47,661.76 per year and over a two year plan, he expected to have this sum returned to his new company. He also estimated the cost of building and transporting a rail car to come in under $30,000, so the lease operation would net $17,000 over the cost of the car for the new Edwards company.

The new company would issue 500,000 shares of common value stock. Edwards would get 75,000 shares to acquire his option on the Sanford plant and his patent rights. Another 150,000 shares were to go to the syndicate who assisted in the formation of the new company and subscribe the first capital at $1.00 a share. A third set of 25,000 shares were to go to individuals selected as "associate directors" in various cities who could be of assistance in selling cars, such as railroad officials at $3.00 per share. One hundred thousand shares were to be sold to the general public at $1.00 a share. The last 150,000 shares would be unissued and remaining in the treasury.

Edwards had hoped to raise $1,025,000 to start the new company and to finance the move to Birmingham. This particular location was chosen because it was located near several large railway systems and because of a low water rate to Mobile, Alabama, which would serve as a convenient port for exporting cars to Latin America. In addition, all of the materials needed to construct the cars could be easily obtained in the local area since Birmingham was a prosperous steel center at the time.

The plan never came to fruition and soon enough Edwards found himself back at the ERwyMCC.

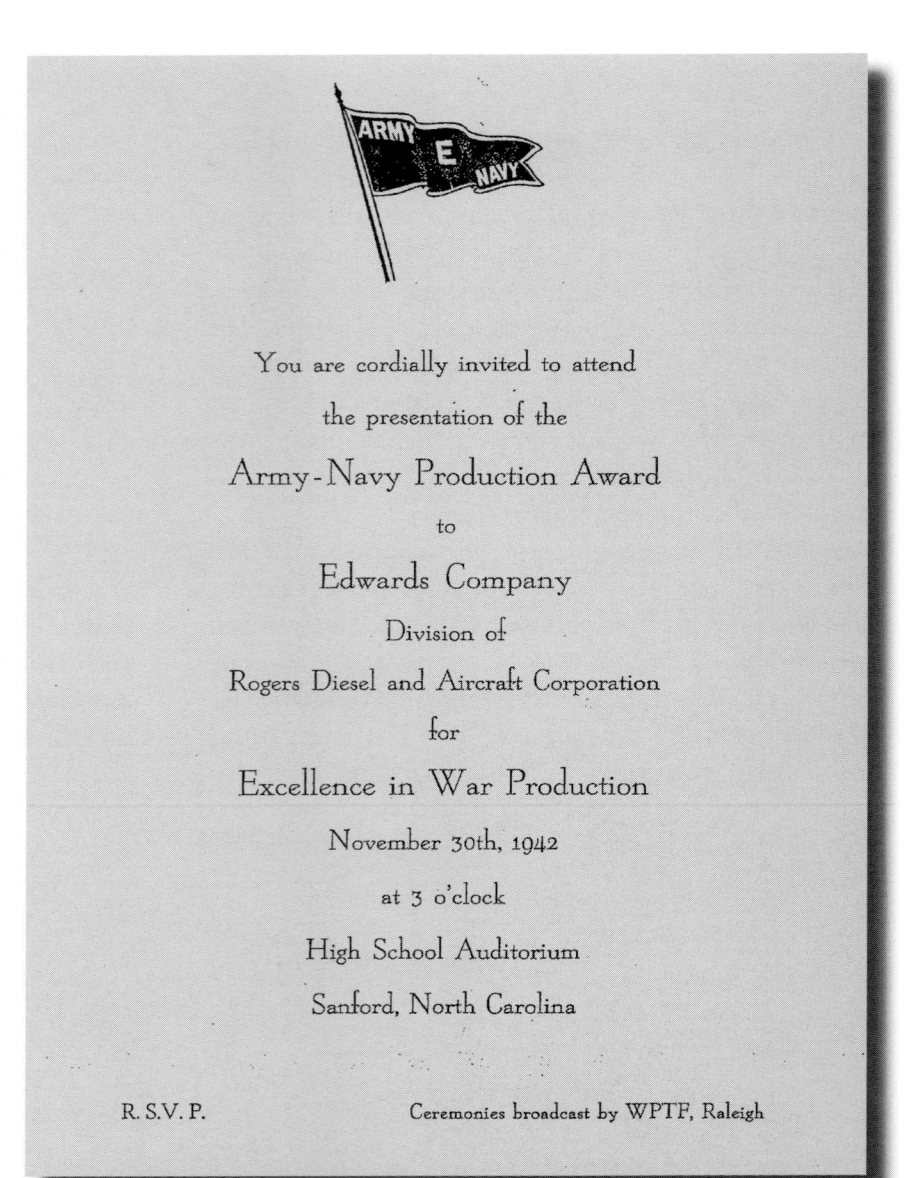

You are cordially invited to attend
the presentation of the
Army-Navy Production Award
to
Edwards Company
Division of
Rogers Diesel and Aircraft Corporation
for
Excellence in War Production
November 30th, 1942
at 3 o'clock
High School Auditorium
Sanford, North Carolina

R.S.V.P.   Ceremonies broadcast by WPTF, Raleigh

A copy of the invitation to a ceremony awarding the wartime Edwards Co. an Army-Navy production award. **Collection of the author.**

Post ERwyMCC

The ERwyMCC and its manufacturing facility would proceed through a quick succession of transformations. In 1940 the ERwyMCC was bought by Ralph B. Rogers who held a number of companies that manufactured diesel and gasoline engines. Mr. Rogers had the distinction of holding the dual title of president of the Edwards Railway Motor Car Company and of the Indian Motorcycle Company. The ERwyMCC soon became a division of the Rogers Diesel and Aircraft Corporation.

A limited number of cars was produced between 1940 and 1942. This included the four built for the U.S. military. The supply of steel had been curtailed prior to the war, which would have limited railcar production. However, with the Declaration of War by Congress on December 8, 1941, the plant quickly geared up for wartime production.

During World War II, the Edwards Company, as it was now known, reached a peak employment capacity of nine hundred employees, operating over three shifts and even reaching one thousand-one employees at one time. A full third of the employees were women, since a large number of men were away at war. In 1946, the employment was scaled back to two hundred employees, still considerably larger than the thirty or so employees of the ERwyMCC era. The Edwards Company was awarded a total of five Excellence in War Production Awards during World War II for its contributions to the war effort.

Two hundred of these machines were produced at the Sanford plant. They were used to wrap cellophane around Camel cigarette packs for the R.J. Reynolds Company. **Collection of Bill Parrish.**

The first war contract the Edwards plant was awarded was to manufacture landing gear struts and retracting gear for the British Wellington bomber. In 1942, the plant produced hydraulic cylinders for the Curtis Wright Hell Diver plane, which was a combination pursuit and light bomber plane. ("Edwards Hell Divers" was the name of the Edwards plant's baseball team, which, in 1945, had an impressive record of 18-6-1 and played visiting service teams throughout the state.)

The Edwards plant went on to produce a wide array of items used for the war effort, including hydraulics for flap controls, and landing gear struts for B-24 Liberator bombers. Landing gear parts for P-40 Tomahawks were also produced. One of the buildings was informally called the "Gun Shop," and there parts were made for Chrysler to be used in a .40 caliber gun, which was mounted in the nose of certain aircraft. Other products included rockets and rocket launch pads for the Redstone Arsenal. For the Navy, the plant produced 150 bilge pumps, which could handle fifty gallons per minute.

In addition to the aircraft parts, a limited number of parts used in the manufacturing of atomic weapons were manufactured at the plant. After the war, the R. J. Reynolds Company used the plant to manufacture cigarette cellophane wrapping machines, with approximately two hundred units being built. Also produced were dental burrs, which were openly sold to the public. This product was produced well into the thousands.

The plant produced approximately seven hundred-fifty diaphragm type shallow well pumps. The pump was a joint collaboration between Gates Huff and William F. Parrish. Another type of pump, also a collaboration between Huff and Parrish and marketed for farm use, was a rotary gear type pump powered by a one horsepower gasoline engine. Approximately three thousand of the pumps were produced during the production run.

Next came a Chenille sewing machine to stitch bedspreads. The sewing machine heads were designed to handle eight-, ten-, or twelve-stitch attachments. The heads were designed by Huff, Parrish and Tom Forbes. The plant also produced two hundred eight-inch table saws.

Later the plant manufactured New Holland farm combine and Ford tractor parts. The plant produced four thousand gear boxes for a New Holland model hay baler. The facility was sold to the Saco-Lowell Corporation in 1948 and continued its long history of manufacturing by turning out machines used in cotton mills. The Saco-Lowell Company later merged with the Platt Company to form the Platt Saco Lowell Company, which closed operations in Sanford, when the plant and machinery were purchased by Liberty Furniture in 1979. The plant has remained in sporadic operation since then.

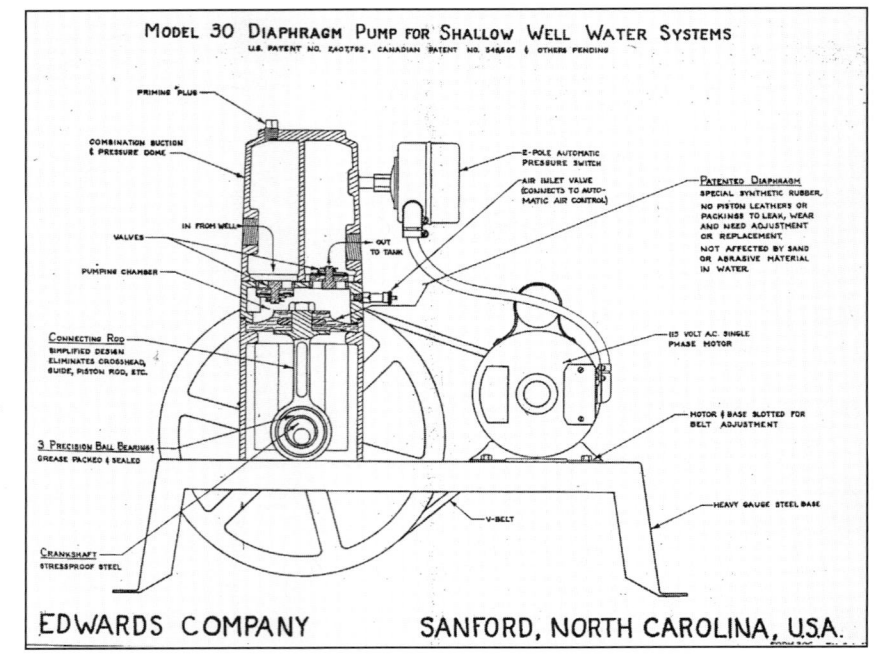

Top, plans for the Gates Huff and William F. Parrish shallow well pump. **Above**, The Saco-Lowell shop occupied the ERwyMCC plant in this 1952 era photograph. The shot is taken in the milling machine section of the plant. Note the rail still embedded in the floor. ***Top, courtesy of the Railroad House Collection, collection of Calvin Harward. Above, Collection of John D. Porter.***

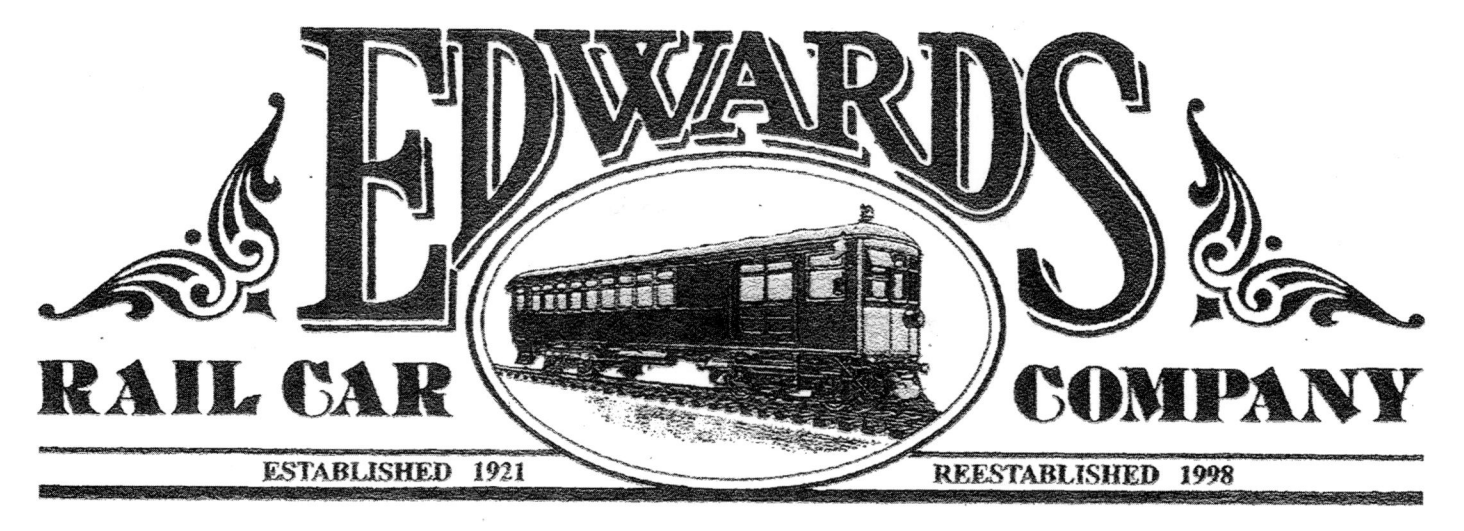

2. REBIRTH

The original Edwards Railway Motor Car Company survived through the turbulent era of the Great Depression, but by the late 1930s, the company had all but ceased production. In fact, few companies were building gasoline-powered motor cars, preferring rather to concentrate on either gas-electric drive or diesel-electric drive. These were two concepts Harry P. Edwards had not pursued to any concentrated extent, and it may have doomed the ERwyMCC in the tight market that lay ahead. The idea of a gasoline powered motor car remained dormant for several decades until 1997.

In the fall of 1997, lifelong railroader and consultant Steven Torrico saw and rode on his first Edwards car, ex-CB&Q no. 507, a Model 20 that had been refurbished by Dave Miner for his Ft. Madison, Farmington & Western Railroad (FMF&W). On this trip, Torrico was impressed with the style of the car and began an extensive research of the company to determine everything he could about the Edwards motor cars. Torrico saw an opportunity and resurrected the ERwyMCC, now calling it the Edwards Rail Car Company (ERCC) and based it out of Mt. Dora, Florida.

In 1998, the new Edwards Company contracted with Dave Miner, to build a replica of an Edwards car through his Miner Rail Services, which is a for profit outgrowth of **the FMF&W**. The FMF&W is a volunteer operated railroad, which owns two ex-CB&Q ERwyMCC Model 25s. Miner has also rebuilt some Brill cars into Edwards style cars and also works on rolling stock restoration.

For the Edwards replica car, Miner used as a base a 1928 Brill interurban car once used on the P&W (ex-Philadelphia & Western) division of Septa (Southeastern Pennsylvania Transportation Authority). Miner rebuilt the mechanical drive using an automatic transmission and a Fairmont reversing gear box (a´la Edwards), and employed the use of a jack shaft, sprockets, and chain drive. To transform the Brill car so that it would resemble an Edwards car, the front and rear ends were chopped off and look alike Edwards front and rear ends were fabricated. The new car was designed to seat forty-eight passengers.

This replica car was then sold to Bill McDonald, of Rutland, Vermont. McDonald in return leased the car to a new tourist railroad, the Mount Dora,

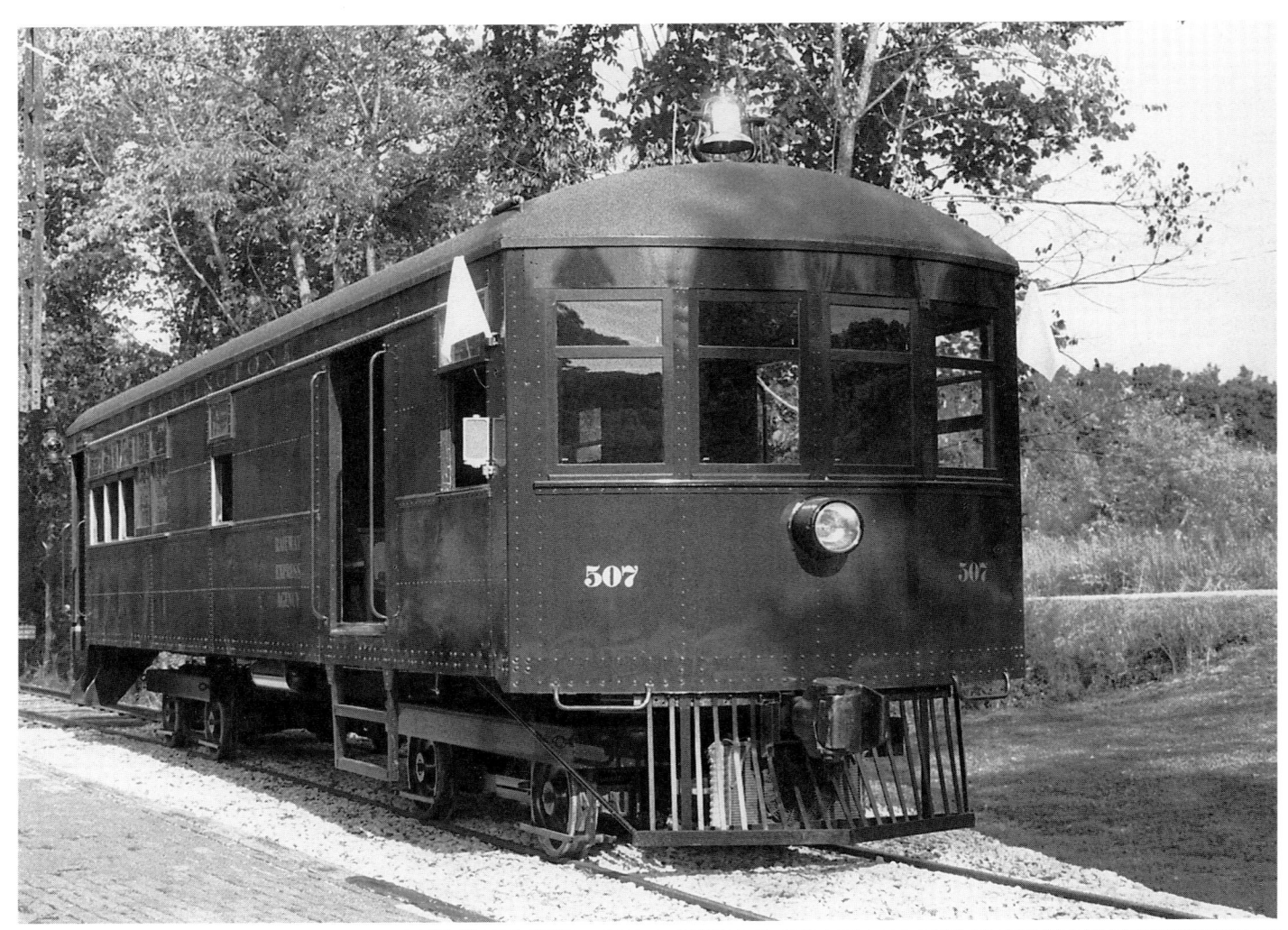

CB&Q no. 507 **(top)** is the car that first inspired Torrico to resurrect the Edwards company. No. 507 is a Model 25 built in 1926. After retirement the car was used as a private residence for fifty years before being refurbished by Dave Miner and placed in service on the Ft. Madison, Farmington & Western Railroad in Iowa. No. M 201 **(above)** is actually a former Brill car refashioned to look like an Edwards Model 20. The car operates on the Mt. Dora, Tavares & Eustis Railroad in Florida. No. M 201 was a guinea pig of sorts which led the ERCC to conclude that further production of such cars was feasible. *Top, FMF&W RR photograph, collection of Dave Miner. Above, photograph by Tom King.*

Tavares and Eustis Railroad, which now runs out of Mt. Dora, Florida. The car, numbered M-201, was placed in service on December 18, 1998, and has performed very well for the task it was intended, hauling passengers on a scenic line.

The next project for the new Edwards company was to restore an original Edwards car, which was built in 1923 for the Washington & Lincolnton Railroad, before being sold to the Birmingham & Southeastern Railroad (B&SE) in 1929. The B&SE operated the car until March 1965 when it was retired. It was purchased by Royce Kershaw and sat in Montgomery, Alabama for many years awaiting restoration. In 1999 the ERCC was hired by Mr. Kershaw to restore no. 500. Owing to the early Edwards design according to which the chassis and coach body were built as separate units, the car was sent in two pieces from Montgomery to Mount Dora. The restoration was a complete rebuild from the ground up and allowed the workers at the new ERCC to learn how early Edwards cars were constructed.

Much like the original Edwards Motor Car Company, which farmed out car construction and major components in the beginning, so did the new ERCC. This didn't last long as it was soon determined by Torrico that a shop and regular crew were needed in order to facilitate all work and restoration "in house." Local Mount Dora carpenter Rick Hansen became the project manager for the no. 500 project, and all subsequent projects, and was the individual largely responsible for the entire restoration of B&SE no. 500

Upon arrival of the car to Mount Dora, all remaining wood was removed and certain pieces were saved in order to make copies. As received, no. 500 was missing the entire front end and rear platform. These were fabricated using photographic evidence. The seats were

B&SE no. 500 in various stages of reconstruction at the Edwards Railcar Company shop in Mt. Dora. **All photos by Steven Torrico.**

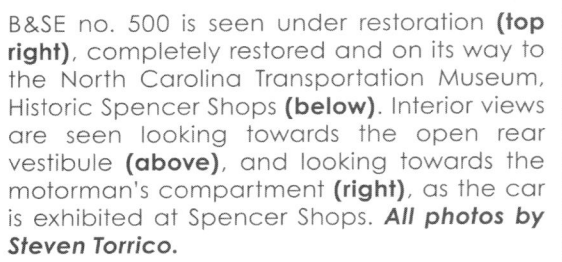

B&SE no. 500 is seen under restoration **(top right)**, completely restored and on its way to the North Carolina Transportation Museum, Historic Spencer Shops **(below)**. Interior views are seen looking towards the open rear vestibule **(above)**, and looking towards the motorman's compartment **(right)**, as the car is exhibited at Spencer Shops. *All photos by Steven Torrico.*

also fabricated from scratch using photographs of the originals. Upon the completion of the restoration, in the spring of 2004, no. 500 was transported to the North Carolina Transportation Museum's Historic Spencer Shops to participate in its annual "Rail Days" event. The Spencer Shops are also home to an original 1926 Edwards Model 20, Hampton & Branchville's (H&B) M-200. B&SE no. 500 stands today as the oldest operating example of an original Edwards rail car.

In the fall of 2000 the ERCC was engaged to build a forty-eight seat passenger car from the ground up. It was to be a modified hybrid Model 25, which had one engine, but applied power to both trucks. This car was built for the West Virginia Central Railroad (WVC). The car has a diesel engine and a mechanical drive supplying power to both front and rear trucks, with the engine mounted in the car frame, similar to an original Model 10. The steel frame of the car was built according to historic Edwards blueprints and mechanical drawings. The ERCC contracted with Irwin Car & Equipment for the construction of the trucks. The car was delivered in June, 2001 to operate as the Cheat Mountain Salamander and is numbered M-3. It should be noted that this is the first actual Edwards car built from scratch since 1940-1942.

In 2001, the ERCC was awarded a contract to restore the 1924 streetcar no. 754 for the McKinney Avenue Transit Authority (MATA) in Dallas, Texas. As of 2005 work is still in progress. An Edwards restoration can take some time to complete as all work is done by hand to the highest of standards. "Historically the Edwards Company has an outstanding reputation in the construction of reliable rail cars" writes John Landrum, chief operating officer at MATA "The re-founded firm is carrying on with the traditions of fine craftsmanship and workmanship associated with the name Harry P. Edwards. We here at MATA are excited to have

B&SE no. 500 can be seen in the final stages of restoration to the left and West Virginia Central no. M-3 is seen to the right in the early stages of construction. *Photograph by Steven Torrico.*

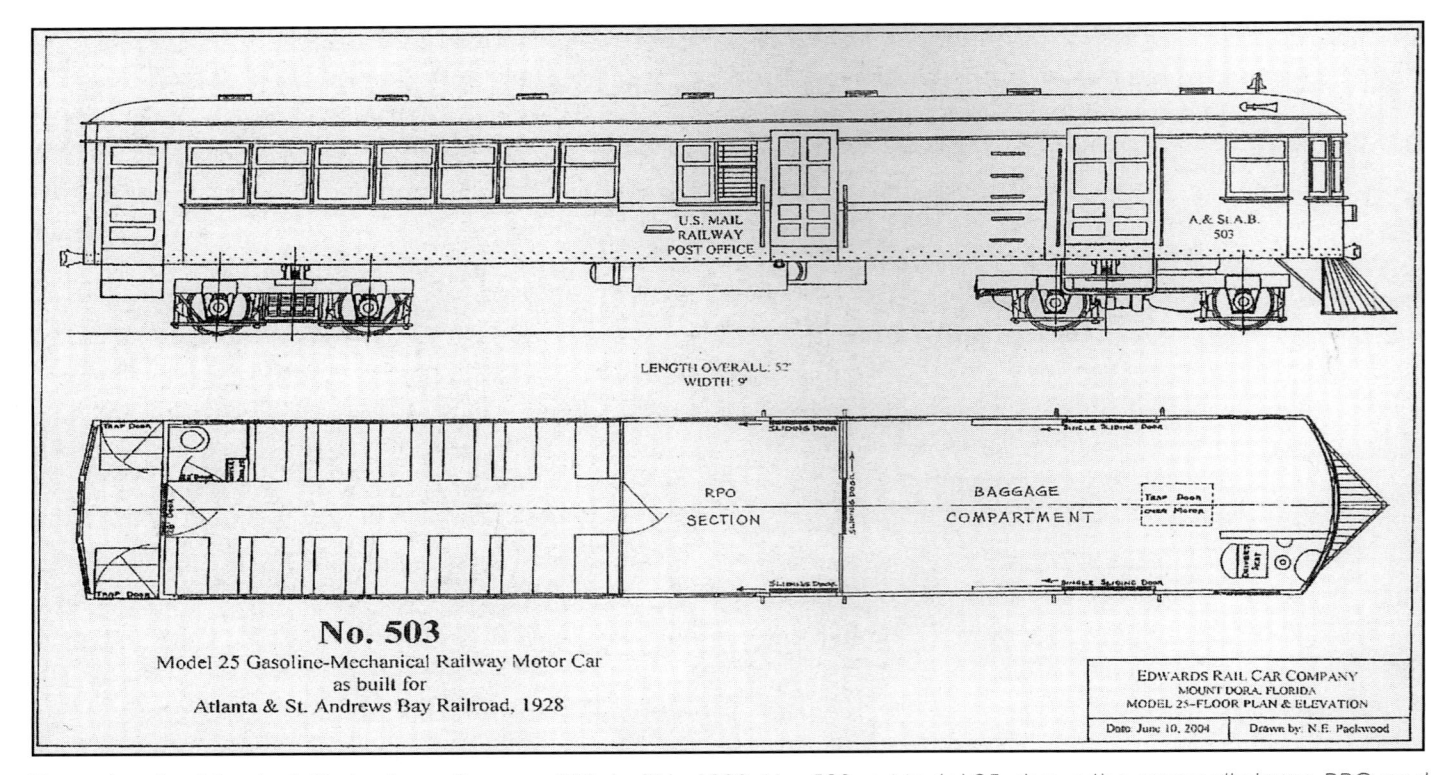

No. 503
Model 25 Gasoline-Mechanical Railway Motor Car
as built for
Atlanta & St. Andrews Bay Railroad, 1928

Floor plan for Atlanta & St. Andrews Bay, no. 503, built in 1928. No. 503, a Model 25, shows the unusually large RPO and baggage compartment. The car was eventually sold to the Tallulah Falls Railroad and the RPO compartment was removed. No. 503 awaits restoration by the ERCC. **Collection of the Edwards Rail Car Co..**

our car restored by the folks at Edwards." When completed, no. 754 will return to the streets of Dallas and operate once again in daily service as a streetcar propelled by electricity from an overhead wire.

In 1928 the Atlanta & St. Andrews Bay Railway purchased no. 503, a Model 25 from the ERwyMCC. This car was unique, having been built with a passenger section, baggage compartment, and an RPO section complete with mail hook and a mail slot for walk-up repository of letter mail. No. 503 was sold to the Tallulah Falls Railway in the late 1930s and renumbered 201. It was extensively re configured by the removal of the passenger section and the addition of another pair of baggage doors. The passenger section was not needed, for the car was to be used for freight, mail, and express service. When the railroad shut down in 1964 the car body was sold to a resident of Clayton, Georgia, where it was turned into a private residence. In 2002 the car was purchased by the ERCC and is scheduled for restoration. Included in the restoration will be the removal of the later-added baggage compartment and the addition of windows to restore the rear passenger section.

In the Spring of 2003 the ERCC sold a J.G. Brill Model 55, built in 1930, to the Black River & Western Railroad for its recently added Belvedere & Delaware excursion train operating out of Philipsburg, New Jersey. The car was originally built for the Sperry Rail Car Company and used as a test car until the early 1940s. It was then sold to the Remington Arms Factory and was used to haul ammunition around the plant. The car was sold in the early 1980s to a New England museum group who had hopes of restoring the car for operation at the Valley Railroad in Essex, Connecticut. The group started the restoration and got about a third done. It is presumed that time and funding ran low and the car sat for years on a side track at the Valley Railroad.

The Edwards firm purchased the car from the Valley Railroad and in turn sold it to the Black River & Western. Along with the sale the ERCC was awarded a contract to fully restore the car. A new engine and transmission were installed, new interior wood work applied, partitions constructed, and a new floor and controls were added. In the spring of 2004 the car was loaded on a low boy trailer and shipped north to its new home. It now operates on the Belvadere & Delaware as their "Delaware Turtle" rail car.

In the summer of 2003, the ERCC was contracted by Bill McDonald to transform the first ERCC replica car, Mt. Dora, Tavares and Eustis Railroad's M-201, from an all-passenger car to a thirty seat, self propelled dining car. Extensive work was required which included the replacement and manufacture of all windows and doors; all new interior wood work and ceiling; installation of a sound system and air conditioning; construction of a forward partition replete with art glass depicting an orange leaf and blossom; removal of old floor covering and installation of an Art Deco style carpet; and reconstructing the forward baggage compartment into a galley. A major rebuild was also done to the power truck with an upgrade to the mechanical propulsion equipment. As a result of all this work, in November, 2003 the car emerged as the Orange Blossom Dinner Train.

It is the idea of the ERCC that the use of a self propelled rail car, modified and outfitted for use in dining car service, is an inexpensive way for an operator to start a dinner train ride at a fraction of the cost associated with standard equipment. It is also believed that a self propelled dining car would be a great addition to an existing dinner train operation for use on days when traffic is lower than normal or for smaller group booking.

In October of 2003 ERCC was selected by the city of Corsicana, Texas, to restore its 1913 Southern Traction Company interurban car no. 305. This car will be on static display in the town square, open for visitors to see as the only Southern Traction car restored to its original appearance. It was built by the St. Louis Car Company for the Southern Traction Company, which ran an extensive interurban line out of Dallas, eventually becoming the Texas Electric. In 1932 the car was heavily modified and "modernized" and lost its entire Victorian splendor. The biggest part of the restoration involved removing these modifications and bringing the car back to its original condition. A great number of parts and hardware had to be replicated and great

An interior view shows the frame of West Virginia Central no. M-3. *Photograph by Steven Torrico.*

research was done in order to get all of the original paint colors matched correctly. Long time Southern Traction/Texas Electric historian Ron Maxfield was assigned as project manager by the city of Corsicana, thus insuring complete accuracy in the restoration process.

After the Texas Electric shut down in the late 1940s, no. 305 was sold to an individual to become part of a cottage in a mobile home park. The car sat under a shed until the owner sold the property. The city of Corsicana purchased the car and moved it to a city compound and finally in October of 2003, it was loaded up a trailer and shipped to the ERCC in Florida. The East Troy Electric Railroad will supply the proper trucks for this car. At the time of this writing in 2005, restoration is half complete.

The fall of 2004 brought a new project to the ERCC. It was awarded the contract to restore a business car, built in 1905 for John Ringling of circus fame. This car, the "Wisconsin," is seventy-three feet in length and completely made of wood. Upon completion of the car it will be placed on exhibit at the John & Mabel Ringling Museum located in Sarasota, Florida.

The year 2006 saw the ERCC relocate to Montgomery, Alabama, where it leases space from Royce Kershaw (for whom the ERCC restored B&SE no. 500). Kershaw's company, Kershaw Manufacturing, manufactures railroad track maintenance equipment. The ERCC is located in the original manufacturing plant of Kershaw where the ERCC can contract with the shop crew for work and to provide equipment, such as trucks, propelling machinery and car bodies. This arrangement also helps to facilitate the manufacture of replica streetcars.

Although the original Edwards Railway Motor Car Company never progressed to the use of anything other than a mechanical drive, the new Edwards Rail Car Company has now branched out and is making available to customers an option of cars with traction motor trucks which include prime movers that power an electric generator. The firm is now able to build vintage electric streetcars in order to increase its customer base. Although the original plan was to sell cars to tourist railways, the major response has come from shortline railroads and cities that want to start light rail programs with vintage-appearing but entirely modern cars. Interest has been expressed through a number of inquires from England and Eastern Europe. In addition, the new firm is planning an aggressive campaign to market cars once again in Latin America, much as Harry P. Edwards did in the late 1930s. Recently the "new" Panama Canal Railway has expressed an interest in the ERCC build streamlined replicas of their original car no. 6, complete with its trailer, no. 6-A.

With the resurgence of shortline and tourist railroads, Torrico was looking for a marketing niche which would provide an alternative for steam with an economically operated railroad motor car. Current production models include the Model 10, Model 20 and Model 21. The ERCC also makes available new "old style" reversible seats for streetcars or standard rail cars as well.

The goal of Steven Torrico and the ERCC is to keep as authentic as possible to the original design and concept of the cars, but to allow them to be modernized whenever possible. The cars resemble the original designs and match the original craftsmanship, but coupled with modern refinements, the durability of the cars has been increased.

The 2005 Edwards Rail Car Company's catalog is reproduced here. Compare with the experts from the original catalogs reproduced in the previous chapter.

RAIL MOTOR CAR:

The standard Edwards Rail Car is designed and recommended for branch line service where traffic requirements are within its capacity, for high speed operation, on roadbeds where the grades are not too severe. The standard rail car is ideally suited for passenger runs where the schedule speed does not exceed 45 miles per hour and have seating requirements for 30 to 50 passengers, express and sack mail where mail requirements do not demand a regulation mail compartment.

Although the standard model was primarily designed to operate as a single unit, it will successfully handle an especially built trailer over roadbeds where the grade conditions are not too severe (2 ½%), and where high speed is not an important factor.

Each and every newly constructed Edwards Rail Car is designed and built especially for the service for which they are recommended. Each and every component and the smallest detail pertaining to its operation have been worked out and time proven. Using surviving blue prints, mechanical specifications and employing modern technology where ever possible, each unit is designed and constructed upon ideas and decisions gained by over 25 years of building successful, economical and dependable rail cars.

Our cars are not only constructed with perfectly balanced and matched components, but the whole line of drive is arranged so as to produce the best possible results, both in performance and efficiency, by utilizing the maximum percentage of the gross horse power produced. The horse power of a motor car, regardless of whether it is straight mechanical drive, gasoline-electric, or diesel-electric can very well be classed in two parts, i.e.

1st. The GROSS HORSE POWER PRODUCED IN THE CAB, a large percentage of which may be lost in inefficient transmission to the rails.

2nd. The NET EFFECTIVE HORSE POWER DELIVERED TO THE RAILS, which is the only and all the power available for tractive effort.

Therefore, the horse power produced in the CAB is of little importance to the car's performance, but if it is transmitted inefficiently to the rails, it reflects most unfavorably in the cost of operation. Now, it must be agreed that to produce power costs money;

therefore, to waste power is a waste of money. A motor car so designed that a considerable amount of the gross power produced in the cab is absorbed or lost in the transmission of the power from the engine to the rails, or is out of balance in weight with its horse power and passenger capacity is inefficient and expensive equipment to operate. Actual tests made in comparison with other designs has proven beyond all doubt, that our standard car is one of the most efficient, economical and dependable means of transportation for passengers, express and mail.

We offer three types of propulsion systems, mechanically, electrically or hydrostatic driven. The mechanically driven car employs the use of engine, transmission, final drive gear box with sprockets and chains to deliver power to the driving wheels. Cars equipped with electric propulsion have an engine which turns a generator for providing electricity for the traction motors. Hydrostatic propulsion employs the use of diesel engine to power a hydraulic pump which supplies pressurized fluid to two 50 H.P. hydraulic motors on the front truck, in place of the final drive gear box as per the mechanical set-up for the standard Model-20.

MECHANICAL SYSTEM:

The power plant consists of a gasoline or diesel engine, a semi-automatic transmission, and final drive. An outstanding feature in this car's construction, which puts it in a class to itself, is the mounting of the complete power plant in the front truck. The engine, transmission, final drive, air compressor and all propelling machinery are mounted in perfect alignment on a sub-frame forming the complete power-propelling unit. The connection from the power plant to the drive axle is made with two double roller chains which are enclosed in oil tight housings and run in a bath of oil.

This method of mounting permits the frame, containing the power plant, to move vertically or horizontally as there is no ridged connection between the driven axle and power plant. It has been time proven that in order to obtain long life and low maintenance cost in a direct mechanically driven car, it is absolutely essential that there be considerable flexibility in the drive mechanism to absorb the rail shock and in starting. This is perfectly accomplished with the Edwards Patented Power Truck for motor car service.

ELECTRIC PROPULSION:

Edwards Rail Cars equipped for electric propulsion will employ the use of newly built trucks and traction motors. This truck is based on established Master Car Builder (MCB) design standards. MCB truck designs have been in service for over 80 years, providing passengers with superior comfort and ride quality. MCB trucks are capable of speed in excess of 60 mph (depending on gearing and motor specifications) and are regularly operated on tracks with centerline radii of 50 feet. The materials used in the manufacture of the truck are of the highest quality and fabricated new.

NO RECYCLED OR SALVAGED parts are employed in the construction of the SRA-MCB Medium Duty Truck. Teflon inserts, precision welding and roller bearings are just a few of the modern features adopted to improve truck performance while maintaining the classic appearance and ride quality associated with the MCB design.

Each truck is equipped with two 50 hp traction motors operating on 600 volts DC electricity provided by a gasoline or diesel driven generator of ample proportion for service to be provided. Traction motors, pinion gears, and electric, solid-state control system provided by Clayton Equipment, Ltd.

Trucks, wheel sets and bolsters are fabricated new and provided by Irwin Car & Equipment, an established company with over 80 years experience.

The many distinctive mechanical features and unusual efficiency transmission of power between the engine and rails insures that these rail cars will carry-

First: The same tonnage the same mileage at less cost.

Second: The same tonnage more miles for the same cost.

Third: More tonnage the same miles for the same cost.

These cars are unquestionably the world's most economical means of transportation with the exception of the sailing vessel

MODEL 10
Condensed Specifications

POWER PLANT:

MOTOR: Chevrolet, 454, V-8 220 horse-power gasoline engine or 200 horse-power Cummins B-T four cylinder diesel engine. 35 miles per hour capability.
TRANSMISSION: Three speed automatic with torque converter.
FINAL DRIVE: Edwards Final Drive unit. Power is transmitted from the transmission to the rear truck. Power is then transmitted from the main drive axle, (rear axle on rear truck), via a double roller chain to the front axle of rear truck. Power is applied to all four wheels of the rear truck.

TRUCKS:

GAUGE: This car can be made for standard, narrow or meter gauge tracks.
WHEELS: Four to each truck, 24 inch diameter, made of steel, pressed on axles.
AXLES: Four inch in diameter made of chrome nickel steel.
JOURNALS: Equipped with standard railway roller bearings.
SPRINGS: One coil spring over each journal box and two half elliptic springs on each truck to support the car body.
BRAKES: Brakes are of the "straight" air type with emergency application feature. "Automatic" type are applied when motor is employed to pull trailer car.
TRUCK FRAME: Made of fabricated steel, outside side frames in one solid piece.

BODY OF CAR:

DIMENSIONS: Length over body is 33 ft. Height from rail to top of roof is 10 ft. 7 in. Width of body is 8 ft. Height top of rail to floor is 3 ft. 5 in. Height of floor to ceiling is 7 ft. 2 in. Bolster centers are 19 ft. Weight of car 22,000 pounds.
CONSTRUCTION: Substantially built of steel with hardwood interior, doors, window sash and T&G floor. Roof is covered with tongue and groove boards, dressed and covered with heavy canvas and painted.
BAGGAGE COMPARTMENT: 8 ft. in length. Has two 38 in. sliding doors, one on each side. Interior ceiling is ¼ inch Agasote, walls are tongue & groove and painted a light buff. Partition between baggage and passenger compartment.
PASSENGER COMPARTMENT: 20 ft. 2 in. in length. Seats are spring cushions and backs upholstered in a heavy grade Naugahyde. Seats are provided for 30 passengers. Passenger compartment is provided with one water closet.
REAR PLATFORM: Open type with steps on each side, iron railing on rear.
OTHER EQUIPMENT: Car is heated by a propane forced air system. 30 gallon fuel tank; air whistle; signal bell; air sanders; 12 volt electric lights; complete set of controls; steel pilot; tool box; fire extinguisher.

This car will make 10 to 15 miles per gallon of gasoline.

MODEL 10-C
Condensed Specifications

This rail car is identical in out-fittings and mechanical arrangements as our standard Model-10 rail car with the exception that the coach employs a "center" door for entrance and egress. The rear of the coach is also easily adapted for a "rear" control stand for dual end operation.

Floor plan for a Model 10. *Collection of the Edwards Rail Car Co.*

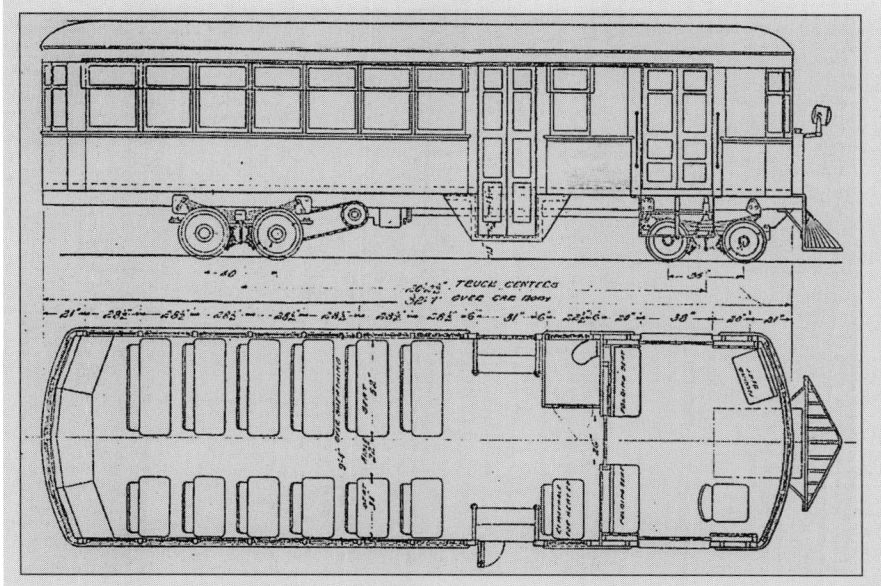

MODEL 20
Condensed Specifications

POWER PLANT:

MOTOR: Chevrolet, V-8, 220 horse-power gasoline engine or 200 horse-power, Cummins B-T four cylinder diesel engine. 45 miles per hour capability.
TRANSMISSION: Allison CRT- 3331 Toromatic Transmission.
FINAL DRIVE: Edwards especially constructed gear box. From this unit to the drive axle the power is transmitted by two double 100 roller chains.
POWER PLANT: The complete power plant is mounted on a inner sub frame, sprung and suspended in the forward truck of the car. The engine is below the floor level, leaving the entire floor space inside the car for revenue purposes.

TRUCKS:

GAUGE: Standard gauge of 4 ft. 8½ in.
WHEELS: Four to each truck. 28 inch in diameter.
AXLES: Five inch diameter made of chrome nickel steel.
JOURNALS: Standard railway roller bearings.
JOURNAL BOXES: Made of fabricated steel, located on outside of wheels.
SPRINGS: One coil spring over each journal box. Elliptic springs in each truck to support car body.
BRAKES: "Straight" type air brakes with emergency application feature. When car is equipped to handle trailer "automatic" type brakes are employed. Conductors valve on rear vestibule and handbrake.
TRUCK FRAME: Edwards special patented design made of steel channel, plates and fabricated shapes.
WEIGHT: Weight of car complete is 48,000 pounds.

BODY OF CAR:

DIMENSIONS: Length over all is 50 ft. Height from rail to top of roof is 11 ft. 3 in. Width of body 9 ft. 6 in. Height from rail to floor is 48 in. Height of floor to ceiling 7 ft. 2 in.
CONSTRUCTION: Substantially constructed of steel throughout with harwood doors, window sash and tongue & groove floor. Roof is covered with T&G boards covered with a heavy weight canvas and painted.
BAGGAGE COMPARTMENT: 12 ft. 9 in. in length, 9 ft. wide. Has two 36 in. sliding doors on each side. Interior is tongue & groove walls painted a buff color. Operators controls are located in the right, front corner. Seating for 4 passengers with accommodations for two wheel chairs.
PASSENGER COMPARTMENT: 30 ft. 4 in. in length. Seating for 44 passengers on reversible type seats upholstered with heavy grade Naugahyde. Water closet with toilet and wash basin. Total seating for this car is 48.

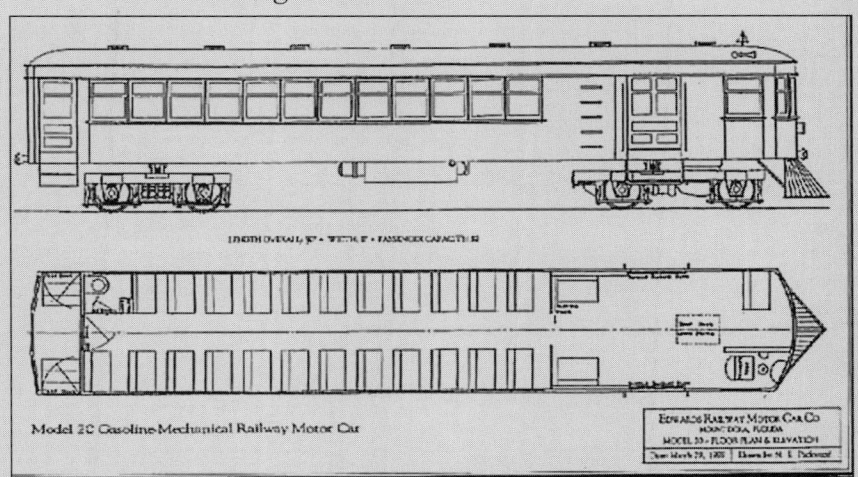

Top, floor plan for a Model 10-C. **Above**, floor Plan for a Model 20. **Both, collection of the Edwards Rail Car Co.**

MODEL 20 DINER CAR
Condensed Specifications

POWER PLANT:

MOTOR: Chevrolet, V-8, 220 horse-power gasoline engine or 200 horse-power, Cummins B-T four cylinder diesel engine. 45 miles per hour capability.
TRANSMISSION: Allison CRT- 3331 Toromatic Transmission.
FINAL DRIVE: Edwards especially constructed gear box. From this unit to the drive axle the power is transmitted by two double 100 roller chains.
POWER PLANT: The complete power plant is mounted on a inner sub frame, sprung and suspended in the forward truck of the car. The engine is below the floor level, leaving the entire floor space inside the car for revenue purposes.

TRUCKS:

GAUGE: Standard gauge of 4 ft. 8½ in.
WHEELS: Four to each truck. 28 inch in diameter.
AXLES: Five inch diameter made of chrome nickel steel.
JOURNALS: Standard railway roller bearings.
JOURNAL BOXES: Made of fabricated steel, located on outside of wheels.
SPRINGS: One coil spring over each journal box. Elliptic springs in each truck to support car body.
BRAKES: "Straight" type air brakes with emergency application feature. When car is equipped to handle trailer "automatic" type brakes are employed. Conductors valve on rear vestibule and handbrake.
TRUCK FRAME: Edwards special patented design made of steel channel, plates and fabricated shapes.
WEIGHT: Weight of car complete is 48,000 pounds.

BODY OF CAR:

DIMENSIONS: Length over all is 50 ft. Height from rail to top of roof is 11 ft. 3 in. Width of body 9 ft. 6 in. Height from rail to floor is 48 in. Height of floor to ceiling 7 ft. 2 in.

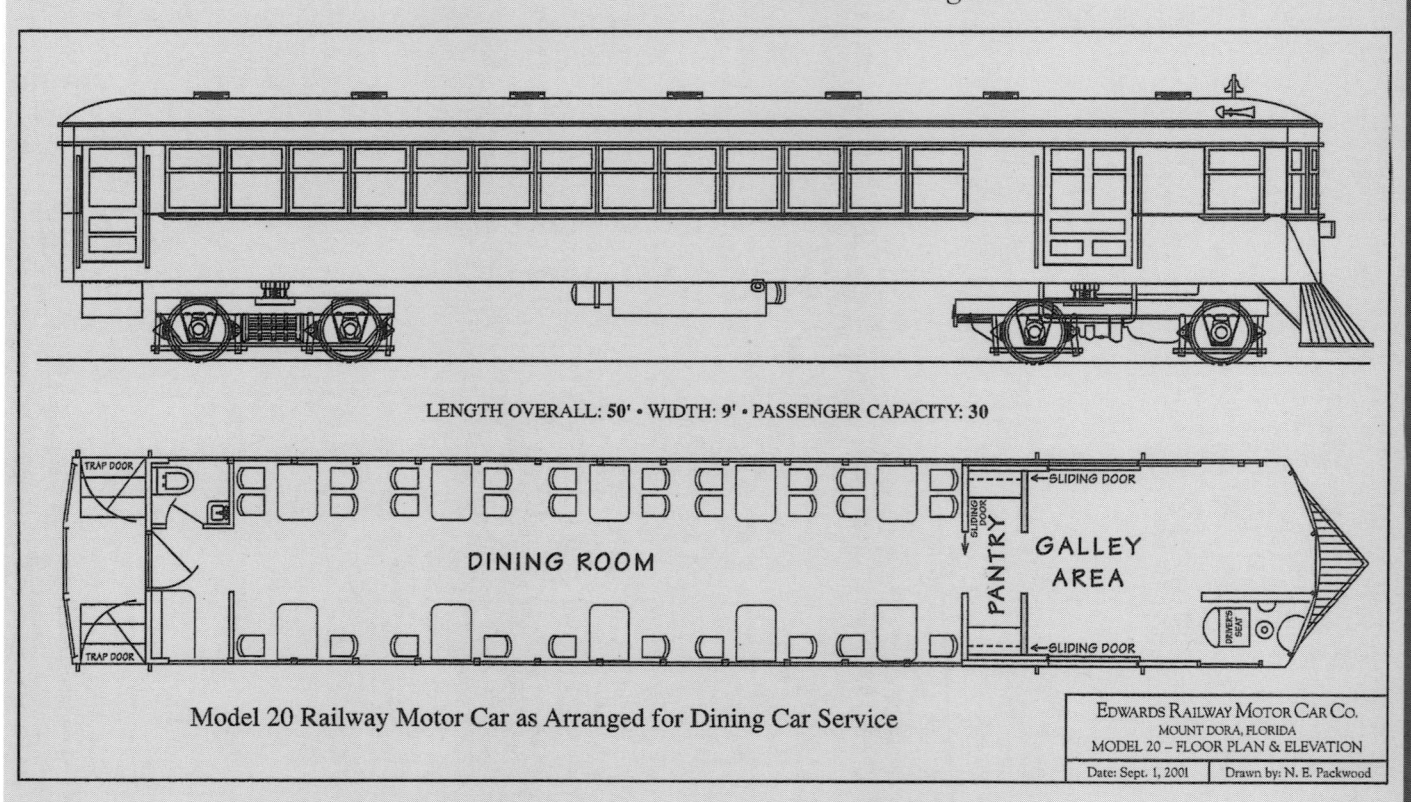

LENGTH OVERALL: 50' • WIDTH: 9' • PASSENGER CAPACITY: 30

Model 20 Railway Motor Car as Arranged for Dining Car Service

Edwards Railway Motor Car Co.
MOUNT DORA, FLORIDA
MODEL 20 – FLOOR PLAN & ELEVATION
Date: Sept. 1, 2001   Drawn by: N. E. Packwood

A modern Model 20 configured as a dining car and intended for use on tourist lines is one of the many options available from the ERCC. **Collection of the Edwards Rail Car Co.**

MODEL 21
Condensed Specifications

POWER PLANT:

MOTOR: Chevrolet 454, V-8 220 horse power gasoline engine or 200 horse power Cummins B-T four cylinder diesel engine. 45 miles per hour capability.

TRANSMISSION: Allison CRT-3331 power shift three speed forward and reverse.

FINAL DRIVE: Edwards special design, unusually massive and substantial. From this unit to the axles the power is transmitted by two roller chains.

TRUCKS:

GAUGE: Standard gauge 4 ft. 8½ in.
WHEELS: Four to each truck. 28 inch in diameter, made of steel.
AXLES: Five inch in diameter made of chrome nickel steel.
JOURNALS: Roller journal bearings of the railroad type.
JOURNAL BOXES: Made of steel, located on outside of wheels.
BRAKES: "Straight" type with emergency application feature. Equipped with standard "Automatic" type when equipped to pull trailer car.
TRUCK FRAME: Edwards special patented design made of steel channel, plates and fabricated shapes.

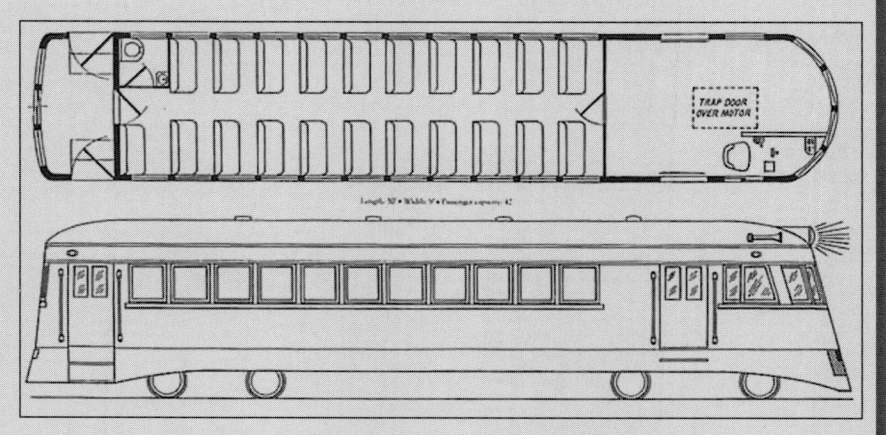

CONSTRUCTION: Substantially constructed of steel throughout with harwood doors, window sash and tongue & groove floor. Roof is covered with T&G boards covered with a heavy weight canvas and painted.

GALLEY COMPARTMENT: 12 ft. 9 in. in length, 9 ft. wide. Has two 36 in. sliding doors on each side. Interior is tongue & groove walls painted a buff color. Operators controls are located in the right, front corner. Seating for 4 passengers with accommodations for two wheel chairs.

DINING COMPARTMENT: 30 ft. 4 in. in length. Seating for 30 passengers at 10 tables. On one side of the car there are 5 tables that seat four each, the other side has 5 tables that sit two each. Water closet with toilet and wash basin. Total seating for this car is 32.

REAR PLATFORM: Enclosed vestibule type; trap doors over steps, dutch side doors with upper portion glazed. Operators controls in right corner.

OTHER EQUIPMENT: Car is heated by propane forced air system; 60 gallon fuel tank; air whistle; engine bell mounted on roof; conductors signal bell; tool box; 12 volt electric lighting system.

Top, Interior of a modern Model 20 diner car. **Above**, floor plan for a Model 21. ***Both, collection of the Edwards Rail Car Co.***

95

MODEL 30
Condensed Specifications

GENERAL DESCRIPTION: The diesel-electric car described here consists of a light weight carbody of special design and construction mounted on MCB traction motor trucks and equipped with a 220 H.P. diesel engine to which is connected a 180KW generator that supplies the current for four 40 H.P. traction motors and other electrical power needs.

BODY OF CAR:

DIMENSIONS: Length over body is 50 ft. Height from rail to top of roof 10 ft. 8 in. Width of body 9 ft. 6 in., height from rail to floor is 46 in.

CONSTRUCTION: Substantially built of steel throughout except floor and roof which are of hardwood construction. Roof is covered with heavy canvas and painted.

BAGGAGE COMPARTMENT: 13 ft. in length, has two 34 in. sliding doors on each side of car and seating for 4 passengers. Operators compartment located in right front corner.

PASSENGER COMPARTMENT: Seating for 46 on reversible walk-over type seats; one water closet with toilet and wash basin. Window sash and interior moulding made of aluminum or brass. Ceiling is ¼ inch Agasote paneling painted with high gloss enamel.

REAR PLATFORM: Enclosed vestibule type with dutch or solid type doors, trap doors over steps.

OTHER EQUIPMENT: Car is heated by a propane forced air system; 60 gallon fuel tank; air sanders; air whistle; 12 volt electric system; headlight; steel pilot; air conditioning. Total seating of car is 50 passengers.

WEIGHT: Weight of car complete is 50,000 pounds

POWER PLANT

ENGINE: 220 horse-power diesel engine. 60 miles per hour capability.
GENERATOR: Westinghouse type, self ventilated, DC of 180 KW capacity.
CONTROL: Located in the right front area of the car. Solid state electrical control system and Westinghouse, straight-air type air brakes with emergency application feature.

TRUCKS

GAUGE: This car can be made for standard or narrow gauge tracks.
WHEELS: Four to each truck, 30 inch diameter, made of rolled steel.
AXLES: Five inch in diameter, made of chrome nickel steel.
JOURNALS: Equipped with railroad type roller bearings.

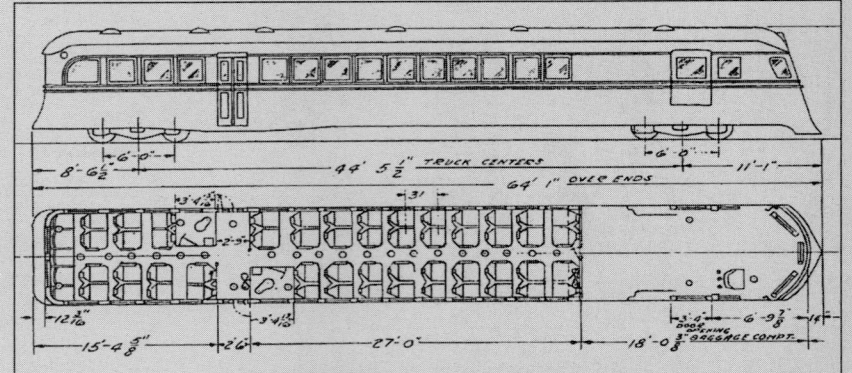

Top, the cab of an original Model 21. Note trap door on floor. Above, floor plan for a Model 30. **Both, collection of the Edwards Rail Car Co.**

SPRINGS: One coil over each journal box and two full elliptic springs on each truck to support coach body.

BRAKES: Brakes are of the "straight" air brake type and applied to all eight wheels of the car.

TRUCK FRAME: Made of fabricated steel, side frames in one solid piece.

MOTORS: Four 40 H.P. electric traction motors. Two motors axle mounted on each truck.

BODY OF CAR:

DIMENSIONS: Overall length is 65 ft. Width of 8 ½ ft. Top of the rail to top of the roof is 10 ft. 5 in. Truck centers: 44 ft. 5 ½ in. Wheel base of trucks: 6 ft. Length of Engine/Baggage Compartment: 18 ft. Passenger Section: 45 ft in length.

PASSENGER COMPARTMENT: Seating capacity for 56 passengers and equipped with two toilets, air conditioning and entrance to car on either side by folding doors.

OTHER EQUIPMENT: Fuel capacity of 130 gallons, air tanks, water tanks, air horn, signal bell; air sanders. Fully equipped this car weighs 54,000 pounds.

MODEL 5
Condensed Specifications

This car will pull a load of fifty to three hundred tons, according to conditions and speed desired. It is designed to pull one standard passenger coach at a speed of 35 miles per hour or will pull three Edwards Model T-10 trailer cars. Can be used efficiently for switching purposes or ideal for use as a line car on electrified railways or for use as a maintenance-of-way car.

POWER PLANT:

MOTOR: 200 horse power Cummins B-T four cylinder diesel.

TRANSMISSION: Allison CTR-3331 Toromatic.

FINAL DRIVE: Edwards Final Drive. Power is transmitted to all four wheels of the rear truck.

GAUGE: This car can be made for narrow or standard gauge.

WHEELS: Four wheels to each truck, 24 inch diameter.

AXLES: Axles are 5 inch in diameter made of chrome nickel steel.

JOURNALS: Equipped with railroad type roller bearings.

BRAKES: Brakes are of the "straight" type. "Automatic" type will be employed when car is used as locomotive.

DIMENSIONS: Length over all is 31 ft. Width of body is 8ft. 6 in. Height from top of rail to top of roof is 10ft. 5 in.

CONSTRUCTION: Substantial steel construction throughout with hardwood interior, floor and roof covered with canvas.

OTHER EQUIPMENT: Car is heated by a propane forced air system; fuel tank of 30 gallons; air whistle; engine bell; air sanders; 12 volt electric lighting.

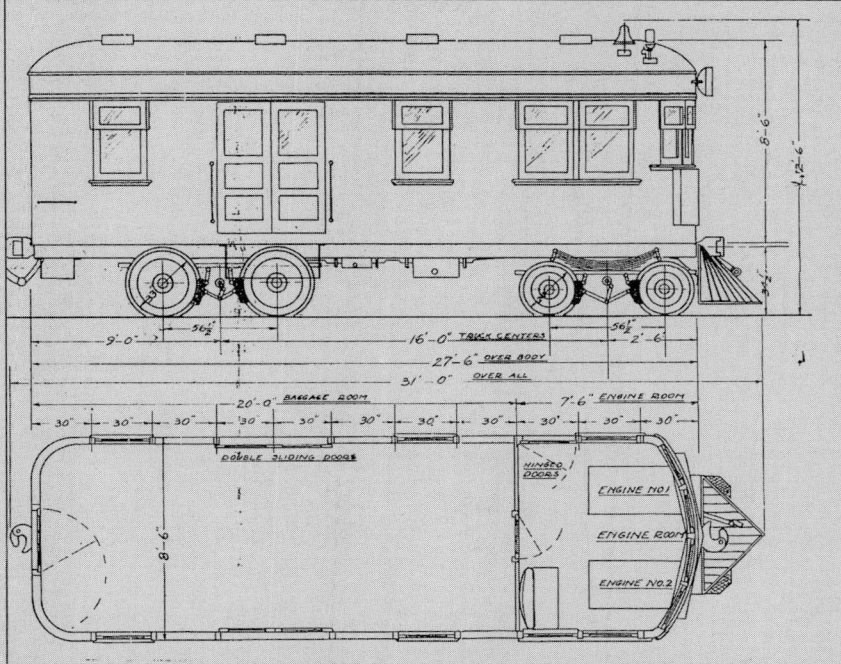

Elevation plan for a Model 5. *Collection of the Edwards Rail Car Co.*

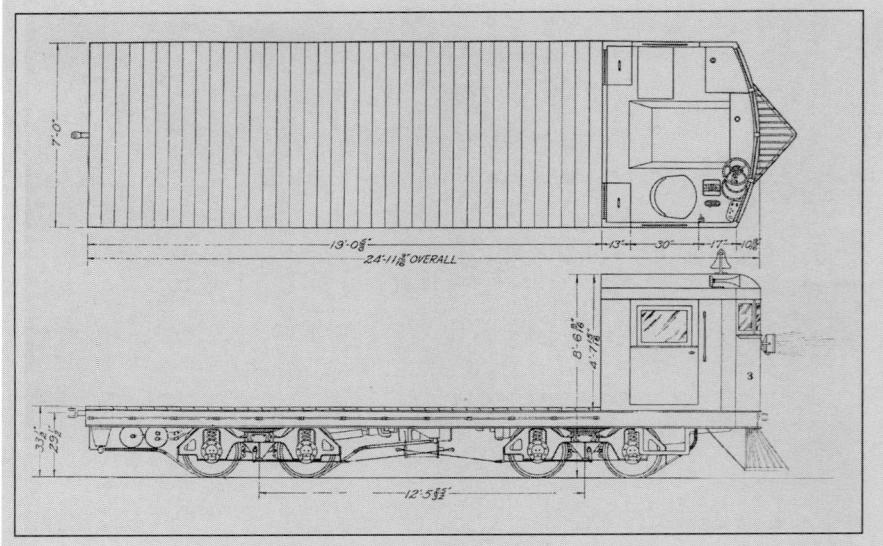

MODEL FM 10
Condensed Specifications

This Edwards "special" is well suited for use as a maintenance-of-way vehicle. With the addition of side railings, benches and canopy, this car is ideal for use as a open air excursion car.

POWER PLANT:

MOTOR: 200 horse power Cummins B-T four cylinder diesel engine.
TRANSMISSION: Allison CTR-3331 Toro-matic.
FINAL DRIVE: Edwards Final Drive. Power is transmitted to all wheels of the rear truck.
GAUGE: This car can be built to narrow or standard gauge.
WHEELS: Four wheels to each truck, 24 in. diameter wheels made of steel.
AXLES: Axles are 5 inch diameter made of chrome nickel steel.
JOURNALS: Equipped with roller type bearings.
SPRINGS: One coil spring over each journal box and two full elliptic springs on each truck to support the body.
BRAKES: Brakes are of the "straight" type with shoes applying to all eight wheels.
TRUCK FRAME: Made of fabricated steel, side frames in one solid piece.
DIMENSIONS: Length over all is 25 ft. Height rail to top of car is 8ft. 6 in. Width of car is 8ft. 6 in. 12ft. 5 in. truck centers with 19ft loading space. Capacity is 15 tons. Also furnished with 20ft. truck centers and 26ft. loading space.
FRAME & BODY: Frame is of all steel construction. Body is steel with hardwood window sash. Roof on cab is turtle back style made of tongue and groove, dressed and covered with canvas and painted. Deck is a hardwood of tongue and groove securely attached to the chassis. Can be outfitted with removable sides or stakes.

MODEL S 10
Condensed Specifications

POWER PLANT:

MOTOR: Chevrolet, 454, V-8 220 horse-power gasoline engine or 200 horse-power Cummins B-T four cylinder diesel engine. 35 miles per hour capability.
TRANSMISSION: Three speed automatic with torque converter.
FINAL DRIVE: Edwards Final Drive unit. Power is transmitted from the transmission to the rear truck. Power is then transmitted from the main drive axle, (rear axle on rear truck), via a double roller chain to the front axle of rear truck. Power is applied to all four wheels of the rear truck.

Top, elevation plan for an FM 10. **Above,** floor plan for an S 10. **Both,** collection of the Edwards Rail Car Co.

TRUCKS:

GAUGE: This car can be made for standard, narrow or meter gauge tracks.
WHEELS: Four to each truck, 24 inch diameter, made of steel, pressed on axles.
AXLES: Four inch in diameter made of chrome nickel steel.
JOURNALS: Equipped with standard railway roller bearings.
SPRINGS: One coil spring over each journal box and two half elliptic springs on each truck to support the car body.
BRAKES: Brakes are of the "straight" air type with emergency application feature. "Automatic" type are applied when motor is employed to pull trailer car.
TRUCK FRAME: Made of fabricated steel, outside side frames in one solid piece.

Front of an S 10. **Collection of the Edwards Rail Car Co.**

BODY OF CAR:

DIMENSIONS: Length over body is 33 ft. Height from rail to top of roof is 10 ft. 7 in. Width of body is 8 ft. Height top of rail to floor is 3 ft. 5 in. Height of floor to ceiling is 7 ft. 2 in. Bolster centers are 19 ft. Weight of car 22,000 pounds.
CONSTRUCTION: Substantially built of steel with hardwood interior, doors, window sash and T&G floor. Roof is covered with tongue and groove boards, dressed and covered with heavy canvas and painted.
BAGGAGE COMPARTMENT: 8 ft. in length. Has two 38 in. sliding doors, one on each side. Interior ceiling is ¼ inch agasote, walls are tongue & groove and painted a light buff. Partition between baggage and passenger compartment.
PASSENGER COMPARTMENT: 20 ft. 2 in. in length. Seats are spring cushions and backs upholstered in a heavy grade Naugahyde. Seats are provided for 30 passengers. Passenger compartment is provided with one water closet.
REAR PLATFORM: Open type with steps on each side, iron railing on rear.
OTHER EQUIPMENT: Car is heated by a propane forced air system. 30 gallon fuel tank; air whistle; signal bell; air sanders; 12 volt electric lights; complete set of controls; steel pilot; tool box; fire extinguisher.

1938 SPECIAL
Condensed Specifications

In 1938 the Edwards Company finished construction of a very unique and special Business Car for the General Manager of the United Fruit Co.

This one of a kind ERC was complete with bedroom, water closet with shower, galley, office furniture, dining arrangements, air conditioning and all the modern comforts and luxuries that would be found on any standard private rail car.

This car was in service until the early 1970's and was recently located on an over grown siding in Guatemala. Records and mechanical reports from the International Railways of Central America indicate that until its retirement, this Edwards Rail Car proved to be a reliable and mechanical sound machine.

Today, as in 1938, Edwards can build this same car with all the unique Art Deco features found in the original. This is accomplished by using the original erection drawings, mechanical and interior specifications as produced in 1938.

Without the need for a locomotive to pull the standard rail car, railroad officials may now travel over their roads in the most unique and reliable fashion. Most importantly the Edwards Rail Car provides the least expense in maintenance and operation. Edwards self-propelled rail cars are the most economical means of rail transportation available TODAY!

MODEL T 10 Trailer Car
Condensed Specifications

BODY OF CAR:

DIMENSIONS & CONSTRUCTION: Same as Model-10 motor car.
PASSENGER COMPARTMENT: Seats 38 passengers on comfortable reversible walk-over type seats. One water closet equipped with toilet and was basin. Ceiling is of ¼ inch Agasote and painted with gloss enamel. Doors are of the swing type with upper portion glazed.
CAR ENDS: Open type platform with steps on each side, iron railing across end.
OTHER EQUIPMENT: Car is heated by propane forced air heating system; conductors valve each end of car; hand brake; 12 volt electrical system. **BRAKES:** Brakes are of the "Automatic" type with emergency application feature.
WEIGHT: 19,000 pounds empty.

TRUCKS:

GAUGE: This car can be made for standard, narrow or meter gauge tracks.
WHEELS: Four to each truck, 24 inch diameter, made of steel, pressed on axles.
AXLES: Four inch in diameter made of chrome nickel steel.
JOURNALS: Equipped with standard railway roller bearings.
SPRINGS: One coil spring over each journal box and two half elliptic springs on each truck to support the car body.
BRAKES: Brakes are of the "straight" air type with emergency application feature. "Automatic" type are applied when motor is employed to pull trailer car.
TRUCK FRAME: Made of fabricated steel, outside side frames in one solid piece.

MODEL T 20 TRAILER CAR
Condensed Specifications

BODY OF CAR:

DIMENSIONS & CONSTRUCTION: Same as the Model-20 motor car.

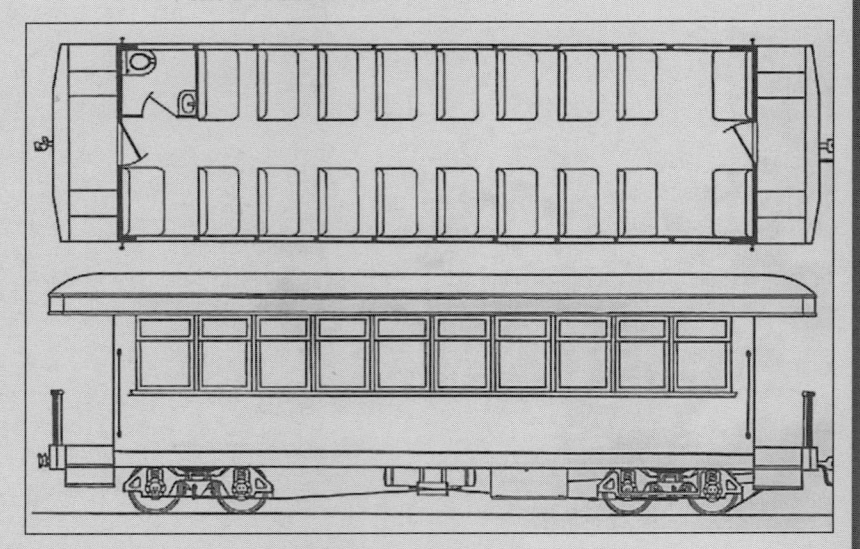

Top, the original "1938 Special." **Above**, floor plan for a Model T 10 trailer car. **Both, collection of the Edwards Rail Car Co.**

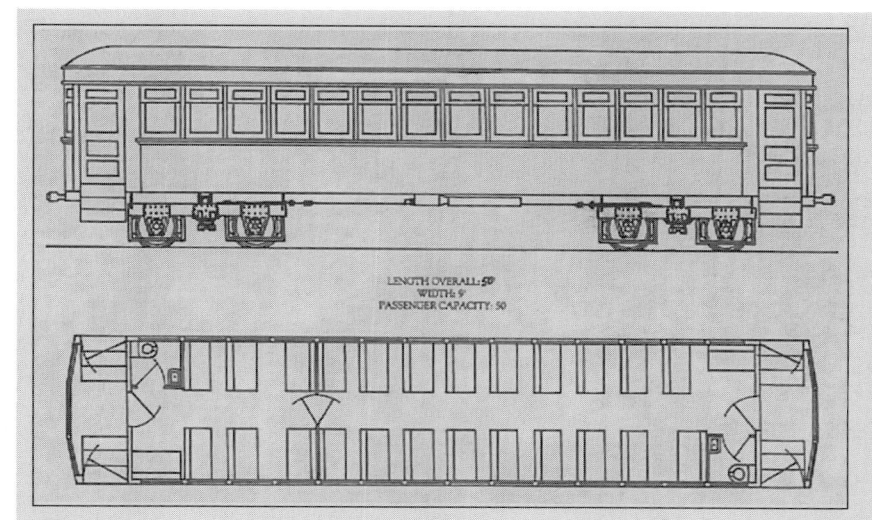

PASSENGER COMPARTMENT: Seating for 50 passengers on reversible, walk-over type seats upholstered in a heavy grade Naugahyde, equipped with two water closets with toilets and wash basins.
CAR ENDS: Enclosed vestibule type with dutch style side doors, with upper portion glazed; trap doors over steps.
OTHER EQUIPMENT: Car is heated by a propane forced air system, conductors valve on each end; 12 volt electric system when used as trailer; hand brake at one end.

TRUCKS:

GAUGE: Standard 4 ft. 8½ in.
WHEELS: Four to each truck, 28 in. diameter, rolled steel.
AXLES: Five inch diameter made of chrome nickel steel.
JOURNALS: Roller journal bearing of the railroad type.
JOURNAL BOXES: Made of fabricated steel, located on outside of wheels.
SPRINGS: One coil spring over each journal box, 2 full elliptic springs in each truck.
BRAKES: "Automatic" type air brakes with emergency application feature.
TRUCK FRAME: Made of steel channel, plates and fabricated shapes.
WEIGHT: 34,000 pounds.

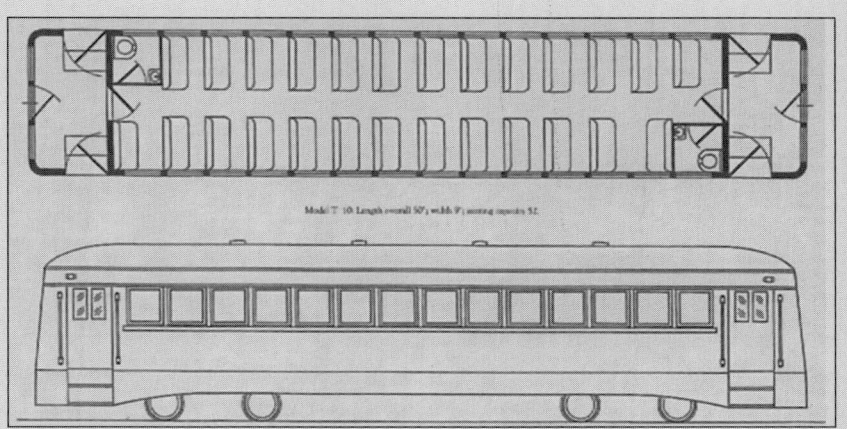

MODEL T 21 TRAILER CAR
Condensed Specifications

BODY OF CAR:

DIMENSIONS & CONSTRUCTION: Same as Model-21 motor car.
PASSENGER COMPARTMENT: Seats 50 passengers and has two water closets with toilets and wash basins. Interior same as motor car appointments.
END PLATFORMS: Enclosed vestibule type, trap doors over steps.
OTHER EQUIPMENT: Car is heated by a propane forced air system; conductors valve on each end; hand brake; air conditioning.
WEIGHT: Weight of car complete is 32,000 pounds.

TRUCKS:

GAUGE: Standard gauge 4 ft. 8½ in.
WHEELS: Four to each truck. 28 inch in diameter, made of steel.
AXLES: Five inch in diameter made of chrome nickel steel.
JOURNALS: Roller journal bearings of the railroad type.
JOURNAL BOXES: Made of steel, located on outside of wheels.
BRAKES: "Straight" type with emergency application feature. Equipped with standard "Automatic" type when equipped to pull trailer car.
TRUCK FRAME: Edwards special patented design made of steel channel, plates and fabricated shapes.

Top, floor plan for a Model T 20 trailer car. **Above**, floor plan for a Model T 21 trailer car. **Both, collection of the Edwards Rail Car Co.**

[The 2005 Edwards catalog also includes the following non-Edwards related streetcars]

MODEL ES 700 SERIES
Condensed Specifications

Edwards Rail Car Company has chosen the modified Peter Witt streetcar design to fulfill the demands of new heritage street railway systems. The Witt Design presents the pinnacle of lightweight streetcar technology and classic early 20th century styling. Steel truss wall construction, mahogany interior trim and nickel plate fixtures combine with modern, efficient traction motors and proven Master Car Builder (MCB) design trucks to offer a reliable, attractive streetcar for use on today's demanding heritage systems.

The car design has its origins with Peter Witt, the Street Railway Commissioner of Cleveland, Ohio. The commissioner specified front and center doors to allow quick loading of rush hour passengers and fare collection at the center of the car to prevent delayed starts due to passengers clogging the front entrance. Edwards offers the traditional Witt design with or without the center doors to allow for solo operation of the car.

Every newly constructed Edwards Electric Streetcar is designed and built to provide the experience of an old-fashion streetcar ride while minimizing the efforts of the shop department to keep the cars in service. Modern allowances provide for safety, ADA accessibility and comfort, while maintains the historical integrity of the car. Edwards employs NO RECYCLED OR SALVAGED PARTS in the construction of our cars.

CAR DESCRIPTION:
Type: Steel truss-wall construction
Seats/Capacity: 56 Walk-over style of wooden slatted style or upholstered.
Length: 50 feet
Width: 8ft. 6 in.
Height: 11 ft.
Weight: 28,000 lbs.
Motors: Four 40 HP Electric Traction Motors
Speed: Approximately 30 m.p.h.
Window Sash and Interior Trims and Doors: Oak.
Outer Woodwork: Ash and Oak.
Roof: Tongue and Groove Oak covered with heavy weight canvas.
Floor: Plymetal sub floor with tongue & groove top floor of hardwood. Rubber traction matting down isle way.
Controls: Solid state electrical control system on both ends of car.

Edwards Rail Car Company is currently engaged by the McKinney Avenue Transit Authority of Dallas, Texas in the rebuilding of a Peter Witt car. The MATA interior demonstrates the finish and general arrangement of the Edwards Electric Streetcar.

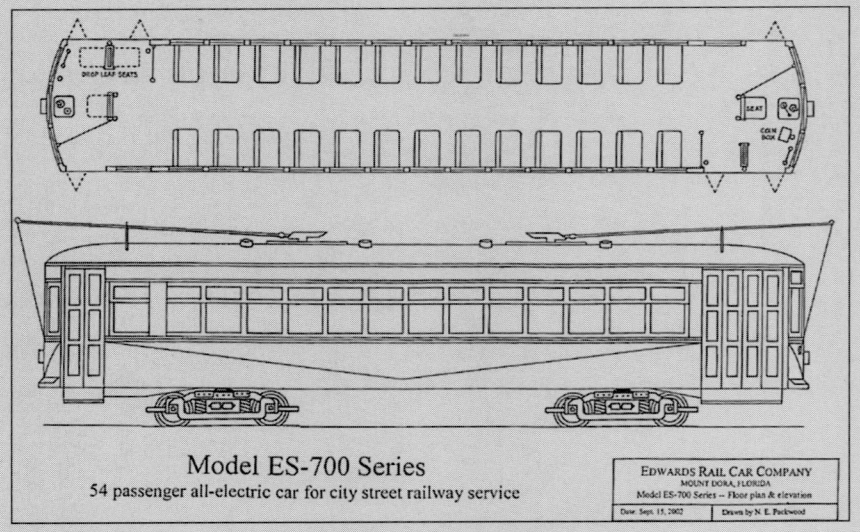

Above, floor plan for a Model ES 700 Series streetcar. **Top**, drawing of an ES 700. **Both, collection of the Edwards Rail Car Co.**

Plans are in the works to offer a "Model ES-Standard Series" electric streetcar to the catalog soon. Other items include an original Edwards slated wood reversible bench.

Above, company drawing of a Model ES Standard Series streetcar. **Below**, drawing showing the Edwards wooden slated reversible seat. The seat is made of hardwood and sealed with durable marine spar varnish. **Both, collection of the Edwards Rail Car Co.**

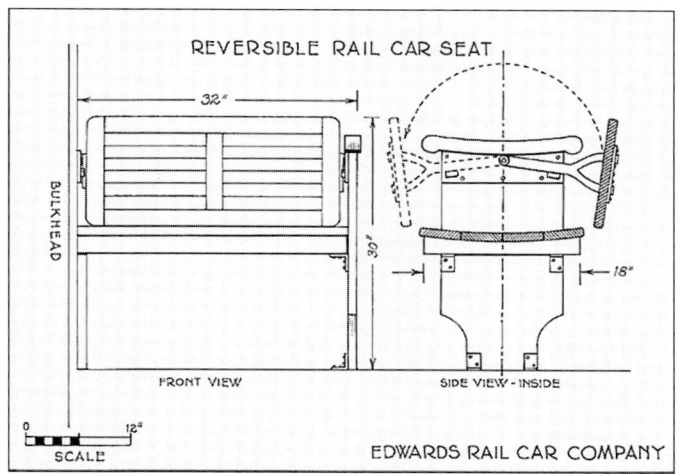

Where are they now?

Of the over 120 cars and trailers built by the Edwards Railway Motor Car Company, sadly only a small handful of cars is known to exist.

Listed below are the known surviving Edwards cars and their current conditions and dispositions.

1. CB&Q no. 505, a Model 20, built in 1926. The body exists in Iowa and awaits restoration on the Ft. Madison, Farmington, & Western Railroad.

2. CB&Q no. 507, a Model 20, built in 1926. The body was sold by the CB&Q for fifty dollars and served as a private residence for over fifty years. The car is currently in service hauling workers to a job site on the Mississippi River.

3. Birmingham & Southeastern no. 500, a Model 10, built in 1923. The car is privately owned and restoration was completed in May 2004 in Florida. Before going home to Montgomery, Alabama, no. 500 was shipped to the North Carolina Transportation Museum in Spencer, North Carolina to participate in the 2004 Spencer Shops annual "Rail Days" event.

4. Morehead & North Fork Railroad, no. 200, Model 20, built 1926. Sold to California Western as their no. M 100. This car was dieselized in 1954. A mid 1960s crash caused major damage and the frame was extended on the rear and a school bus body was applied to the original frame. Nothing of the original coach has survived. The M-100 continues in tourist service on the "Skunk Train," operating out of Ft. Bragg, California, which was sold in 2004 to the Sierra Railroad.

5. Hampton & Branchville Railroad, no. M-200, a Model 20, built in 1926. One of the most unusual of preservations, it operated until

Birmingham & Southeastern no. 500, shortly after its restoration. The car is seen in service at the North Carolina Transportation museum's "Rail Days" at Spencer Shops in 2004. **Photo by John D. Porter.**

California Western "Skunk train" M 100, a 1926 Model 25, was originally built for the Morehead & North Fork. In the image at **top** the car is seen in its signature yellow livery on June 27, 1948. By this time the car had been heavily modified with its capacity reduced to thirty-six from forty-one, and the addition of a chimney, air tanks, air horns, number boards and a large headlight that partially obscured the window. Two years previous to this photo, in 1946, a single 150 hp Cummins diesel engine replaced the dual Buda gasoline engines. After a 1964 head on collision which totaled a second railcar, the M 100 was rebuilt by a local bus company into an extremely unusual piece of equipment. A 2004 photo **(above)** shows the M 100 in its new maroon paint scheme. *Top, photo by R.W. Biermann. Collection of Arnold Menke (Arn's Rail Photos). Above, courtesy of Sierra Railroad's Skunk Train.*

the 1950s, at which time it suffered a transmission/drive shaft failure. Since the ERwyMCC had been shut down for over ten years and no replacement parts were available from the manufacturer, it was deemed too great of an expense to have the needed parts fabricated in a machine shop. With the advent of bus competition and privately owned automobiles dominating the roads, there was not enough passenger traffic to warrant the expense of the repair. The car was pushed into a storage shed and left unattended for decades except for the occasional railfan who would seek permission to peek inside the shed. Eventually the tracks were removed, and few knew of the existence of the car. It was eventually sold to the North Carolina Transportation Museum in Spencer where it currently awaits restoration.

6. Atlanta & St. Andrews Bay/Tallulah Falls Railroad, no. 503, a Model 25, built in 1928. Originally sixty feet in length, the car served the A&SAB with a baggage/RPO compartment and a passenger compartment with seating for twenty-seven. When the car was sold to the Tallulah Falls Railroad in 1939, the passenger section was removed. The car was a longtime private residence until recently and is currently under restoration by the ERCC.

7. Tucson, Cornelia & Gila Bend, no. 401, a Model 10, built in 1926. This car is currently at the Nevada State Railway Museum in Carson City and is operated on a regular basis.

8. FC Panama Nacional, no. 202, a non powered open-platform trailer, built around 1936. The car is preserved in the town square of Boquete, Panama and is protected with a shelter built over the car.

9. FC Panama Nacional, no. 102, a Model 20, built in 1927. The engine was removed in the mid 1950s and the car was used as a trailer. Anecdotal reports indicate that the car still exists.

10. Tennessee Central Railroad, no. 16, a non powered trailer, built in 1923. The car is currently in Oneida, Tennessee, but is scheduled for restoration by the ERCC.

Top, H&B no. 200 at its home at the North Carolina Transportation museum on March 6, 2004. Interior view **(above)** shows the vintage unrestored condition of the car. This shot was taken shortly before the car was sold to the NC Transportation Museum. **Top, photo by John Jones. Above, photo by Steven Torrico.**

Tucson, Cornelia & Gila Bend no. 401 **(above)** seen at Traveltown in Los Angeles, California in 1961. No. 401 is an eight window, thirty passenger Model 10 built in 1926 for the Tucson, Cornelia & Gila Bend railroad of Ajo, Arizona. It logged over 783,000 miles while running the forty-three miles between the copper mine at Ajo and Gila Bend before being retired in 1947 and donated to Travel Town. The original Continental engine was replaced in 1943 by a six-cylinder White gasoline engine which was in turn replaced by a 75 hp Cummins diesel engine in 1997. After being repainted in the 1970s, the car was restored to its original appearance in 1999 and received a new fluid drive transmission at the same time. The car is preserved today at the Nevada State Railroad Museum in Carson City, Nevada, where it is in running order and sees excursion service over the museum's right-of-way. A recent photo shows the interior of the car **(Below left)**. The interior of the M-3 Cheat Mountain Salamander **(Below right)** is seen prior to delivery on the West Virginia Central. ***Above, photograph by Wilbur T. Golson, collection of the Edwards Rail Car Co. Below, both photos by Steven Torrico.***

11 Butte, Anaconda & Pacific (BA&P), no. M-10. Built in 1925, its original design was that of a small locomotive. Edwards promoted that this car would pull one standard coach or three especially designed Edwards trailers. Only one of these Model 5 cars was built. The BA&P bought it to use as a self propelled line car. The car is preserved at the World Mining Museum in Butte, Montana. It is a matter of some speculation as to whether Edwards built the entire car or just the chassis. The speculation centers on a board of director's minutes which refer to just a chassis being built, but the entire car resembles an Edwards product. The car was modified by placing a large platform on the roof, which could extend upward and allow inspection of the overhead centenary lines.

12 United Fruit Company no. 1150. Built as a streamlined Model 10, the car served as a company officer's inspection car. The car was furnished with galley, air conditioning, and wardroom. The car and its original running gear has been salvaged and awaits restoration in Guatemala.

With the number of units sold to Central and South America, it is hopeful other examples have survived.

Butte, Anaconda & Pacific, no. M-10 is seen in September, 2005 at its present lodgings at the Anselmo Mine in Butte, Montana. The mine, about one mile from the World Mining Museum, also houses some other BA&P rolling stock. As of this writing, the car is exposed to the elements and only visible through a chain link fence. The car appears to have deteriorated badly at its present home. Note the "Neversweat & Washoe" livery. The car operated on the Mining Museum's "Neversweat" railroad, rolling past several mines for a brief time when first acquired. **Photograph by Thornton Waite.**

United Fruit Company no. 1150 **(top)** now sits protected as it waits for restoration in Guatemala in 2005. A&SAB/Tallulah falls no. 503 **(above)** awaiting restoration in Montgomery, Alabama in 2006. The car served for many years as a private residence. ***Both photographs by Steven Torrico.***

Next page, West Virginia Central, no. M-3, the "Cheat Mountain Salamander," was the first Edwards car built from scratch in fifty-nine years. The car operates regularly in excursion service over the WVC. It is seen here following the Shavers fork of the Cheat River near Switchback Curve shortly after its arrival at the WVC in 2001. ***Photograph by Lars Byrne.***

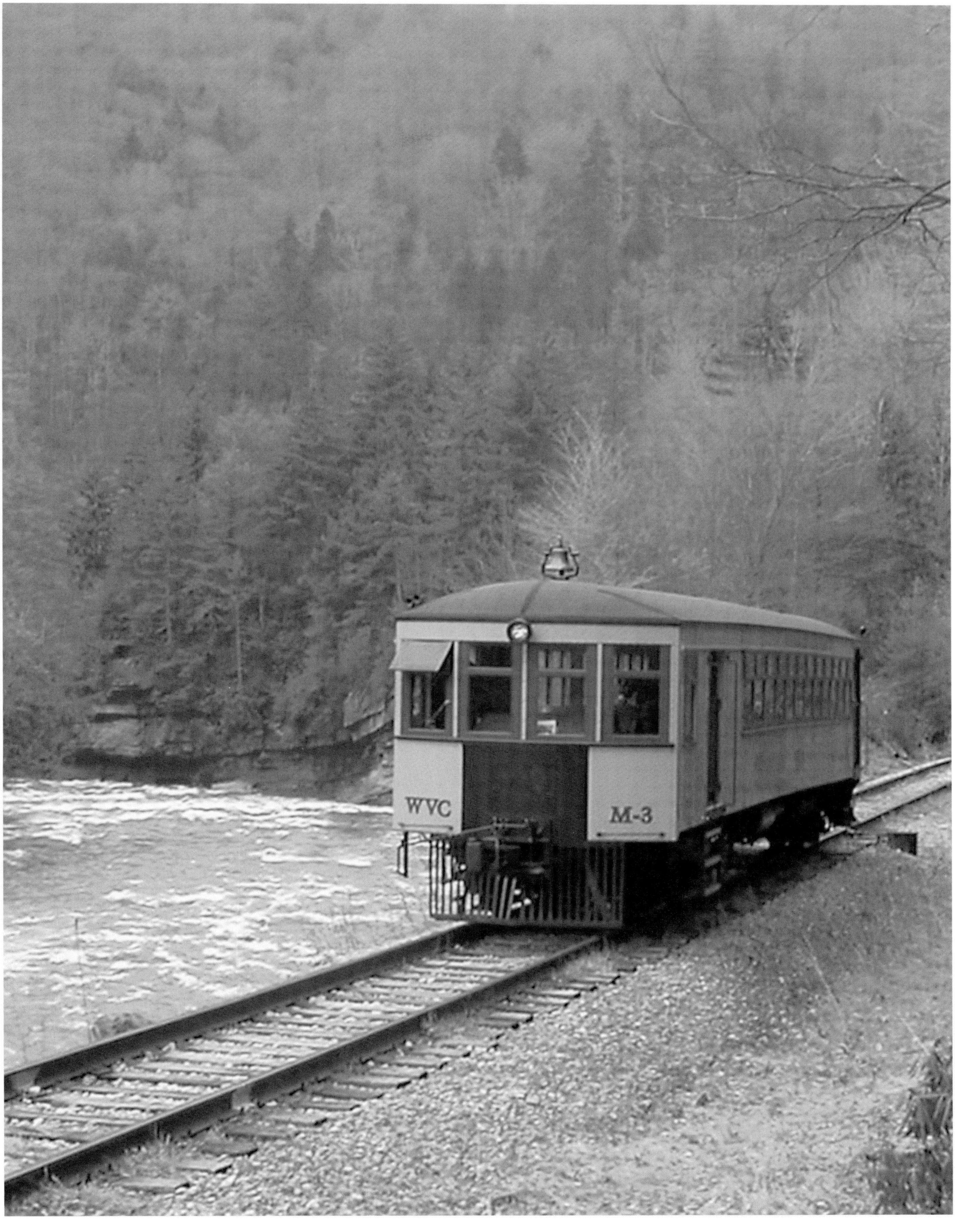
WVC
M-3

Part 2: H.P. Edwards, "The Doctor of Sick Shortlines"

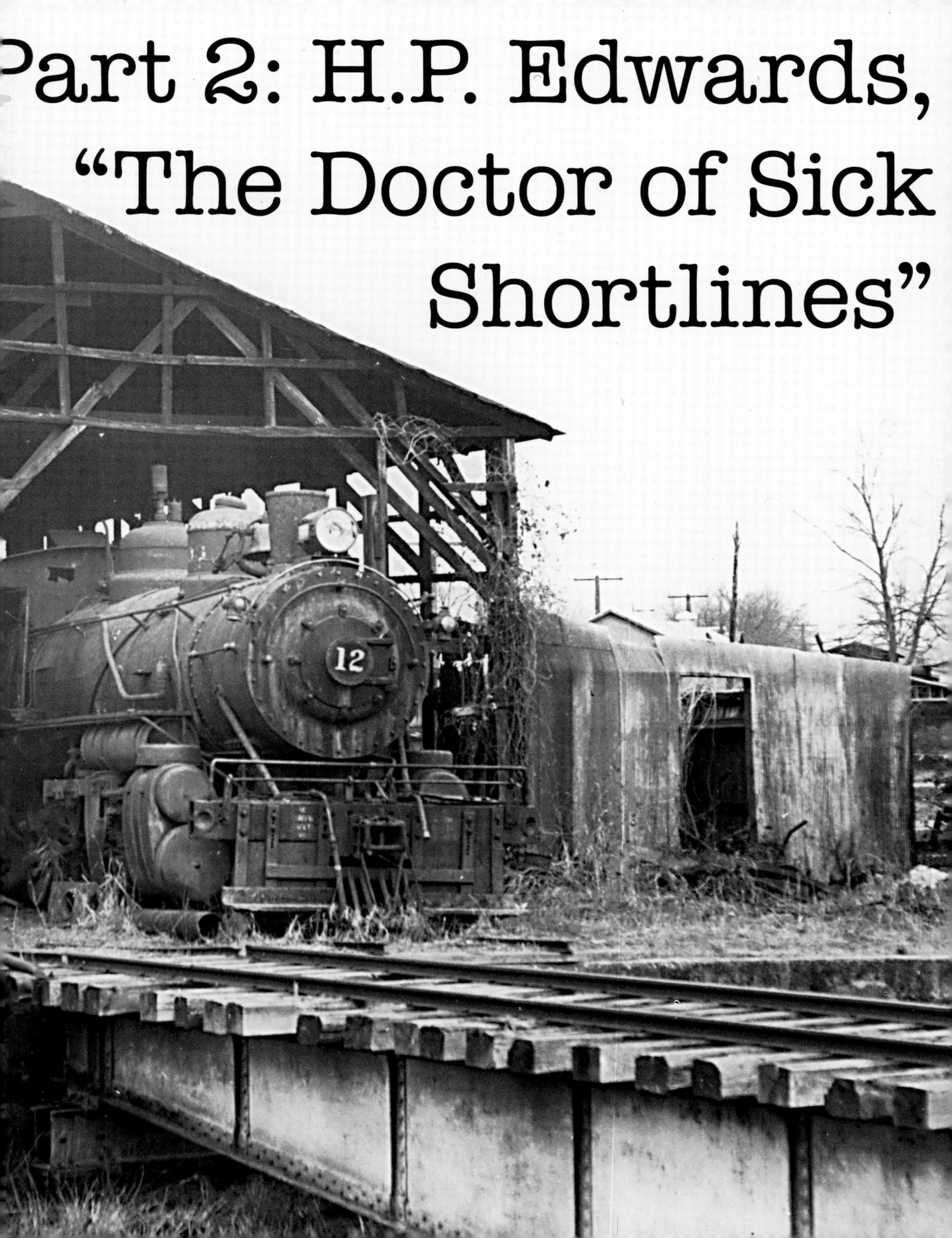

3. Atlantic & Western

The Atlantic & Western Railway is the railroad Edwards "cut his teeth" on. It was where he developed the railroad management skills that eventually lead to his founding of the Edwards Railway Motor Car Co. The A&W was founded by his father, William Joseph Edwards, and was incorporated on March 7, 1899 as the Atlantic & Western Railroad. The charter allowed the line to be constructed from Sanford, North Carolina to Goldsboro, North Carolina, a distance of seventy miles. In actuality, the line never reached a distance of more than twenty-five miles in total length. Joseph Edwards had envisioned a railroad that would stretch from central North Carolina through to the coast.

Though chartered in 1899, the line wasn't started until July 1903. In that year, fifteen thousand dollars in common stock and two thousand dollars of first mortgage bonds were issued to finance the construction. With this money in hand, the senior Edwards constructed three miles of track between Sanford and Jonesboro, North Carolina and the line became operational later in 1903. It should be noted that the Jonesboro stop consisted solely of a purple and white sign mounted on a pole. A connection was made at Jonesboro with the south end of the Cape Fear & Yadkin Valley Railway. The line was constructed according to rather poor standards, which included very light earthwork, several grades of three percent and curves as steep as twelve degrees. The rail used was fifty six pound relay rail, which had been rolled as early as 1879. Later, newer rail, which was forty pound was rolled in 1910.

The next phase of growth occurred later in 1903 when the common stock was increased to $53,400 and the first mortgage bonds to $100,000. The additional capital allowed the line to be extended from Jonesboro to Broadway, a distance of 6.18 miles. This section of track was completed and operational by July 1905. The first year of reporting for the A&W was 1906, in which a gross revenue of $10,410 was reported.

The railroad came under the control of the Meddendorf, William & Company of Baltimore, Maryland when all outstanding stock and bonds were acquired. From September 15, 1913, through April 19, 1915, several sets of additional bonds were issued, though only $3,000 of stocks, and $3,000 of bonds were actually sold.

Joseph Edwards held little or no formal title with the A&W, although he was the principal person responsible for the operations of the line. His son, Harry P. Edwards, served as general manager. Several of the investors were from Europe, and bond holder addresses included, but were not limited to, Paris, France, Basel, Switzerland and several other European cities.

Harry P. Edwards went to work for his father and soon began to learn the career of railroad management from the ground up. As the line began to build east from Sanford and extend toward Lillington, North Carolina, Edwards was placed in charge of the end-of-track crew. Before the tracks reached Lillington, the railroad encountered a handful of angry farmers who were not pleased with the fact a railroad was going to run through their property. Edwards supervised a crew as the line crossed one particular farmer's property, and the local sheriff was called and the crew was arrested for trespassing. Edwards then began a strategic game of cat and mouse in order to continue to push the tracks eastward. As the farmer and sheriff were escorting

ATLANTIC & WESTERN

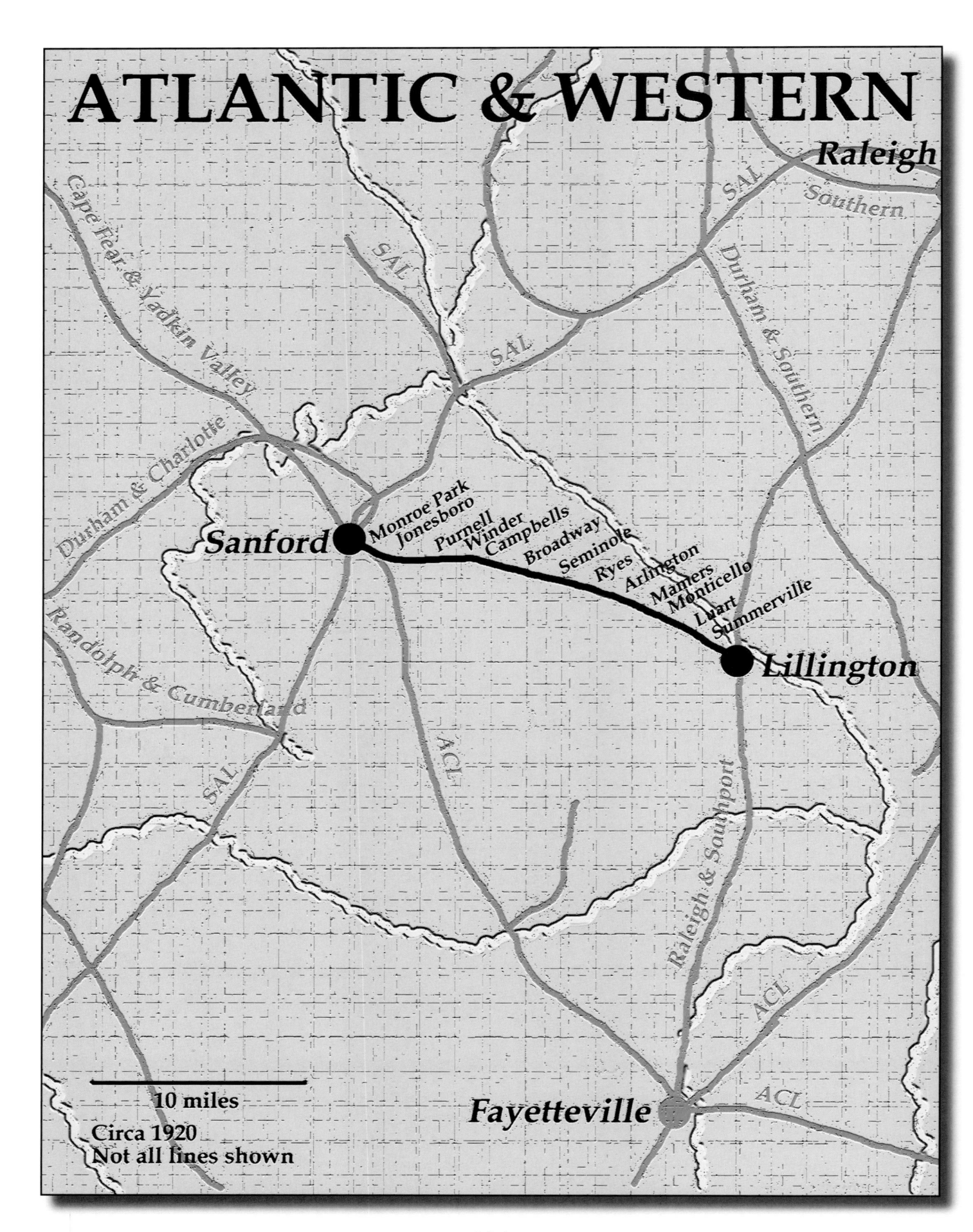

Raleigh

Sanford

Monroe Park
Jonesboro
Purnell
Winder
Campbells
Broadway
Seminole
Ryes
Arlington
Mamers
Monticello
Luart
Summerville

Lillington

Fayetteville

10 miles
Circa 1920
Not all lines shown

the first crew to the local jail, Edwards had a second crew ready and continued laying track. Upon the farmer's return, the sheriff had the second crew escorted to the local jail. Edwards had yet a third crew ready, and this crew was successful in pushing the line across the disenchanted farmer's property. Later on, the same band of farmers thanked both Joseph and Harry Edwards for their perseverance, as they later saw the economic development which the railroad produced.

Joseph Edwards died in April 1916 at the age of fifty-seven, at which time he was actively negotiating to extend the A&W eastward to the town of Swansboro, North Carolina, located on the Atlantic Coast Line Railroad. The line experienced financial trouble during certain periods of its history. The years from 1918 to 1921 were a particularly depressing period during which the railroad operated in a deficit. In an example documented by correspondence, the railroad even had difficulty paying for a caboose it had purchased. In correspondence dated February 19, 1924, Edwards notes the inspection of a caboose at Kearney, New Jersey. In counter correspondence, the Birmingham Rail & Locomotive Company wrote on April 1, 1924 that "our bank has not yet reported collection of this draft of $350.00."

Under Edwards's management, tie replacement was of vital importance. In a board of directors' report filed on December 31, 1924, Edwards noted that 39,442 ties had been replaced between 1921 and 1924. In addition, the report notes that "4 ½ miles of mainline track was covered by 40 lb. rail, which is entirely too light for moving current equipment." During 1924, a full mile of this forty pound rail was removed and replaced with fifty-six pound rail. It was noted in the directors' report that "we will have to replace the balance of this rail just as rapidly as our finances will permit." The report listed total mileage of the railroad as 24 miles of main line with 3.51 miles of sidings and industrial tracks.

A&W 4-6-0 no. 8 was built by the Baldwin Locomotive Works in 1906 for the Cape Fear & Northern as the (second) no. 103. After being sold to the Durham & Southern it found its way to the A&W where it served for fourteen years from 1930 to 1944 when it was retired. *Photo by William Monypeny, Collection of Mac Connery.*

In order to generate additional revenue, Edwards was willing to go after other railroads' business. For example, Edwards was advised in 1923 that a shipper, W. T. Temple, was moving shipments of fish from Norfolk, Virginia to Lillington via express. The express service was furnished by the Norfolk Southern Railroad, but was extremely poor. In order to get the contract, Edwards instructed company auditor E. T. Ussery to bill the shipments of fish from Mamers, North Carolina rather than Lillington, its final destination. The final method of shipment was to send the fish from Norfolk to Sanford via American Railway Express, then to Mamers on Southeastern Express, and finally from Mamers to Lillington on the A&W.

The report of 1924 further states the A&W had acquired a rebuilt sixty ton locomotive, while retiring two of its older locomotives due to age and defective boilers. At this time, the line had two steam locomotives, although one was of a light design and could not be used in heavy freight hauling. The report further noted the railroad had scrapped its three second hand coaches in favor of a gasoline railway motor car. The car was purchased new and replaced an older gasoline unit, which was being retired. The nonchalant method of mentioning the addition of a new gasoline motor car and the retirement of the older car was, in actuality, the announcement of the birth of the Edwards Railway Motor Car Company. Edwards had experimented with Kelly-Springfield built truck frames and motors on the A&W as early as 1917. The first several gasoline motor cars were built in the A&W shops, including one each for the B&O and the CB&Q, and several shortline railroads.

Edwards's two small children, Winslow and Bill, often visited their father at work. Bill remembered one day when he and his older brother

The A&W purchased Brill Car no. 7 in 1939 after considering an Edwards car. The car was nicely trimmed in red and blue with a silver roof. The unit was purchased from the Long Island Railroad and was photographed in front of the A&W station and office. **Collection of Jimmy Haire.**

played "post office" in the A&W freight station. The game consisted of pulling tags off of the freight and using them as "mail" for their post office. Bill remembered that his father came down from his office a short time later and furiously demanded, "Why hasn't this train gone out?" The train crew first told Edwards that the train was delayed due to the mail, which was partly true. Edwards quickly remembered that this particular train did not handle mail and demanded further explanation as to the delay. The crew reluctantly told him that it had taken them two hours to get the freight properly identified after the two boys had rearranged the labels.

On one other occasion, the two boys set a pile of wood shavings on fire in the ERwyMCC, which was located a short distance from the A&W freight office. They started the fire to see how well the new fire extinguishers worked; fortunately, the extinguishers worked as planned and the two boys caused no real damage. They did wonder why their father commented to their mother to "Get those Katzenjammers out of here!"

Edwards continually marketed the railroad and strove to find new sources of revenue. In 1921, he originated an idea to encourage local farmers to diversify their truckable produce and include watermelons in the next year's crop. Edwards went so far as to give free seed away to farmers who would agree not only to grow the melons, but also to ship the melons out via the A&W. It was reported that Edwards had convinced twenty-three farmers to take up his offer of free seed.

While Harry P. Edwards was serving as general manager of the A&W, it was placed in receivership by action of its bondholders on December 8, 1926. The railroad had a deficit of $153,919 and also owed an additional $149,000 in past due interest. On August 1, 1927, the Fidelity Trust Company of Baltimore sold the A&W at public auction, acting on behalf of the stockholders. Effective on September 9, 1927, the reorganized line was formally recognized as the Atlantic & Western Railway Company and was purchased for $122,000. The receivership must have weighed heavily on Harry Edwards's mind, for later in the year he tendered his resignation to accept the vice president and general manager's position on the Atlanta & St. Andrews Bay Railway. Under Edwards's management, he had stressed the importance of maintenance of way (MOW) upkeep, which may have been his undoing. In order to keep MOW upkeep in hand, he had deferred payments to the Seaboard Air Line Railroad and to the Southern Railway. A year later, Edwards was to lose control of the ERwyMCC as well, though he would be brought back in the latter part of the 1930s as vice president for sales.

The loss of the A&W must have been a bitter pill for Edwards to accept, particularly in light of the fact that this was the railroad founded by his father. If any consolation can be found in the situation, Edwards later became known (as he was first referred to in a local newspaper) as an "expert and doctor of ailing shortlines." One can only imagine that many of the lessons he learned on the A&W would be put into practice on the Atlanta & St. Andrews Bay Railway and the Atlantic & East Carolina Railway.

Edwards was replaced by E. T. Ussery, a longtime employee of the A&W. His career started in 1913 and he served as agent at Broadway, Lillington and Sanford. He left the A&W in 1917 to work on the Atlantic Coast Line/Seaboard/Southern joint office as a cashier. He rejoined the A&W for a long and distinguished career again in 1919 as the company auditor. After Edwards's departure, Ussery was named general manager of the reorganized company and would eventually become its president in 1961. The association between Edwards and Ussery had been close, as Ussery had become the ERwyMCC secretary and treasurer in 1924.

Ussery was able to keep the A&W solvent by reversing Edwards's philosophy of upkeep on the track. Instead, he concentrated on paying the back debt to the Seaboard and Southern, while deferring maintenance on the track and equipment. Ussery developed a payment plan in which the Seaboard Air Line was paid two hundred dollar monthly installments in order to erase the debt.

R. Douglas Walker, noted North Carolina railroad and logging researcher, was an observer of the A&W during the mid 1950s. As a freshman at Campbell Junior College in Buies Creek, North Carolina in 1955, he had the unique opportunity to observe several shortlines in the area. To Walker,

A&W depot in Lillington, as it appeared in October 1962. By this time the tracks have already been pulled from in front of the depot as the A&W had abandoned the line to Lillington. *Photograph courtesy of Douglas R. Walker.*

this small college was the absolute end of the state as far as railroads went, or so he thought. The closer he looked, he saw that shortlines actually surrounded him. Walker's observations were indicative of the A&W problems: it was located in an area saturated with shortline rail service, compounded with increased truck freight traffic.

Five miles to the west of Buies Creek was Lillington, the eastern end of the A&W. To the east was Coats, North Carolina, which was served by the Durham & Southern Railway (D&S). The D&S still ran steam locomotives to the south end of the line at Dunn, North Carolina during the mid 1950s. North of Coats was a D&S water tank that was seldom used, and a little further up the road, the D&S crossed the line of the original Norfolk Southern main line at Varina, North Carolina. During 1955, Walker watched a lot of trains on wavy rails with lots of weeds between the tracks that seldom seemed to bother their passage.

The A&W discontinued passenger service in 1949, although correspondence puts the conclusion at an official date of March, 1950. This date included the termination of mail and express service as well. The service had been conducted twice a day via a motor car.

The railroad struggled, yet held on through the Depression and the 1940s. The 1950s were draining on the line, and in 1959, the line lost $1,736.54. Losses continued in 1960 with a net loss of $10,983.45, and in the first seven months of 1961, a loss of $7,151.46 had accumulated. With the losses mounting, the board of directors asked the stockholders to abandon the largest portion of the line from Jonesboro to Lillington.

As a longtime employee of the railroad, Ussery had slowly assumed near total control of the operations of the line. As a case in point, he owned 205 shares of stock, with long time investors such as W. R. Williams owning 206 and H. C. Huffer owning 550. By 1950, Huffer owned only 39 shares, Williams owned 376, yet Ussery's portfolio had jumped to 1238 shares.

During a meeting held on July 3, 1961, the board of directors voted to abandon 20.62 miles of track from Lillington extending westward to a point halfway between mileposts four and three just east of Jonesboro. The Interstate Commerce Commission approved the abandonment on November 1, 1961, and the service order was effective for November 1, 1961. Operations discontinued on December 15, 1961, and ever since that date, the entire length of the Atlantic & Western Railway has been 3.38 miles of track. In 1963, the rails and other materials were dismantled and the abandonment was completed. A November 1963 issue of the Official Guide of Railways listed the official mileage as 3.36 miles in length. Several years later, the same publication listed the A&W as serving Sanford and Jonesboro and "beyond." The "beyond" was a two-mile extension that crossed North Carolina Highway 42 and ran to an industrial park that never seemed to have any rail customers.

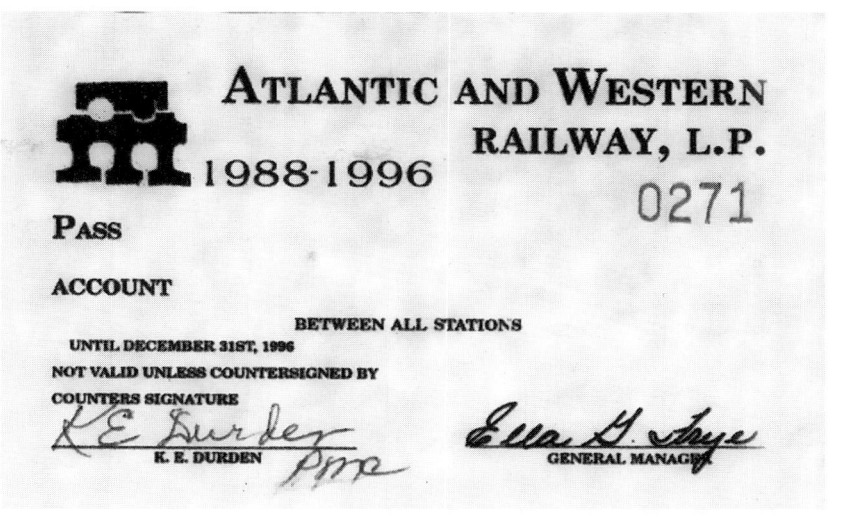

On December 15, 1967, the Atlantic & Western Corporation purchased all stock with the exception of 302 shares. On January 1, 1970, the Atlantic & Western Railway Company was merged into the Atlantic & Western Corporation. In May 1988, K.E. "Earl" Durden's, Rail Management & Consulting Corporation purchased the A&W and reorganized the company as the Atlantic & Western Railway, L.P. Ironically, the Atlanta & St. Andrews Bay Railway, another line once managed by Harry Edwards, was also owned and operated

Top, Atlantic & Western pass as issued by Earl Durden. **Above**, Atlantic & Western roundhouse as it appeared in February, 1954. No. 9, a Baldwin 4-6-0 can be seen at left; no. 12, a Baldwin 2-8-0, is at center; at right is no. 6, a derelict Edwards car. **Top, collection of the author. Above, photograph by Bob Drake, collection of John D. Porter.**

by the Rail Management & Consulting Corporation, which reorganized that road as The Bay Line Railroad, L.L.C. Along with his other shortlines, Durdan sold the Atlantic & Western Railway, L.P. and The Bay Line Railroad, L.L.C. to Genesee & Wyoming Inc., a shortline conglomerate, in 2005.

During the late 1990s, the A&W acquired the south end of the Atlantic & Yadkin Railway, which had become part of the Norfolk-Southern Railway system. The Atlantic & Yadkin was built just before the Civil War. Cumnock was a coal mining town and was in the Deep River coal fields. The railroad was built to haul coal from the Cumnock mine to Fayetteville. From Fayetteville it was shipped on the Cape Fear River to the port of Wilmington. The Confederate Navy used this coal in its war ships. The Cumnock mine was worked up to about 1928. The acquisition added a distance of 9.3 miles of track from Sanford to Cumnock, North Carolina. The additional nine miles, combined with the three miles of original line, gave the A&W a combined mileage of twelve main line miles of track. A large source of income for the railroad is the rental and lease of freight cars, of which in 1996, it had over twenty-one hundred revenue cars in service. It has been jokingly said that if all the boxcars made their way home at the same time, the original track could never handle the traffic, as their combined length would exceed the length of the track mileage.

Atlantic & Western no. 12 **(top)** is preserved beside the Railroad House in Sanford. The locomotive was originally built by Baldwin for the Raleigh & Southport. The unit was acquired by the A&W in July 1948, but retired when the line dieselized in 1950. A&W no. 109 **(above)** is seen on switching duty outside the Atlantic & Western office in Sanford. No. 109 was built originally as a GP-9 for the Denver & Rio Grande Western, but was rebuilt as a GP-10 by the Illinois Central Gulf where it was no. 8323. It was then sold to the Meridian & Bigbee and became no. 109 before migrating to the A&W. **Both photographs by the author.**

4. Bay Line

Harry P. Edwards spent his third longest tenure of railroad employment on the Atlanta & St. Andrews Bay Railway (A&SAB), behind that on the Atlantic & East Carolina and the Atlantic & Western railroads.

The Atlanta & St. Andrews Bay Railway, known as the Bay Line, was a relatively late railroad as construction dates go. Begun in 1905, the line eventually extended from Dothan, Alabama, south to Panama City, Florida. From the time of the very first European settlements in the Florida panhandle, it was recognized the region had a seemingly unlimited supply of forest products.

The backbone of the industry related to forest products was the harvesting of pine and related items to be made into naval stores. The term "naval stores" is a comprehensive term referring to rosin, turpentine, talk oil, and pitch, which were used for sealing and caulking wooden naval ships. In addition to the naval store products, the panhandle pine trees were used for the paper industry and for lumber.

In 1904, A.B. Steele, a railroad builder from Georgia, arrived in Panama City at the invitation of developers R.L. McKinney and G.M. West. McKinney soon founded the Gulf Coast Development Company and immediately served as the community's first mayor.

The area where the Gulf Coast Development Company began operations had been virtually unsettled, and it was quickly realized that a railroad was needed to connect with the rest of the country. As first president of the new railroad, Steel had to overcome several obstacles in completing the line. As the line was constructed south of Dothan, progress was hampered by an east-west Louisville & Nashville Railroad (L&N) line and a few separate logging lines. The L&N opposed the construction of the A&SAB line and went so far as to issue a refusal for a right-of-way passage and took the even more extreme step of placing a locomotive on their own main line over the spot where the A&SAB line would cross the L&N tracks at Cottondale, Forida. A.B. Steele and his superintendant, P. J. Dogner, stockpiled all necessary materials for construction and proceeded south when the locomotive was temporarily moved to allow passage of a train.

Three additional logging lines had to be crossed as well. To negotiate a quick settlement with one of the lines, the A&SAB had to install gates to protect the crossing. The crossing gate was at the highest elevation on the line, and if the gate was closed, the trains often stalled after losing their momentum.

Dealings with a third logging line ended in court with issuances of criminal trespass. The German-American Lumber Company filed a suit to prevent the A&SAB from crossing their tracks near

No. 107, a Baldwin built 4-6-0, poses for its builder's photo in October 1908. No. 107 was produced at Baldwin's Eddystone plant. *Collection of Donald Hensley.*

ATLANTA & ST. ANDREWS BAY

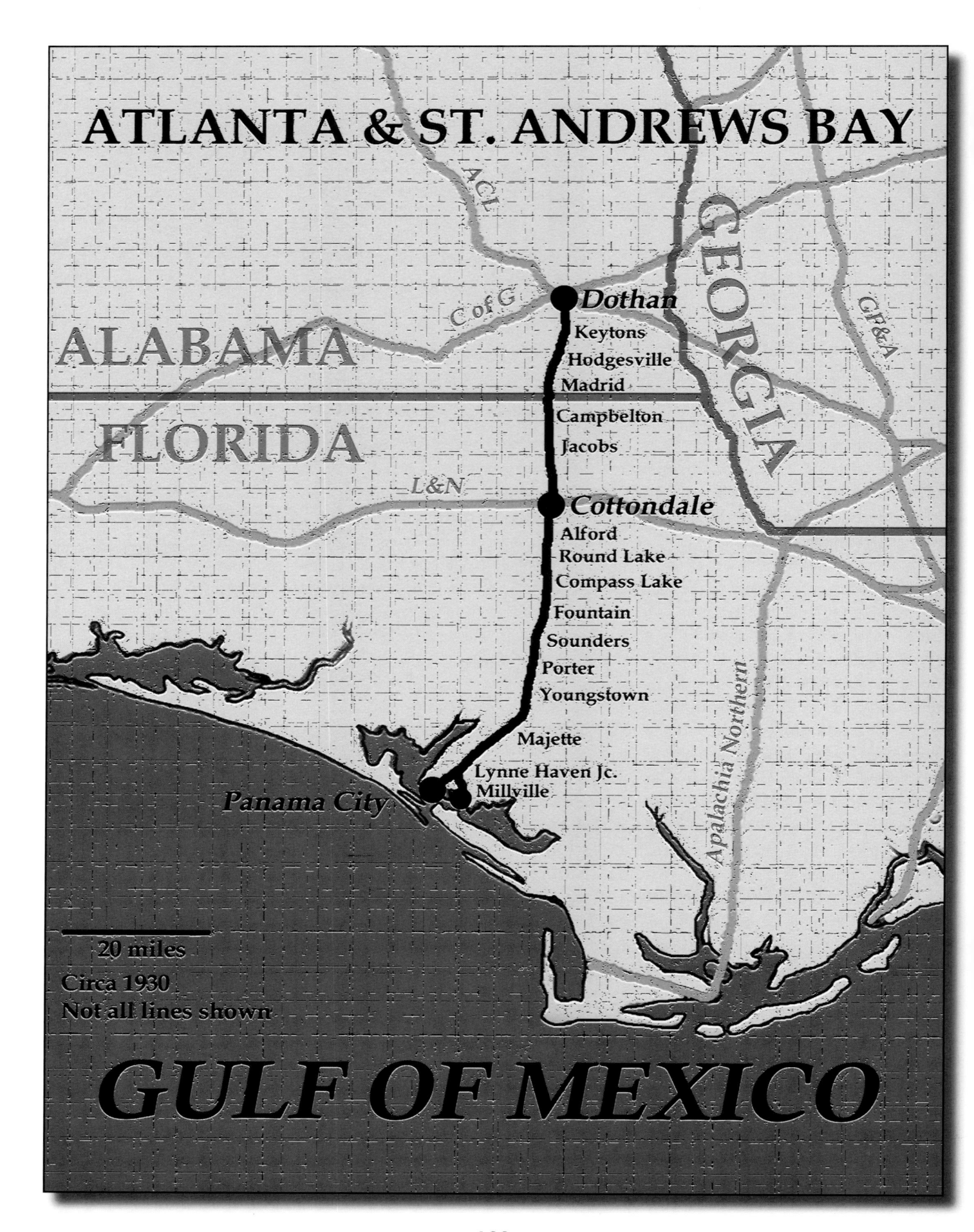

ALABAMA

FLORIDA

GEORGIA

ACL

C of G

GF&A

L&N

Apalachia Northern

- Dothan
- Keytons
- Hodgesville
- Madrid
- Campbelton
- Jacobs
- Cottondale
- Alford
- Round Lake
- Compass Lake
- Fountain
- Sounders
- Porter
- Youngstown
- Majette
- Lynne Haven Jc.
- Millville

Panama City

20 miles
Circa 1930
Not all lines shown

GULF OF MEXICO

Bayou George, Florida. R. L. McKinney and associate A. J. Gary took matters into their own hands and pulled up a section of the German-American Lumber Company tracks. Their bold move resulted in both being charged with trespassing, but the crossing was completed, and the construction proceeded south to Panama City. The first train pulled into Panama City in June 1908, and the first passenger train arrived on the 25th of the same month. It was estimated that 250 passengers made the first trip, pulled behind a second hand Baldwin built locomotive.

Interchanges would eventually include the L&N connection at Cottondale and both the Atlantic Coast Line Railroad and the Central of Georgia Railroad at Dothan. A four mile spur was begun in 1911 from Millville Junction on the line to Lynn Haven, Florida. The spur was completed June 10, 1913, with the first actual train making the trip on July 1, of that year. At 9:30 A.M., hundreds of well wishers cheered as the train headed toward Panama City, at a cost of thirty-five cents per passenger.

Shortly after the completion of the line, A.B. Steele passed away, and the line was sold to Asa G. Chandler, who had marketed and made Coca Cola a household name. Chandler purchased the line for fifty thousand dollars and intended to utilize the railroad to ship Coca Cola south to port as well as to ship seafood north to southern cities. Chandler had intended to push construction north to Columbus, Georgia which is ironically where the Coca Cola formula was developed by Dr. Robert Pemberton, a Confederate officer and local pharmacist.

In 1910, an excursion train filled with conventioneers to the Alabama Rural Carriers Association derailed south of Youngstown, Florida, when two cars jumped the tracks. No serious injuries were reported; however, it made for an overnight trip for the conventioneers as a jacking crew took until the next morning to re-rail the two cars.

In 1917, a wooden trestle over Bayou George was destroyed by fire and the railroad had to turn to an old nemesis, the German-American Lumber Company, and negotiate to permit their trains to operate over the logging line via Millville until the Bay Line's trestle could be restored.

The most notable train wreck on the line occurred on September 16, 1923, at Cottondale and involved an L&N train and a Bay Line excursion train. Both railroads usually stopped their trains before the intersection and allowed passengers to purchase food and refreshments. The L&N train was due at 10:45 P.M., and since the Bay Line train was approaching after 11:00 P.M., it is assumed the engineer thought the L&N train had previously passed. The L&N train was running late and engineer N. L. Boghie could not stop his train in time before colliding with the Bay Line train. Three were killed instantly, and three others were severely injured and died a few days later. An additional twenty-five passengers were injured in the collision.

Lack of debt payments sent the line to the State Trust, which in turn sold the line to the United Fruit Company. Co-

No. 131 **(top)** was a Schenectady 4-6-2 built in 1917 for the Florida East Coast. It was sold to the A&SAB in 1935 and later found its way to the National Railway of Mexico. No. 120 **(above)** was a Baldwin 4-6-0 built in 1913. No. 120 was later sold to the Sandersville Railroad, a Georgia shortline. ***Both, collection of Donald Hensley.***

founded by Minor C. Keith, the United Fruit Company was one of the largest conglomerates in the world.

Born January 19, 1848, Minor C. Keith was the son of Minor Hubbell Keith, a successful lumber merchant and Emily Meiggs, who was the sister of railroad builder Henry Meiggs. Keith began his railroad career with his uncle Henry when the pair began work on the Callao-Lima Railroad and the Oreja Railroad in Peru. Later the two landed a contract by the Costa Rican government to build a railroad from San Jose to the port of Limon on the Caribbean coast. By 1882, the line reached seventy-five miles, but it was running out of money and the Costa Rican government was defaulting on some promised payments. Keith pushed the line through, even though he was obligated to take on 1.2 million British pounds of debt to complete the construction. Once completed, the line did not have enough passengers to sustain it, so the solution Kieth arrived at was to start transporting bananas. Out of his desperation to secure capital, he would inadvertently develop one of the most powerful companies Central and South America had ever witnessed. By 1883, Keith owned three banana export companies, and their combined value exceeded the net worth of the railroad. Keith soon organized the Tropical Trading and Transport Company to handle all his banana business

Keith merged his company with that of two of his rivals; Andrew Preston and his partner, Lorenzo Baker. The combined companies were incorporated on March 30, 1899, as the United Fruit Company (UFC). Keith served as vice president of the new company, but quickly returned to his railroad interests when he bought the Western Guatemala Railroad. In 1911, Keith organized his railroad network in Central America as the International Railways of Central America (IRCA). The combined lines covered eight hundred miles of track and had a net value of eighty million dollars. One German historian referred to Minor C. Keith as the "uncrowned King of Central America."

Keith hired W. C. Sherman as vice president of the railroad, which allowed Keith to return to his aggressive expansion in Central America. Keith had used New Orleans, Louisiana and Tampa, Florida as ports of entry for his banana shipments, but soon became alarmed when tariffs continued to increase at those two ports. It can be argued that Keith was looking to develop Panama City into another port of entry and control the costs of the tariffs. It is known that Keith began developing the Port of Los Angeles as another entry way for his products. From 1927 through 1936, the UFC had a facility at Berth 188 at the Port of Los Angeles that was extremely labor intensive and involved storing the bananas before they could be loaded onto railcars. The delay meant that some spoilage occurred. In 1935, the UFC developed a new facility, which allowed moving the banana shipments directly from the transport ship to railroad cars. This new facility eliminated the need for the development of other ports of entry for Keith's banana crops in the western United States.

It was during Keith's ownership that Harry P. Edwards was brought in as vice president and general manager in July

No. 206 **(top)** was an Alco 0-6-0 built originally for the Florida East Coast as no. 140. No. 403 **(above)**, originally built as a 2-8-0 for the New York Central in 1920, was rebuilt as a 2-8-2 by the Brooks Locomotive Works. No. 403 came to the A&SAB in March, 1937. **Both, collection of Donald Hensley.**

No. 510 (**right**), an Edwards car built in 1928, could carry twenty-eight passengers and was photographed at Dothan in 1939. The same unit completely overhauled and renumbered (**below**) as no. 550. No. 550 served as a track inspection car and included a bedroom suite and kitchen. *Right, photograph by Henry C. Dubal, collection of Don Hensley. Bellow, collection of Quinton Bruner.*

1927. At the time, the A&SAB was headquartered in Panama City and had eighty-two miles of mainline track and eight miles of branch lines and sidings.

A November 19, 1929, public timetable gave several reasons passengers might want to patronize the Bay Line Railroad. The advertisement touted the gasoline passenger cars that produced "No Smoke, Cinders or Dust." The fine print stated: "Ride these cars and avoid the dust, dirt, the danger, crowded seats and close contact with diseased and undesirable persons encountered by traveling by buses over the highway." The advertisement featured a photo of A&SAB gasoline passenger car no. 503, which Edwards had helped design when employed by the ERwyMCC.

The 1929 public timetable boasted of paying thirty thousand dollars annually in county, city and federal taxes. It further stated that the annual payroll contributed to the county amounted to one hundred thirty thousand dollars and that the railroad spent ninety thousand dollars for materials and supplies that were purchased locally. The advertisement listed the following services: "Double daily main train service, double daily express service, double

125

daily passenger service and daily freight service." The railroad went so far as to inform the public that they provided "free taxi service at Dothan and Panama City to take passengers to and from their trains and their hotels and home." The 1929 public timetable appears to be one of the advertisements developed under the management of Harry P. Edwards.

Edwards realized that a percentage of his ridership was being siphoned off by bus lines as well as by some freight taking to the highways. Newly constructed highways paralleled a good portion of the line from Dothan down through Panama City. To combat his freight and rider loss, Edwards formed the St. Andrews Bay Transportation Company. This new company was given the mission of operating a bus and truck line over the highways from Panama City to Marianna to Pensacola and through to Dothan. Edwards personally served as president and general manager of the company, which was a wholly owned subsidiary of the A&SAB.

On July 14, 1929, Minor C. Keith died in an automobile accident. His death spelled a period of uncertainty for the railroad and its continued role in the importation of bananas. In the meantime, Edwards, in his role as vice president of the local Chamber of Commerce, helped lure the International Paper Company to locate a major plant in Panama City. One of Edwards's concerns was that the once vast forests in the region were being depleted. Before the days of conservation and replanting, the clear cutting methods of timber harvesting were laying bare broad tracts of land. Edwards saw the critical need to develop a new industry that would continue to use wood products but also help replenish the local forests. He probably also recognized the declining importance of banana shipments and the need for the industrial base to be more diversified and less dependent on one industry.

While employed on the A&SAB, Edwards and his two small sons entered into a somewhat idyllic life. The children often played on the beach and Edwards even purchased a thirty-foot cruiser to tour the islands around Panama City. Edwards employed a man named Captain Caswell to serve as his boat captain, and the small children viewed him as a great hero. This was partly due to his knack for coming up slowly on a shark and then jumping on top of the shark's back and dispatching it with his knife. In order to keep operating costs from rising, the captain was dismissed and the boat was eventually sold.

During this time Harry P. Edwards is generally credited with designing the first steel bulkhead pulpwood flatcars. In 1930, he purchased fifty flat cars from the Gulf, Mobile & Northern Railroad and had the cars sent to the Bay Line shop in Panama City. There, the steel bulkheads were attached to the flat cars and the cars were returned to service. The Bay Line thus became the first U.S.

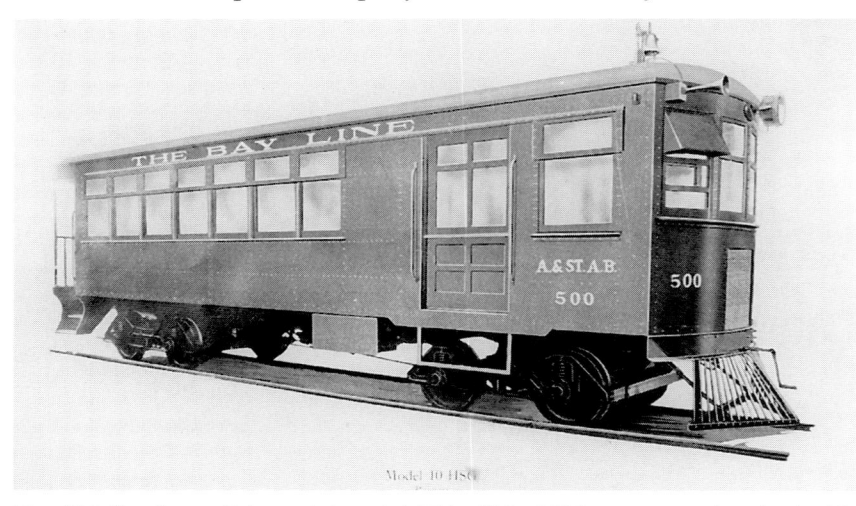

No. 503 **(top)**, an Edwards Model 25 built in 1928, was constructed with a large RPO compartment and seated only twenty. No. 503 was later sold to the Tallulah Falls Railroad of Georgia, where it was also used as a traveling post office. The car survives as of 2005 and awaits restoration. No. 500 **(above)**, the first of four units ordered by the A&SAB in 1928, was a Model 10 seating twenty-eight. **Both, collection of John D. Porter.**

railroad to haul pulp wood logs in such a manner. Today, similar cars are common on Class 1, regional and shortlines alike.

In 1931, the A&SAB was sold to the St. Andrews Bay Holding Company, a wholly owned subsidiary of the International Paper Company. This was the very company Edwards had earlier lured to locate in the Panama City area. After serving as general manager for a few months with the new ownership, Edwards left his employment with the A&SAB Railroad. He was promptly replaced by J. H. Frank as first president.

Edwards's departure is somewhat clouded, particularly since few concrete facts have come to light regarding his sudden resignation. Since Edwards had managed so well, one would question the need for his departure after the sale to the new owners. One line of speculation is that the International Paper Company had asked for a general reduction in traffic rates, which would impact the profitability of the A&SAB Railroad. It is thought that Edwards refused and was asked to resign his position. A document filed with the ICC for Edwards's proposal to manage the Atlantic & East Carolina Railway, attributed his resignation to the fact that "The paper company wanted to put their own men in charge of this railroad, therefore, Mr. Edwards resigned." It was a gentleman's way of putting this chapter in his life behind and moving on to new challenges.

A look at Edwards's accomplishments on the line during his five year tenure would convince most people that he was not let go for a lack of performance. Edwards facilitated the construction of a new port at Panama City which increased revenue and diversified traffic. He constructed new modern railway shops in Panama City and constructed an additional 10 miles of branch lines to serve new industries. Edwards also reduced operating costs by eighty-two thousand dollars during the first year of his administration and achieved a transportation ratio (train operating costs to operating revenues) of 19.65% during his tenure, which made the A&SAB one of the most efficiently operated railroads in the U.S. He secured a location at Panama City for construction of a large International Paper Company plant, which provided over one hundred carloads of freight per day for the railroad. Finally, bringing his own technology to the A&SAB, Edwards began the early conversion from steam to internal combustion locomotive power by purchasing five Edwards Railway Motor Cars for the road.

In 1934, A. Strayer became general manger and moved the headquarters to Dothan. The move was short lived, and Panama City soon once again became home to the A&SAB.

Edwards founded the St. Andrews Bay Transportation Company, which served as both a bus and over the highway freight company (top). The company was a direct subsidiary of the A&SAB and operated from Panama City to Dothan. Above, a builder's photo of a bulkhead flatcar used for hauling pulpwood. It is speculated that Edwards was the first to design such a car when he purchased fifty flatcars from the Gulf, Mobile & Northern and converted them into the design illustrated above. *Top, courtesy of Duke University Library, Edwards family archives. Above, collection of M.B. Connery.*

The Bay Line became one of the first railroads to dieselize. During the railroad's steam days, it used second hand engines, usually of the 2-8-2 or 4-6-2 classes. In March, 1941, the Bay Line purchased three new ALCO RS1 road switchers. The units served for several months with great success, only to be requisitioned by the Maritime Commission in January 1943 for the war effort. The units were then equipped with C-C trucks (which spread the weight of the locomotive out over more wheels enabling it to be used on lighter rail), had their cabs narrowed, and were placed in service on the Trans Iranian Railroad.

The Bay Line was also one of the few lines to acquire diesels during the war. ALCO S2 switchers were received in November 1942, and five more RS1s arrived in April 1943 to replace the requisitioned units. A third order of five RS1s arrived in October 1947. The fact that the A&SAB received highly sought after diesels during the war was no doubt because the line served as a strategic connection for moving war related materials. The Lynn Haven terminal was the origination point for oil trains, which headed north to their eventual destination of Churchland, Virginia. It is estimated that over sixty thousand tanker car loads of Bunker C oil were carried over the line, helping to feed the war effort. In addition to the rail contributions, the Wainwright Ship Yards of Panama City constructed 108 Liberty and Victory ships to help in the Allied war effort. Rail traffic had increased to such a degree that thirteen trains a day were run between Tyndall Field, Wainwright Shipyard, and the Naval Countermeasures Station.

On January 1, 1947, the Bay Line was designated a Class 1 railroad by the Federal Railroad Administration. The line had the distinct privilege of being the first Class 1 to become totally dieselized by June of 1947. In addition to its ALCO products, the railroad purchased its first EMD product, a steam boiler-equipped F3A, which it employed in passenger service. The passenger service ran from Panama City to Dothan and continued on to Albany, Georgia on the Central of Georgia tracks. Passenger service was discontinued on July 15, 1956. Local highways had cut heavily into the passenger revenues and the railroad chose to focus on freight service from that point onward.

By 1955, all new locomotive purchases would be EMD. The EMD units obtained over the next few years would be a general mixture of whatever EMD was producing at the time, including GP7s, SD9s, a single SD40, GP38s, a single GP39, and GP38-2s.

Trailer on flatcar traffic began in 1962 as the line continued to modernize. On July 14, 1971, the A&SAB completed construction of a branch form Campbellton, Florida, to a connection with the L&N at Graceville, Florida, a distance of seven miles. The branch enabled the A&SAB to haul a large volume of pulpwood from the Graceville area to the International Paper Company plant at Panama City. Other revenue traffic on the branch came from a large lumber mill and the Golden Peanut processing plant, thus diversifying the traffic base even more. After the pulpwood traffic from that area was depleted, the L&N abandoned its branch line into Graceville from the west and the A&SAB abandoned its branch between Graceville and Campbellton.

In 1979, the A&SAB was sold to Southwest Paper Industries. The line was later sold to the Stone Container Corporation, which on January 1, 1994, sold it to the Rail Management & Consulting Corporation which changed the name to The Bay Line Railroad, L.L.C. In 2005 the line was sold to Genesee & Wyoming Incorporated.

Current operations include a connection at Dothan with CSX, Norfolk Southern, Abbeville & Grimes Railway (a wholly owned subsidiary of the Bay Line of twenty-six miles which runs from Abbeville, Alabama to Grimes, Alabama) and the Hartford & Slocomb. An additional connection is with CSX at Cottondale, Florida. The rail is generally listed at 90 to 115 pounds, of which over thirty thousand cars travel per year. Commodities shipped include wood chips, chemicals, and agricultural, petroleum and paper products.

5. Marianna & Blountstown

Calhoun County, Florida, is a relatively inaccessible tract of land located in the state's panhandle. Before the construction of the Marianna & Blountstown Railroad (M&B), the Apalachicola River was the area's only dependable source of transportation. The railroad ushered in a boom for the isolated county. After the railroad, though, came the highways, which eventually spelled doom for the shortline railroad.

Incorporated in June 1908, the M&B Railroad started construction from its Louisville & Nashville Railroad connection in Marianna, Jackson County, Florida, and ran its right-of-way south to Blountstown, Calhoun County, Florida. The first train traveled the twenty-nine miles of track and arrived in Blountstown in September of 1909. Eventually the line constructed an additional eleven miles of track and reached Scotts Ferry, a logging community located south of Blountstown.

Rufus Pennington was a prominent businessman who wanted to develop the area. He needed the railroad to haul out timber and related products. He also theorized that the railroad would provide an important link to the outside world for the residents of Calhoun County. His theory was proven correct when residents came from Marianna to the north and from the Gulf coast to see the first train steam into Blountstown in September 1909. With a play on the M&B initials, the railroad quickly developed a couple of distinctive nicknames. For many locals, the line was referred to as the "Many Bumps," probably largely due to the fact that the line was never ballasted, like most other similar railroads. Other residents, recognizing its importance in the scheme of the local economy, referred to the railroad by a more fitting name, "Meat & Bread."

The isolation of the area was evident during World War I, when the M&B served as one of the few transportation arteries connecting the local citizens with the outside world. In 1917, a successful Army recruiting trip resulted in a full passenger train of recruits headed north out of Blountstown. By all accounts, it was a very emotional scene, most of the young recruits never having been outside of Calhoun County in their entire lives. On another trip, the M&B brought in a piece of war history to help with the local war bond drive. The railroad hauled in what was supposed to be a captured German tank on a flatcar for the locals to view. Study of existing photographs indicate the tank was more likely an Allied French Renault light tank. Even so, the tank was probably the first type of weaponry of this nature anyone in the county had ever viewed.

No. 70, a Baldwin built 4-6-0, was photographed in August, 1940, in Blountstown. **Photograph by C.W. Witbeck, collection of Louis Saillard.**

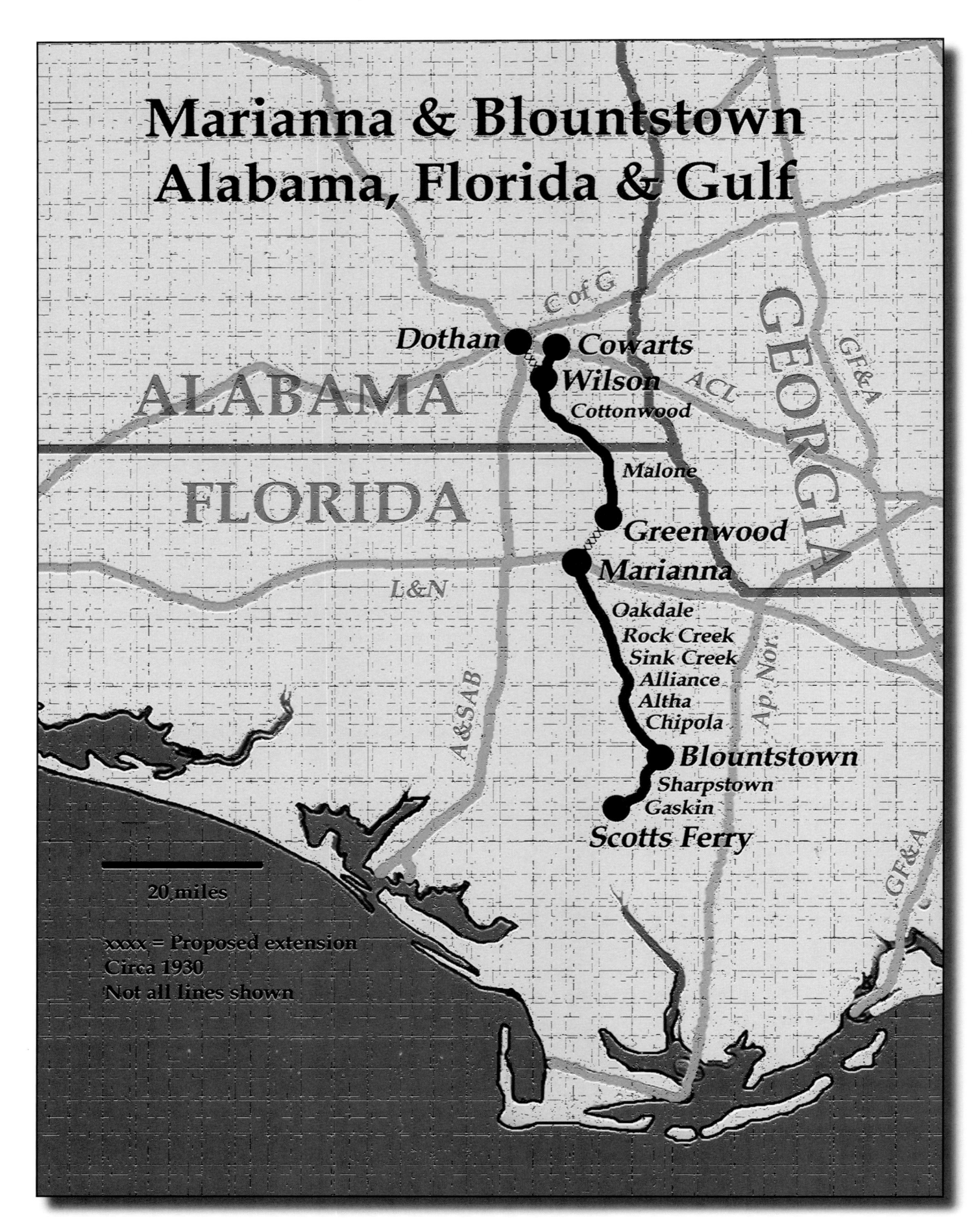

Marianna & Blountstown
Alabama, Florida & Gulf

Dothan
Cowarts
Wilson
Cottonwood
Malone
Greenwood
Marianna
Oakdale
Rock Creek
Sink Creek
Alliance
Altha
Chipola
Blountstown
Sharpstown
Gaskin
Scotts Ferry

ALABAMA
FLORIDA
GEORGIA

C of G
ACL
GF&A
L&N
A&SAB
Ap. Nor.
GF&A

20 miles

xxxx = Proposed extension
Circa 1930
Not all lines shown

The Scotts Ferry section of line supported several lumber mills and turpentine producers. Due to the timber being played out, operating the line ceased to be profitable, and the eleven mile section was abandoned in August 1938.

In March 1927, the line was sold to A. Felix duPont of Wilmington, Delaware. DuPont became de facto owner by accident when he purchased a large tract of land during the land boom of the mid 1920s. Of 1200 shares of stock, 1197 had been held by timber interests of the Pennington & Evans Company. The duPont family represented the largest manufacturer of explosives in the United States. In 1913, the company was broken up into three separate companies, but the duPonts remained one of the wealthiest families in the country. J. C. Packard, a native of Marianna, became the general manager for the duPont interests. Packard eventually acquired ownership when the timber track and railroad interests were later separated.

The railroad served as a passenger line until December 3, 1929. Increased competition from better roads, automobiles, and buses spelled doom for continued passenger service. From that date forward the railroad continued as a freight service only. It was under Packard's general managership that passenger service was discontinued.

In September 1930, O.O. Miller became general manager; he became president of the line on May 30, 1939. By July 23, 1947, Miller had acquired sole ownership of the railroad and had overseen the transition from steam to diesel when, on October 1, 1947, the last surviving steam engine was retired in favor of a 70-ton diesel-electric locomotive, no. 75, which was purchased new from General Electric. A second seventy-tonner, no. 99 was purchased from the L&N in 1969. No. 75 still operates on the Dakota Southern Railroad in South Dakota (as of 2005).

In 1932, after the International Paper Company replaced Harry P. Edwards as general manager on the Atlanta & St. Andrews Bay Railroad, he went searching for other suitable employment. Finding full time management jobs scarce with the Great

A busy day in Blountstown as one locomotive prepares for switching duties and another is serviced in the engine shed.
Photo by C.M. Clegg, California State Railroad Museum Library, Lucius Beebe & Charles Clegg Collection.

Depression raging, he turned to a series of "consulting engineering" jobs, as he called them, later in life. The first such position was on the Marianna & Blountstown Railroad.

What Edwards found on the M&B was a mainline, which ran north from Blountstown for a distance of twenty-nine miles to its connection with the L&N at Marianna. On the line were sixteen stations, along with both namesake towns and McNeil, which served as agency stations. McNeil served as an agency station for the eleven miles of logging line running south of Blountstown to Scotts Ferry and Myron, which was the end of the line and was as far south as the tracks were ever constructed.

In early 1931, the M&B began to prepare a case to be presented before the Interstate Commerce Commission by which it proposed to acquire another shortline which ran just north of the M&B tracks and to construct connecting tracks to make the railroad one single north-south line. Edwards was employed by the M&B to help develop the plan and to testify before the ICC for the proposed construction. The dual purpose of the plan was to purchase the Alabama, Florida & Gulf Railroad and to construct additional track to connect the disjointed segments of the two merged lines.

The AF&G was a contemporary line of the M&B and would have been a good fit as far as expansion went. W. S. Wilson and E. L. Marbury founded it on August 16, 1910, as a logging line. Originally called the Alabama, Florida & Southern, the line ran north from Malone, Florida, to a connection with the Atlantic Coast Line Railroad at Ardilla, Alabama, east of Dothan in Houston County. Wil-

No. 81, a Taunton, New Jersey built 4-6-0 **(top)**, was constructed in 1881. The M&B paid $4,541.36 for no. 81 in 1910. Baldwin built 4-6-0 no. 444 **(above)** had a long and colorful history. It was originally built for the Brinson Railroad in 1911, then went to the Savannah & Northwestern Railway, then to the Savannah & Atlanta Railway in 1917, and finally to the M&B in 1935. No. 444 survives today as a memorial to the M&B in Blountstown. ***Both photos from the collection of Louis Saillard.***

son became the sole owner and purchased a second logging road, which operated between Cowarts, Alabama and Cottonwood, Alabama. The combined line was incorporated as the Alabama, Florida and Gulf in 1917 as track had been constructed in the direction of Greenwood, Florida. By 1931 the AF&G was a combined twenty-nine mile line which ran from Cowarts to Greenwood. Its motive powered consisted of two steam locomotives as well as an Edwards Motor Car, Model 10 no. 500, which had been purchased second hand.

The AF&G had entered into receivership under the Dothan National Bank, which was also insolvent. Albert L. Lohn, the court appointed receiver, had earlier tried to sell the line to both the A&SAB and the Atlantic Coast Line, but both railroads rejected the proposal.

In the M&B's statement of its case before the ICC, filed on June 4, 1932, it outlined the following objectives:

1) To acquire by purchase from Albert L. Lohn, receiver for the Dothan National Bank, for $40,000, the name and assets of the Alabama, Florida & Gulf Railroad.

2) To construct and operate a line of railroad between Marianna and Greenwood, a distance of nine miles, to connect the present railroad with the property now operated by the AF&G.

3) To construct and operate a line extending from Wilson in the County of Houston, Alabama, on the present AF&G, to the City of Dothan, a distance of five miles.

The objective for the M&B was to reach Dothan, at that time the largest community in southeast Alabama and the Florida panhandle. With a population of sixteen thousand, the town was the center for a large agricultural and lumber producing area. It was also noted that the area served by the AF&G was surrounded by thirty million board feet of standing short-leaf and yellow pine. In addition, another one hundred million board feet of hardwood were also in the area.

No. 101, a Baldwin built 4-6-0, is seen hauling a mixed freight. No. 101 was originally built in 1919 for the Giles Bay Lumber Co. as No. 1. She went to the Georgia Northern in 1925 and from there to the Georgia, Ashburn, Sylvester & Camilla Railroad in 1937 and finally to the M&B sometime after that. Photo by Lucius Beebe, California State Railroad Museum Library, Lucius Beebe & Charles Clegg Collection.

Stiff opposition from the AS&B, the ACL, and the L&N lines met the proposed expansion by the M&B. While general manager of the A&SAB, Edwards had noted that the timber reserves along the tracks of the Bay Line were beginning to play out. It is possible the Bay Line wanted to tap into the reserves and continue to fuel the nearly insatiable appetite of the International Paper plant in Panama City.

The hearing was held in Marianna on April 1st, 2nd, and 4th 1932. H. C. Davis served as examiner for the ICC to hear and adjudicate the case. The M&B presented H. E. Stewart, a civil engineer for over thirty years, as a chief witness. Stewart estimated that the connection to Dothan, a distance of five miles, and the connection to the M&B, a distance of nine miles, would cost $89,970. He also hoped to replace much of the lightweight rail which was currently in place with heavier 70 lb. rail to be leased from an outside source. The earlier issue of a proposed sale of the M&B to the ACL system became a bitterly contested issue during the hearing. Under advice of counsel, the M&B was offered for sale under two premises. The first was to "attach the railroad to a strong truck line so as to insure its permanence and secondly to build it up to a point where it was not in danger of abandonment." In two letters dated September 15, 1931, and October 3, 1931, the offer of a proposed sale was listed in detail. During the ICC hearing, the L&N chose to introduce into testimony only portions of the proposed sale, rather than producing the entire documents. The M&B bitterly protested that either all of the documents be submitted as evidence, or that none of the letters be used in testimony.

Harry P. Edwards was brought in as a witness for the applicant and began his testimony by stating that for twenty-five years he had experience in all branches of railroading, and especially in shortline railroads, "having examined, inspected and made reports on twenty-five different shortlines located in various parts of the United States." From 1919 through 1921, Edwards had served with the United States Railroad Administration under W. H. King. It was in this capacity that Edwards had toured and inspected numerous shortlines around the country. He further testified that in 1931, he made a thorough inspection of the AF&G, in which he "interviewed citizens, gathered statistics in regard to traffic and made up an estimate of earnings, with an approximate estimate of the investment required to extend the line to Marianna and Dothan."

Edwards knew he would be going up against his former employer, the A&SAB. It was noted in the ICC report that the Bay Line was "very familiar to the witness," seeing as he served four years as the executive vice president and general manager for that railroad. To counteract any criticism, Edwards stressed to the ICC that no railroad would lose significant traffic because of the merger. His testimony included the following statement in which he stressed his point, "The traffic taken from the L&N at Marianna will be given to the other lines including its owner, the (Atlantic) Coast Line, and the traffic that will be taken at Dothan will be given back to the L&N, and it will not injure but would greatly benefit the national railway system as a whole. In addition, thereto, whatever traffic might be taken from the L&N would be given to the (Atlantic) Coast Line, which owns the L&N, at Dothan."

When asked his opinion regarding the sale and the price being asked for the AF&G, Edwards responded that in his opinion, "the forty thousand dollars was a fair and conservative price and value for the property of the AF&G." Further testimony on his part revealed a tenet of his true management style, which was known for cutting costs and improving the efficiency of his railroads. He proposed to the ICC that the merger of the railroads would greatly improve customer service and eliminate delays exchanging freight between two separate railroads. He also promoted the cost savings of eliminating one executive department and one accounting department, and eliminating the keeping of two sets of books and two separate locomotive shops.

On the other side of the ICC hearing, H. W. Woolf, Secretary and Auditor of the Bay Line, represented the A&SAB. In his testimony, Woolf readily admitted the land just south of Dothan was largely cut over timberland and was not currently being developed by his railroad.

Harry P. Edwards was recalled for additional testimony during the ICC hearing. He was asked to confirm the amount of revenue — thirty thousand dollars a year — derived by the Bay Line from all intermediate stations other than Panama City and Dothan and the interchange at Cottondale. In the course of this argument, it was established that the revenue area did not extend more than ten miles on each side of the right-of-way of the Bay Line. In effect, Edwards was arguing that from Cottondale south, there would not be any significant competition from the merger of the M&B and the AF&G. He further argued that "if the application is granted,

AF&G railbus no. E-1 at Cowarts in June 1940. Under Edwards's guidance, the AF&G and the M&B won ICC approval to merge into one operating system. *Photograph by J. E. Junas, collection of F.E. Ardrey, Jr., courtesy of Louis Saillard.*

the Bay Line would not lose any traffic at all, other than at Cottondale and a small amount in Dothan." It would seem extremely difficult to argue against a witnesses who just months earlier was privy to the most confidential revenue data.

In his second round of testimony, Edwards admitted that the L&N would lose some of the interchange at Marianna, but pointed out that this traffic would then go to the ACL and the Central of Georgia in Dothan. With the ACL owning the L&N, he theorized that little overall traffic would be lost because additional traffic would be gained from new businesses that would locate on the newly created tracks of the merged railroads.

In an interesting turn of events, Edwards used his intimate familiarity with the A&SAB to compare the two railroads and their perspective operating costs. He testified that the Bay Line "has forty trestles totalling 7,000 feet, while the proposed new line would have only 3,700 feet of trestles and there will only be 1,000 feet of trestle on the portions to be constructed." His next statement could be viewed as the coup de grace; he argued before the ICC examiner, "the operating expense of the Bay Line is much heavier than the operating expense of the proposed new line, because the trestle mileage is much greater and heavier."

When asked under testimony about the association of the Bay Line with the International Paper Company, Edwards responded that "A. R. Graustein was president of the International Paper Company and Mr. Friend was vice president of the Southern Kraft Corporation, which is owned by the International Paper Company, with both companies operating the plant in Panama City, Florida." He then identified Graustein as recently being elected president of the Bay Line and Friend as executive vice president of the Bay Line, a title Edwards had held earlier while employed by that railroad. Edwards's last piece of testimony was to place a $2,500 scrap value on the sole locomotive and an additional $400 on a motor car and some company buildings of the AF&G. The motor car was an Edwards Model 10.

The ICC denied the Bay Line a hearing in which to continue its protest and the merger was approved. In its final decision, a 1921 case in which the AF&G had petitioned the ICC to complete the southern extension into Marianna was cited as a reason for approving the merger plan. Other reasons included having both Alabama and Florida's approval, and by having the approval of the Comptroller of the Currency, who was asking the Commission to grant the application arguing "that otherwise the depositors of an insolvent national bank will suffer tremendous loss."

In a ruling dated October 8, 1931, the ICC found in favor of the Marianna & Blountstown acquiring the Alabama, Florida & Gulf Railroad and commencing with the new track construction. Though the ICC noted the "L&N and St. Andrew Bay line doubtless will lose some traffic under the plan presented, but their loss is more than offset by the benefits to shippers along the lines involved." The ICC ruling made three provisions. The first allowed the acquisition and operations of the AF&G by the M&B. The second allowed for both construction of the extensions from Marianna to Greenwood and construction connecting the now joined lines with a second extension from Wilson to Dothan. The third provision stated the extensions "shall be commenced on or before January 1, 1933, and to be completed on or before January, 1, 1934."

Although they had approval in hand from the ICC and despite the hard work and testimony by Harry P. Edwards and other witnesses, the M&B found it impossible to raise the capital needed to purchase the AF&G from the bank. By the late 1930s, the Alabama, Florida & Gulf had disappeared into bankruptcy and the line was scrapped.

Blountstown became a major truck produce growing area during World War II. In 1945 alone, the M&B shipped 672 carloads of watermelons during the growing season and an additional 92 carloads of cucumbers. A local ice plant supplied ice at its facility to accommodate the around the clock shipping of vegetables to a hungry nation.

In 1958, Miller died and his brother in law, Alton Denby, assumed the general manager's position. In 1959, the line was sold to George Tapper, who wanted to develop another revenue source, crushed rock. Tapper negotiated a contract with the U. S. Corps of Engineers to provide crushed stone to form jetties and rip rap along the Chattahoochee/Apalachicola River. The eventual destination of the crushed rock was Columbus, Georgia and the M&B ran shifts around the clock to meet the provisions of the contract.

The Marianna & Blountstown Railroad Company

TIME TABLE NO. 21
Effective June 15th, 1925.
DAILY EXCEPT SUNDAY

No. 1 A.M.	Mi.	Stations (Central Time)	No. 2 P.M.
6:00		Lv. Marianna	
2:40			
6:18	5	*Oakdale	
2:20			
6:30	8	*Simsville	2:10
6:37	10	*Rock Creek	2:00
6:40	11	*Union City	1:57
6:45	12	*Sink Creek	1:53
6:58	14	*Cox	1:48
7:01	15	*Alliance	1:44
7:05	16	Altha	1:40
7:09	17	*Langford	1:35
7:18	19	*Chipola	1:30
7:30	22	*Leonards	1:18
7:42	25	*Durham	1:08
7:46	26	*Mill City	1:04
7:50	27	Blountstown Lv.	1:00
8:00		Ar. McNeal	

No. 3 A.M.			No. 4 A.M.
8:10		Lv. McNeal Ar.	
8:15	27	Blountstown	10:40
8:35	31	*Flowers Still	10:20
8:50	35	*Sharpstown	10:05
9:10	40	*Gaskins	9:45
9:20	42	*Scotts Ferry	9:35
9:25	43	Myron Lv.	9:30

STATIONS MARKED THUS (*) ARE FLAG STOPS
As Information, Not Guaranteed

CONNECTIONS
AT MARIANNA ---
WITH LOUISVILLE & NASHVILLE RAILROAD.

L. N. SMITH, Superintendent

The round the clock schedule produced a beating on the tracks, and with little proactive maintenance being done, the line was in horrible shape. In the last months of 1970, the line was shut down and Tapper filed for abandonment in January 1971. His abandonment petition came nearly a year after trains last operated over the railroad. The ICC rejected the request for abandonment due to the outcries of local merchants and businessmen who wanted the line to remain open. Locals also accused Tapper of profiteering from the rock hauling contract and deferring all maintenance on the track.

On September 10, 1971, the ICC approved sale of the line to Joseph C. Bonanno, of Essex Falls, New Jersey. Thus began one of the most unique and controversial ownerships in U.S. railroad history.

When Bonanno purchased the line in 1971 for $ 170,000, he promised the shippers on the line that he would rehabilitate the line for freight traffic. The local press went as far as to describe Bonanno as "a man in a white hat," but he later took on the persona of a mobster who refused to allow his face to be photographed. Several questions immediately emerged regarding Bonanno's acquisition of the M&B. His application to acquire the line was approved by the ICC in only three days, a record speed according to most railroad officials. This was at a time in ICC history when acquisitions, mergers, and other transactions took months, if not years, to facilitate. Even then governor Reuben Askew sent a telegram of support, and the customary public hearing was waived in order to expedite the sale approval.

Applause for the sale soon turned to suspicion when the line was not immediately revitalized and operated as had been promised. Bonanno's plan was to use the former vegetable packing facility as a car repair shop. The venture was short lived when Bonanno came under the suspicion of the trustees of the Penn Central Railroad. The Federal Bureau of Investigation alleged that 638 former Penn Central boxcars had their reporting marks covered up and replaced with markings of the LaSalle & Bureau County Railroad (LS&BC), a line owned by Bonanno. The LS&BC was a fifteen mile long shortline located in Illinois and had direct ties with Bonanno. Bonanno had promised to provide an ample supply of cars for shipping on the line in order to lower the rates; the local shippers would probably have never suspected that it was alleged he got his supply of boxcars compliments of another railroad.

A 1925 timetable **(top)** shows the relative slow pace of travel between Marianna and Blountstown. The local vegetable produce shed **(above)** was an invaluable source of revenue for the M&B. **Both, collection of Pat Trammell.**

During the early 1970s, Congress passed a measure which would allow railroads to rebuild their boxcar fleet. At the time, the larger Class 1s had allowed their fleets to decline in number and quality, and shippers were in need of new cars for shipments. The ICC intervened and allowed shortline railroads to substantially build their boxcar fleets to meet this demand. During this time period, shortlines around the country sported new paint schemes and increased fleet size. There was a major stipulation, which led to speculation as to why Joe Bonanno wanted the M&B. A provision in the Congressional measure allowed only currently operating shortlines to participate in the program; hence the reason to purchase an existing operating line.

As the FBI continued its investigation, Bonanno began to search for a buyer for the railroad. He had purchased the line for $170,000, and only a few months later, his asking price was $500,000. This astronomical sum for a twenty-nine mile shortline with a couple of locomotives was considered excessive and kept most serious buyers at bay. The operations along the route were limited by poor track and needed bridge work. It was noted that one observer

A mixed freight can be seen **(top & above)** moving slowly through Altha, Florida, in February, 1960. By this time a GE seventy ton diesel-electric locomotive had replaced the steam units. The caboose still exists as part of a memorial to the M&B in Blountstown. *Both photos by J. C. Hawkins, collection of Louis Saillard.*

had seen a northbound train moving about five miles per hour. The observer asked the conductor when he had left Blountstown, and the answer was "Just after lunch yesterday. We'll probably make it to Marianna today." It was taking two operating days to make the twenty-nine mile run. The conductor was not riding in the train, but following along in his VW Beetle in case he needed to shovel out a crossing ahead of the train. His explanation as to why he drove, rather than ride the engine, was, "You never know when we'll fall in and have to go for help."

Bonanno found a buyer in Alexander Thesharous of Connecticut and Alfred Merolla of New Jersey. The two purchased the line on June 8, 1972. However, the line reverted back to Bonanno when the check failed to clear and the pair were found in default of payment on December 6, 1972.

With the bridge over the Chipola River damaged from flooding, Bonanno filed a petition to abandon the line south of the river on August 22, 1973. On January 16, 1974, he petitioned the ICC to abandon the remainder of the line. The ICC initially decided against abandonment on June 2, 1975; however, it reversed its decision on July 21, 1976, and allowed formal abandonment to take place. On that date, the Marianna & Blountstown Railroad ceased to exist. Bonnanno was never indited by the FBI and an agreement was reached with the Penn Central where all charges were dropped.

Several items relating to the M&B still exist. The small depot in Blountstown is still standing and is being used as an arts and craft store. A locomotive and caboose are also on display, complete with a State of Florida historical marker. How the locomotive, tender and caboose became a memorial is really a story about the depth of pride and civic involvement on the parts of the citizens of Blountstown.

The people of Blountstown rallied around every effort to revitalize the M&B, regardless of who the owner was at any given time. Even after the ICC gave final approval to allow the line to close, the community sought to remember the M&B in some

The undoing of the Marianna & Blountstown occurred when the Chipola River washed out a section of trestle. Without the ability to reach its connection to the outside world in Marianna, the railroad held on for a few years and eventually was abandoned. **Collection of Louis Saillard.**

fashion. The locals noted that the county possessed not a single monument or historical marker. With this in mind, the community sought to commemorate the Marianna & Blountstown Railroad.

A dedicated group of Blountstown citizens organized a committee to establish a proper memorial. State funding was secured and Florida's Secretary of State, Jim Smith, made a trip to Blountstown and presented the community with a check for fifty-five thousand dollars to be used to establish the memorial. Local citizens, Bobby O'Bryan, Hentz McClellan, and David House then looked into the possibility of purchasing no. 444, a 4-6-0 steam locomotive to be used as the centerpiece for the memorial. No. 444 had a stellar career on the M&B and the locomotive would serve as an appropriate memorial. The group had located the locomotive outside Houston, Texas, where a local physician had purchased it as a collector's piece. The engine was scheduled to be cut up for scrap metal after the doctor's death. The committee purchased the engine and tender (the original tender having long since fallen apart to rust and neglect) and began the extensive preparations for its journey back to Florida.

One major hurdle was the State of Louisiana, which was going to charge the local committee the enormous price of thirteen thousand dollars to issue a special permit for the transport vehicle to cross its borders. Due to intense local and state legislative efforts, the fee was reduced to three thousand dollars. No. 444 began its journey home on May 30, 1989.

Today no. 444, along with the new tender and caboose, proudly reminds both residents and visitors of the heritage and history of the Marianna & Blountstown Railroad. The locomotive is painted yellow and green. This particular paint scheme was apparently the result of the wishful fantasies of the Houston doctor wanting to own a locomotive in the distinctive Southern Railroad paint scheme. Today, the memorial, with the salvaged depot not far away, represents one of the more unusual, yet positive attempts by a small community to preserve a bit of its local railroad history. The site was the first in the county to be granted a historical marker.

No. 444 **(top)** was built by Baldwin in 1911 for the Brinson Railway. It was acquired by the M&B in 1935. Upon retirement it found its way to a private collector in Texas and eventually was bought by the town of Blountstown. The Blountstown depot **(above)** now serves as an arts and crafts store. It is the sole surviving structure related to the M&B. **Both photographs by the Author.**

Title: M & B RAILROAD
Location: Railroad and Pear Street
County: Calhoun
City: Blountstown
Description: For 63 years (1909-1972) the Marianna and Blountstown Railroad was Calhoun County's link to the railroads and commerce of the nation. Sometimes known as "Many Bumps" or "Meat and Bread," the M&B had a significant impact on the lives of Calhoun Countians. Until 1929, before automobile travel was commonplace, the M&B provided passenger service. Farmers used the railroad to ship a wide array of agricultural products. In the early years, logging spur lines extended into remote areas of the county and millions of board feet of long-leaf pine lumber were shipped from local sawmills. The M&B also carried mail, manufactured goods and building products. During its operation, the 29-mile-long line was Florida's shortest railroad. Until 1938 it ran 16 miles farther south to Scotts Ferry. Steam locomotive #444 was in operation when the M&B's first diesel engine arrived in 1947 and rests today on the exact location of the M&B roadbed.
Sponsors: Sponsored by Rep. Robert Trammell in cooperation with the Florida Department of State

The citizens of Blountstown and the surrounding area rallied to purchase no. 444 in order for it to serve as the center piece for a memorial dedicated to the M&B. The full text of the marker appears above. *Photograph by the author.*

6. Watauga & Yadkin River

The Watauga & Yadkin River Railroad (W&YR) came into existence as the Watauga and Yadkin Valley Railroad, a feeder line positioned to transport lumber from the Grandin Lumber Company's mill at Grandin to a connection with the Southern Railway. The Grandin Lumber Company was set up to harvest the vast timber resources of western Wilkes County and northeastern Caldwell County, North Carolina. Western North Carolina was known to contain huge virgin stands of timber and other natural resources. The first species sought were black walnut, ash, and cherry and later, poplar and oak. In 1911, W. J. Grandin, a prominent Pennsylvania timber man, came in search of new timber reserves. He purchased sixty thousand acres from former Confederate General Robert Hoke. Hoke had himself purchased the land in an attempt to gain control over two local railroads, the Caldwell & Northern and the Carolina & North-Western.

On December 14, 1911, with state charter in hand, Grandin established his company with $1,950,000 in capital and headquartered it in Lenoir, North Carolina. Pennsylvania native H. C. Landon was brought in both to survey the railroad route and to estimate the timber reserves. The line would begin at the sawmill at what would become known as Grandin. Landon surveyed two very distinct routes—one connecting with the Carolina & North-Western Railway in Lenoir and the second route connecting with the Southern Railway at North Wilkesboro, North Carolina. The first route was only fifteen miles in length but would consist of steep grades. The second route was twice as long, but was chosen because it followed the meandering Yadkin River and had much more manageable grades. The technique of following a meandering river had long been utilized in western North Carolina, the best example being the Southern Railway with its tracks following the French Broad River from Asheville, North Carolina into eastern Tennessee.

The line was constructed by hiring local workers, supplemented by convict laborers hired from the state of North Carolina. While this technique was not unique to the Watauga & Yadkin Valley Railroad, it had not been employed for a number of years. During the 1870s and 1880s, when the Western North Carolina Railroad was being built, it employed large numbers of convict laborers who pushed the line westward towards Asheville. During the construction of that line, the state reported 120 convicts had lost their lives, but most researchers feel the number was much closer to 400. There was a resulting outcry, and the practice of using convict laborers tapered off. Grandin, however, was able to secure the hiring of a number of convict laborers, and there is a record of one such individual being killed by falling stones. It was recorded that he was wrapped in a blanket and buried alongside the tracks, the same practice employed by the Western North Carolina Railroad more than thirty years earlier.

While the Watauga & Yadkin Valley was a subsidiary of the Grandin Lumber Company, it had grandiose ideas of its own. One such idea was to build north along Elk Creek and then into Brownwood, North Carolina, where a connection with the Norfolk & Western Railroad could be established. This would allow the W&YV Railroad to serve as a bridge route between the Southern Railway and the Norfolk & Western Railroad. While the line never made it that far, a branch split at Elkville, North Carolina, where it followed Elk Creek to Darby, North Carolina.

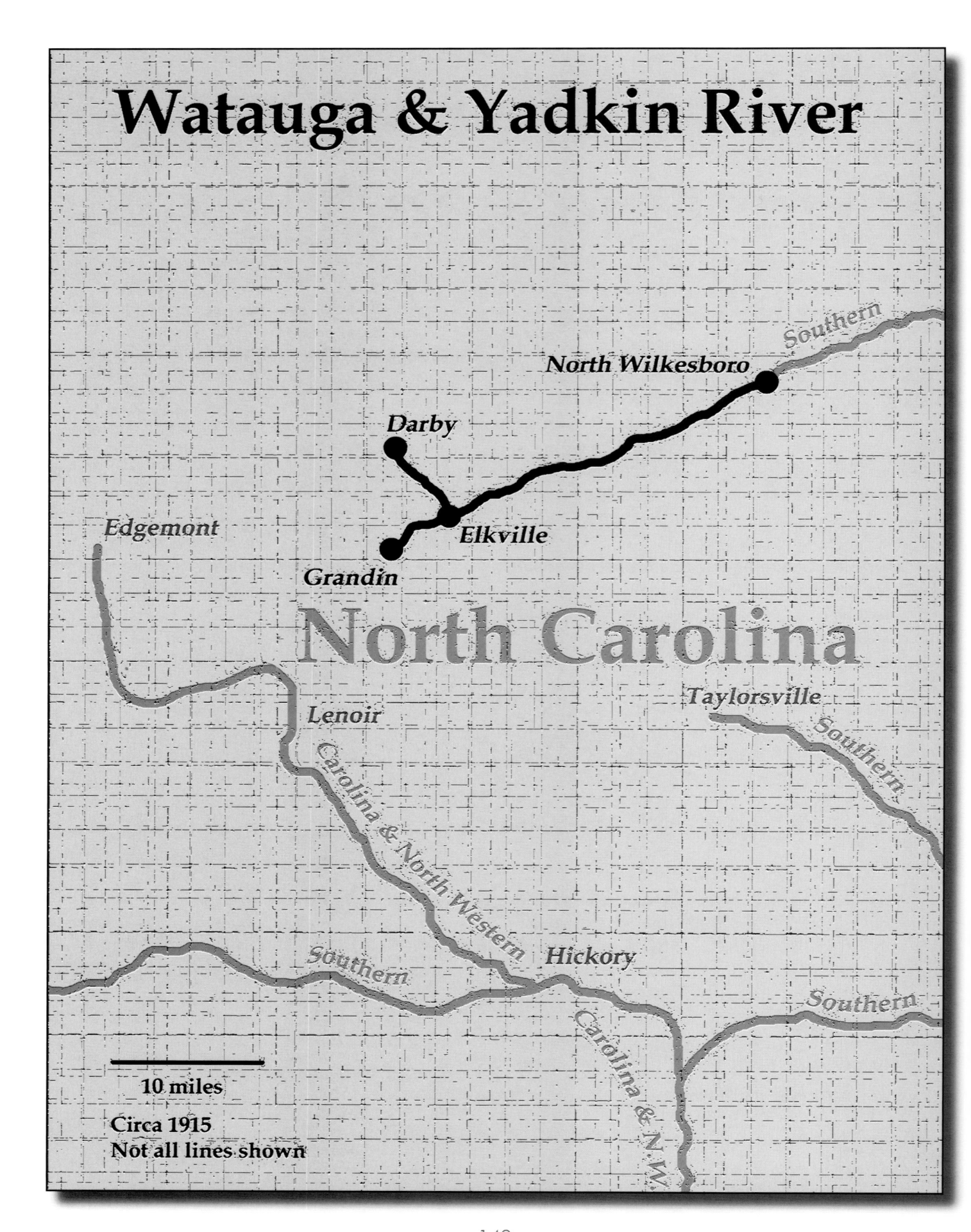

Watauga & Yadkin River

North Wilkesboro
Darby
Edgemont
Elkville
Grandin

North Carolina

Lenoir
Taylorsville
Carolina & North Western
Southern
Hickory
Carolina & N.W.
Southern

10 miles

Circa 1915
Not all lines shown

For locomotive power, the railroad ordered two Baldwin units, new from the plant. The first 2-8-0 arrived in June 1912 and was numbered 101. The second 2-8-0 arrived in January 1913 and was numbered 102.

The line quickly went into receivership and Grandin was appointed the court ordered receiver. Grandin served as the general manager over the twenty-eight mile route and reorganized the line as the Watauga & Yadkin River Railroad Company. The mileage included one tunnel and twenty trestles and was all lain in eighty pound rail.

The line appeared to prosper for a while and additional rolling stock was purchased. In addition, an 0-4-0 Porter locomotive was acquired to help around the mill yard. A community was organized around the sawmill and became known as Grandin, in honor of the founder of the line. The town was the location for the mill company store, where mill hands and members of the local community could purchase needed supplies.

In 1916, two hurricane fronts collided over the southeastern United States and caused major damage to the lines in western North Carolina. The first hurricane came in from the Gulf of Mexico and came ashore near the Alabama and Mississippi state line. The storm hit land on July 5, 1916, and winds of 107 miles per hour were reported in Mobile, Alabama. The weakened hurricane moved slowly across Alabama and into Tennessee, and stalled along the western corner of North Carolina. While the winds had subsided, the front dropped torrential rain on the area. A second hurricane came ashore over Charleston, South Carolina, on July 14, and the two fronts collided over western North Carolina. The combined storms dropped so much rain in the area that all previous flood records were surpassed. In some cases, ten to twenty inches of rain fell within a twenty-four hour period. Survivors told of entire mountaintops "sloughing off" and the snapping trees sounding like gunshots.

In nearby Asheville, the Southern Railway yard was completely under water and a locomotive was swept away, never to be recovered. Three of the four routes into the city were completely destroyed and the restoration of service would take several months to accomplish. It is estimated that eighty people lost their lives, and the United States Weather Bureau assessed property damage at twenty-two million (1916) dollars.

The Watauga & Yadkin River employed a mixture of local laborers and state convicts to construct its line. While the technique of employing state convicts in railroad construction was not unheard of, it had not been employed in years. **Collection of R. Douglas Walker.**

The Yadkin River, which the railroad right-of-way had been built adjacent to, was reported to be twenty feet above its normal level. H. C. Landon, who had surveyed the original route of the line and chose the meandering river route, was horrified to find entire sections of track missing when the floodwaters subsided. Locals had warned Landon that he was turning a blind eye to the high water marks left on trees and rocks from previous floods. Many miles of the track bed were destroyed, and several of the wooden trestles were washed away. One passenger train was abandoned by its crew; a car was washed away and the locomotive was pushed a mile down the tracks by the floodwaters. One can assume, since no record is made of the passengers, that they escaped the floodwaters. An opening of the single tunnel on the line collapsed as well due to the excessive rainfall.

Despite the devastation, the line was rebuilt and reopened for business. H. C. Landon was recognized by the Southern Railway for helping to round up over five hundred men in the local area to help rebuild both the Southern Railway's tracks and those of the W&YR Railroad.

Shortly after rebuilding the line, Grandin placed the line up for sale, along with the largely untapped timber resources. Before the sale was concluded, Grandin was killed in an automobile accident back in Pennsylvania.

In October 1918, several days of continuous rain produced a second round of flooding. Though not as damaging as the flood of 1916, the line was nonetheless severely damaged with several miles and numerous bridges destroyed. In an attempt to keep from losing equipment, Landon summoned a crew that was in Darby at the time to head to North Wilksboro as fast as possible. The crew got within a quarter of a mile of the town before being stopped by a washout on the Reddis River trestle.

On December 24, 1918, Grandin's heirs sold the railroad and resources to the Oil City Trust Company of Oil City, Pennsylvania for $160,000. All railroad activity came to a halt, and the rolling stock and equipment were stored at North Wilkesboro, where they remained for over a decade.

In 1927, Fredrick Fare purchased the assets of the property for $160,000 and held onto them for several years. In 1932, the line was sold to C. E. Jenkins for $350, the price of the back taxes.

Jenkins formed a new railroad company and named it the Wilkes & Western Railroad. He planned to issue $250,000 in stock, but apparently raised little of the amount. Jenkins hired Harry P. Edwards as a consulting engineer to determine if the line could be rebuilt. He made the personal determination that thirty-two bridges and several miles of the track would need to be rebuilt. It was part of his analysis of the line that Jenkins used as the centerpiece for his plan to rehabilitate the line and reopen it for business. It can be speculated that Edwards was looking for a new railroad to manage, but even he had to doubt that the line could ever be put back in order. Simply too much time had elapsed from its last operations, and the fact the road bed had been constructed too close to the Yadkin River meant that it would always be prone to flooding. Jenkins promoted his revitalization plans to both the Works Progress Administration and the ICC. The ICC ruled against the plan due to its being in a sparsely settled area which was already served by trucking companies.

The ICC report, no. 10205, dated 1933, noted that by that date both entrances to the one tunnel on the line had collapsed. It further stated that in some places "the ties have rotted entirely away, and the track washed out in 38 places." It also noted the track bed was in such poor shape that trees "as large as 10 inches in diameter" were growing where the roadbed used to be.

The proposal called for an estimated 1,587 feet of track and twenty-nine girder bridges to be rebuilt. The ICC noted only two local shippers were in attendance at the hearing; citing the apparent lack of interest on the part of the locals, the ICC voted to deny the reopening of the line.

In 1933, the line was formally abandoned, and the rolling stock was cut up for its scrap value sometime after that date. The rolling stock included three passenger coaches, ten boxcars, twenty flatcars, one ex-Pennsylvania Railroad caboose, twelve camp cars, one pile driver crane, and the two Baldwin 2-8-0 locomotives.

The Watauga & Yadkin River rostered only two locomotives and three coaches. Both locomotives were 2-8-0 Consolidations built by the Baldwin Locomotive Works. *Collection of R. Douglas Walker.*

7. Georgia, Florida & Alabama

Originally called the Georgia Pine Railway, the Georgia, Florida & Alabama Railway (GF&A) became an important link between the state of Florida and the Midwest region of the United States. Founded in 1895 by J. P. Williams, the line connected Bainbridge, Georgia, to Arlington, Georgia, a distance of forty miles. This was soon extended north to Cuthbert, Georgia and south to Tallahassee, Florida, an additional forty-one miles of track.

The line rapidly acquired smaller shortlines and soon commanded over two hundred miles of track. Eventually, the line reached as far north as Richland, Georgia, where it connected with the Seaboard Air Line Railroad (SAL), which had four lines radiating from the small community in the directions of Montgomery, Alabama and Columbus, Albany and Savannah, Georgia. The connection in Richland greatly enhanced its position as connecting route between the two east-west mainlines of the SAL, but it also placed the railroad within the grasp of the SAL.

In 1928, the SAL took over operation of the GF&A. From the beginning, the SAL was delinquent in making its rent payments to the board of directors of the GF&A. Unfortunately for the SAL, their "Through the Heart of the South" slogan also placed the railroad squarely between J.P. Morgan's Southern Railway and its wealthy competitor, the Atlantic Coast Line Railroad. Two years after taking control of the GF&A, the SAL went into receivership. The railroad would languish in receivership for fourteen and one-half years. The line was placed under the wardship of the U.S. District Court of Norfolk, Virginia.

Baldwin built 0-6-0 no. 1 poses for its builder's photograph. The unit was purchased new and later sold to the Seaboard Air Line as its second no. 1000 in 1929. **Collection of the author.**

GEORGIA, FLORIDA & ALABAMA RAILWAY

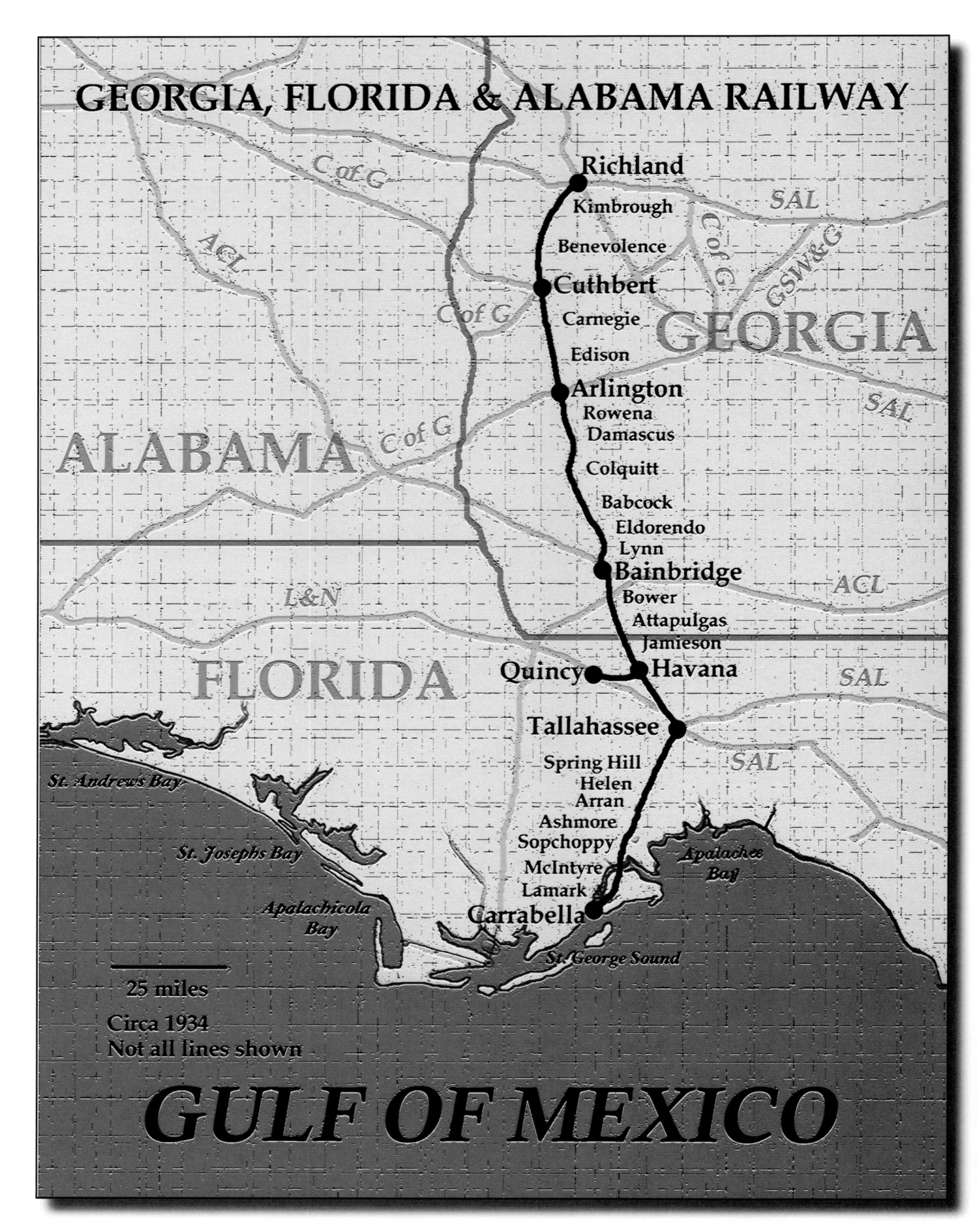

MAIN LINE.

....	No. 1	Mls.	May 6, 1923.	No. 2	....
....	*6 25 A M	0	lve... +Richland ᴆ ..arr.	8 10 P M	....
....	6 39 "	6.7	.......Kimbrough.......	8 57 "	....
....	6 51 "	12.8	........Troutman........	8 46 "	....
....	7 02 "	17.7	.......Benevolence..... ᴆ	8 35 "	....
....	7 20 "	27.5	arr... +Cuthbert ..lve.	8 15 "	....
....	8 00 "	27.5	lve... Cuthbert .. arr.	8 00 "	....
....	8 05 "	....	.....Central Junction.....	7 52 "	....
....	8 20 "	35.5	.........Randolph.........	7 36 "	....
....	8 25 "	37.4	.........Carnegie.........	7 32 "	....
....	8 30 "	39.6	..........Moye..........	7 27 "	....
....	8 40 "	43.8	+.....Edison........ ᴆ	7 17 "	....
....	8 50 "	48.3	..........Turman..........	7 05 "	....
....	9 05 "	53.8	arr.{ +Arlington ᴆ {lve.	6 52 "	....
....	9 15 "	53.8	lve.{ {arr.	‖6 21 "	....
....	9 26 "	57.9	..........Rowena..........	6 10 "	....
....	9 38 "	63.7	+.......Damascus....... ᴆ	6 55 "	....
....	9 43 "	66.3	......Warren's Mill......	5 47 "	....
....	9 48 "	68.4	..........Corea..........	5 41 "	....
....	9 59 "	72.5	+.......Colquitt........ ᴆ	5 32 "	....
....	10 11 "	77.7	........Babcock.........	5 17 "	....
....	10 20 "	82.3	.........Eldorendo.........	5 07 "	....
....	10 31 "	87.1	...........Lynn...........	4 57 "	....
....	10 35 "	89.3	........Whites Mill.......	4 53 "	....
....	10 55 "	93.3	arr.{ + Bainbridge ᴆ {lve.	4 40 "	....
....	10 55 "	93.3	lve.{ {arr.	4 40 "	....
....	11 15 "	101.2	..........Bower..........	4 13 "	....
....	11 25 "	105.5	.........Attapulgus....... ᴆ	4 02 "	....
....	11 30 "	107.7	..........Laingkat..........	3 51 "	....
....	11 40 "	112.3	.........Jamieson......... ᴆ	3 41 "	....
....	11 47 "	115.0	..........Hinson..........	3 34 "	....
....	11 57 A M	116.6	+........Havana......... ᴆ	3 30 "	....
....	12 15 P M	125.1	.......Lake Jackson.......	3 09 "	....
....	12 21 "	127.0	........San Helena........	3 00 "	....
....	12 35 "	133.6	arr.{ +Tallahassee ᴆ {lve.	2 50 "	....
....	2 10 "	133.6	lve.{ {arr.	12 55 "	....
....	2 35 "	142.9	........Spring Hill........	12 32 "	....
....	2 40 "	145.3	..........Helen.......... ᴆ	12 27 "	....
....	2 44 "	147.2	........Hilliardville........	12 22 "	....
....	....	152.2	.........Raker Mill.........	....	....
....	3 01 "	153.8	..........Arran.......... ᴆ	12 07 P M	....
....	— —	156.0	........Mill Grove........	— —	....
....	3 17 "	161.7	..........Ashmore..........	11 47 A M	....
....	3 22 "	164.0	.........Sopchoppy........ ᴆ	11 42 "	....
....	....	168.3	.........Curtis Mill.........	— —	....
....	3 35 "	170.0	..........McIntyre..........	11 28 "	....
....	3 55 "	178.5	..........Lanark..........	11 12 "	....
....	4 10 P M	183.3	arr... +Carrabelle ᴆ .lve.	*11 00 A M	....
....			(Via Wing Boat Line.)		....
....	4 45 P M	183.3	lve.....Carrabelle....arr.	10 30 A M	....
....	7 45 P M	215.3	......Apalachicola......	*7 00 A M	....
....			ARRIVE] [LEAVE		....

HAVANA AND QUINCY.

......	111	109	Ms.	May 6, 1923.	110	112	......
	P M	P M		LEAVE] [ARRIVE	A M	P M	
......	*3 40	*12 01	0	+.....Havana..... ᴆ	11 00	3 12	......
......	3 53	12 15	4.9	......Florence.......	10 45	2 59	......
......	3 59	12 25	6.9	......Littman.......	10 35	2 53	......
......	4 06	12 35	9.4	........Cory........	10 27	2 46	......
......	4 12	12 42	11.3	+.....Quincy..... ᴆ	*10 20	*2 40	......
	P M	P M		ARRIVE] [LEAVE	A M	P M	

THROUGH SLEEPING CAR SERVICE.
Drawing-room Sleepers.
TALLAHASSEE AND ATLANTA, via Cuthbert, Cent. of Ga. Ry.

....	2-12-3		(Central time.)	8-11-1	....
....	2 50 P M	lve.Tallahassee (Ga. Fla. & Ala.)	arr.	12 35 P M	....
....	3 30 P M	lve.Havana..........	" arr.	11 57 A M	....
....	4 40 P M	lve.Bainbridge.....	" arr.	10 55 A M	....
....	6 52 P M	lve.Arlington......	" arr.	9 05 A M	....
....	8 30 P M	lve.Cuthbert..(Cent.of Ga.)	lve.	8 00 A M	....
....	1 10 A M	arr.Macon.........	" lve.	2 50 A M	....
....	6 05 A M	arr.Atlanta.........	" lve.	11 00 P M	....

Open for occupancy at Atlanta 8 00 p.m.

Trains marked * run daily. ‖ Meals. + Coupon stations; ᴆ Telegraph stations. STANDARD—*Central time.*

Principal crops hauled by the railroad were cotton, tobacco, and sugar cane. Numerous sawmills helped fuel logging operations along the route as well. The line also had a Pullman service from Tallahassee to Atlanta, which continued well into the 1930s. The general offices and shops were located in Bainbridge.

Harry Edwards's involvement with the GF&A came in 1934 when he was employed as a consultant engineer. Edwards was employed by Freeman & Company Investment Bankers of New York City to work out the reorganization plans and make up estimates on earnings/expenses that could be expected under a proposed plan to operate the railroad as an independent line. The railroad was 226 miles in length, and the stockholders were furious over the lack of payment on the part of the SAL. The bondholders, under the leadership of the Freeman & Company, were considering taking over the property and operating it again. Edwards worked for a part of 1934 in drawing up plans for the GF&A to return as a separate entity. However, as Edwards finalized his proposal, the SAL paid up all back rents and made satisfactory arrangements to assure continuation of rent payments. The bondholders concluded that this was a better long range decision than running the railroad themselves. The GF&A was eventually completely incorporated in the Seaboard Airline Railroad.

Left, A schedule for the GF&A from 1923 shows through sleeping car service to Atlanta via the Central of Georgia. **Collection of the author.**

8. Atlantic & East Carolina

The Atlantic & East Carolina Railway (A&EC) had as its origin one of the oldest railroads to operate in the United States, the Atlantic & North Carolina Railroad (A&NC). The idea to build a line from Goldsboro North Carolina, to the North Carolina coast was first proposed by Joseph Caldwell in the 1820s to provide a mountains-to-the-sea railway. His proposal was to connect the three state-owned railroads - the Western North Carolina Railroad, the North Carolina Railroad (NCRR) and the Atlantic & North Carolina Railway.

In 1853 Governor John Motley Morehead moved to implement Caldwell's plan. Governor Morehead was doggedly determined to push the line through due to the simple fact that he and his associates owned large tracts of land around Sheppards Point, North Carolina, a deep water port on the proposed line. The new community would soon be renamed Morehead City in his honor. Construction began in earnest in 1856, and the line was operational in June 1858.

When completed, the A&NC would stretch ninety-six miles from Goldsboro through New Bern and on to Beaufort in North Carolina. The connection would be made in Goldsboro with both the North Carolina Railroad and the Wilmington & Raleigh Railroad. The line would be constructed largely with state funds, with the state owning 12,666 of the total 18,000 shares issued.

The line was a fairly prosperous railroad due to Morehead City's being developed into a deep water port. To facilitate traffic being generated at the connection with the NCRR and the Wilmington & Weldon Railroad, a new depot was constructed adjacent to these two railroad lines. However, Morehead City had little in the way of new construction, and the facility for passenger service was referred to as "a railroad depot at the end of a long wharf."

In the fall of 1860, the A&NC was successful in luring a steamship contract to provide three monthly trips to Morehead City from other eastern seaboard ports. Shortly thereafter, however, the Civil War and the Union blockade put an end to what traffic was generated by the contract.

At the start of the Civil War, there were twenty-six locomotives operating within the state of North Carolina, and six of these operated on the A&NC. The line between Morehead City and Kinston, North Carolina fell to Union forces in March 1862. By March 1865, the entire line was totally under Federal control. From March 1865 through Oct. 4, 1865, the line was formally operated by Union forces as a military railroad.

In the days just prior to and during the Civil War, locomotives often were given names rather than numbers. The sheer scarcity of locomotives did not mandate a numbering system; rather the names were symbols of state or local pride. One rostered A&NC locomotive was a 4-4-0 type, named "Scout." The unit was earlier named "Eclipse" and was built by Breese, Keeland & Company. The first nine locomotives of the A&NC were each referred to in such fashion by a name rather than a number.

Union forces also took control of the NCRR from Goldsboro to Charlotte, North Carolina, 233 miles; the Wilmington & Weldon Railroad, 162 miles; and 25 miles of the Raleigh & Gaston Railroad. General D.C. McCallum, military director & superintendant of railroads, reported that 38 locomotives, 422 cars and 3,387 men were employed under his military railroad command.

ATLANTIC & EAST CAROLINA

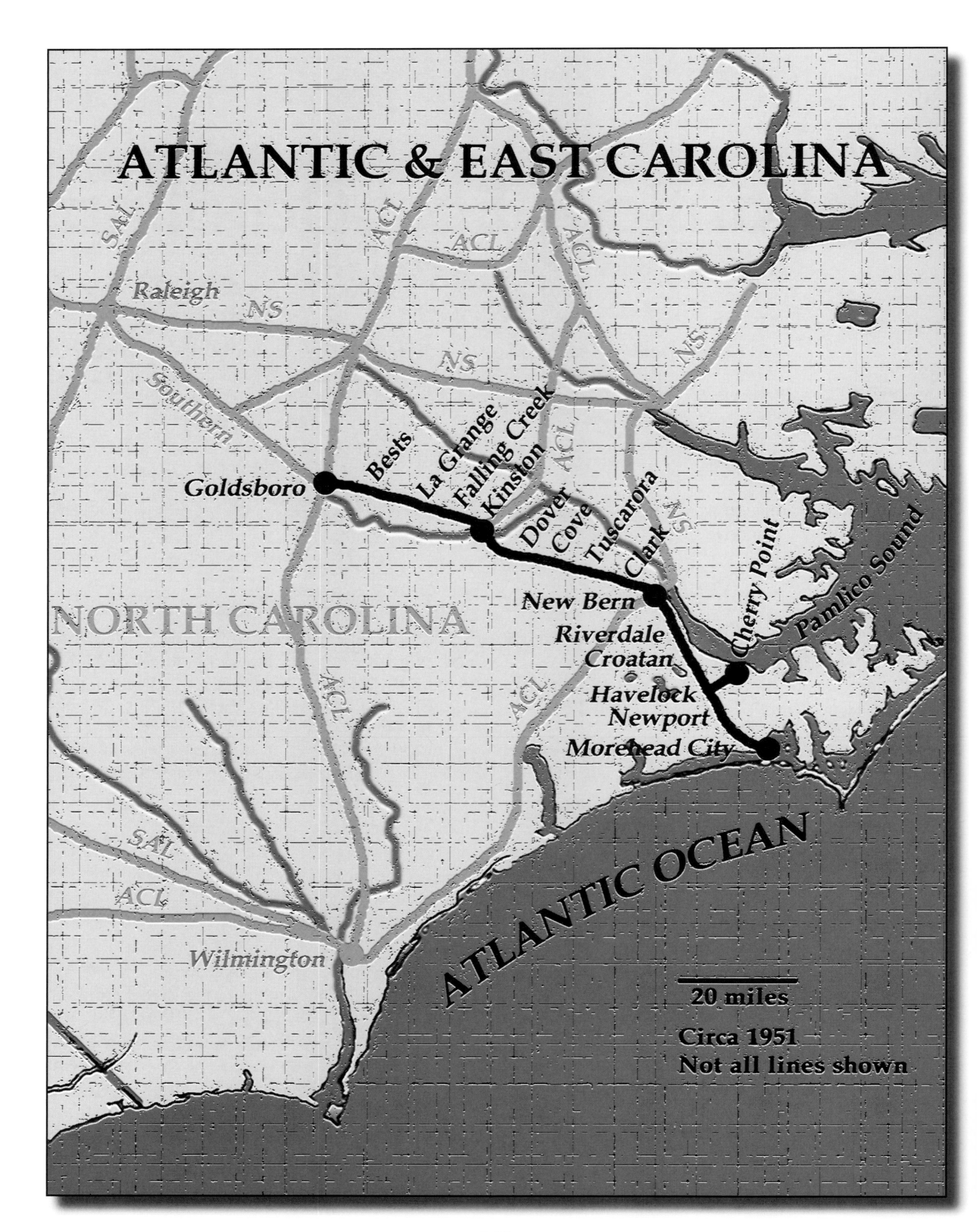

20 miles

Circa 1951
Not all lines shown

Retreating Confederate forces destroyed much of the A&NC track around Kinston and Batchelors Creek. The Union forces then employed large numbers of black laborers to work day and night to restore the line. Union soldiers were also pressed into service to help cut ties, and with the combined work force of freed slaves and soldiers, the tie supply was replenished in two days.

Most A&NC equipment had been moved inland by retreating Confederate forces, and thus saved from initial destruction. Eventually, Union forces raided farther inland and recovered most of the rolling stock and equipment, with the exception of the 4-4-0 locomotive, the "Dr. Hawks," which was stranded behind a burned out trestle.

The military campaign was pressing the capacity of the available locomotive supply to move Union forces around the eastern part of the state. The United States Military Railroad requested additional motive power, and two units were sent to New Bern, North Carolina. However, the "A. A. Bunting" and a New Jersey Locomotive & Machine Workings locomotive, the no. 2, were lost when the ship carrying them sank in the Atlantic Ocean.

As the Civil War wound down and peacetime traffic returned to normal, the A&NC developed a rather unusual nickname, "The Old Mullet Road." The nickname came about from the large quantities of fresh fish that were shipped on the line. The line owned two specially designed cars used in the transportation of the iced, fresh fish. The herald consisted of a mullet jumping out of the water and was displayed on various articles, ranging from boxcars to company letterhead.

In 1904 the A&NC was leased to the Howeland Improvement Company, which was later acquired by the original Norfolk & Southern Railway, which had a connection with the A&NC in New Bern. The Norfolk & Southern was a regional railroad, which stretched from Norfolk, Virginia south to New Bern, and westward to Raleigh, North Carolina. Two years later in 1908, the Norfolk & Southern entered into receivership. In 1910, the Norfolk Southern was reorganized as the Norfolk

Shortly after the turn of the century the Norfolk & Southern operated the state-owned A&NC. In a postcard view the N&S depot in New Bern is host to an A&NC train on the right and a N&S train to the left. **Collection of R. Douglas Walker.**

Southern Railroad, though construction was still proceeding until the line reached just over five hundred miles in length.

With many politicians making profits from the A&NC, it was soon the centerpiece of political joking. *Time Magazine* called the A&NC a "political toy train" and further stated that "it was considered almost as disgraceful to be without an A&NC pass as it was to vote for a Republican."

In 1932, the Norfolk Southern entered into receivership again and in 1935 it was declared in default of its A&NC lease. From November 16, 1935 through September 1, 1939, the state operated the A&NC by itself as an independent railroad. While the line was fairly profitable in its own right, it never achieved the levels of revenue that the stockholders had hoped for. With discontent coming from the stockholders, the governor went in search of a long-term, viable solution to the ailing A&NC needs.

Governor Clyde R. Hoey offered the Southern Railway the use of the line without rental charges with the simple agreement and understanding that the line had to be kept open for existing customers. Southern Railway conducted its own inspection of the line, thoroughly reviewing the physical plant and equipment. A committee of five officials inspected up and down the tracks of the A&NC and issued its rather disturbing report. The committee found the line to be in deplorable shape. Coupled with lack of traffic and other negative possibilities, such as the lack of sustained growth, the Southern Railway refused to issue a lease proposal. The Southern Railway counter-offered the governor by formally requesting the state to make good on any deficits incurred during the operation of the line. Governor Hoey promptly declined. The future of the A&NC was uncertain when Harry P. Edwards returned to North Carolina.

After Harry P. Edwards left the employment of the A&SAB Railroad, he returned to North Carolina and heard news of the A&NC's being in rent default. He later had a conference with Governor Hoey and expressed an interest in leasing the line. Edwards made a personal inspection of the line and found it to be in bad shape, but not impossible to restore. He saw in the A&NC a ray of hope where Southern Railway officials had seen a totally depleted physical plant. Edwards went so far as to compare the new task at hand to his management of the A&SAB Railroad, a line which he found to be in similar shape when he had taken over management of that line in 1927.

Edwards had competition for the A&NC in the form of Henry Page. Page was also interested in the operations of the line and began to put together a bid to compete against Edwards's bid. Edwards felt Page to be a serious threat; however, when the bid opening date drew near, Page withdrew his bid, leaving Edwards as the only serious competitor.

Governor Hoey and Edwards entered into a contract to operate the state-owned A&NC Railroad as the privately managed Atlantic & East Carolina Railroad. Provisions of the contract called for:
- Annual rent to be paid to the state of North Carolina in the amount of $60,500.
- Percentage of gross revenues in excess of $475,000.
- A twenty-five-year lease, to be renewed for an additional twenty years if both parties agreed.

No. 601 **(above)**, a Baldwin 4-6-0 built in 1922 for the Wisconsin & Michigan Railroad, was acquired by the A&NC in 1937. When Edwards took over operating the A&NC two years later, he found that 70% of the locomotives he inherited had an average history of twenty-five years in service. The corporate logo of the newly formed A&EC is seen at **center**. The term "the Tobacco Belt Route" described one of the most important crops carried by the A&EC. *Above, photograph by Roy W. Legg, collection of Tom King. Center, Collection of M.B. Connery.*

- Harry P. Edwards and party to post a $50,000 bond as a performance guarantee.
- Edwards to provide 76% of the necessary operating costs and Edward Buchan, Edwards's brother-in-law, to provide the remaining 24%.
- J. A. Bolich was the third associate named in the contract.

During his meeting with Governor Hoey, Edwards disclosed to the governor that his father had tried to lease the line in 1904. At that time, the lease was awarded to the Howeland Improvement Company for a period of ninety-one years.

Edwards took over formal control of the A&EC on September 1, 1939. What Edwards invested in was a railroad with seventy percent of its ties in rotted condition. He also inherited a fleet of eleven second-hand steam locomotives each with an average age of twenty-five years.

Edwards immediately began to rebuild the line, including coming up with a new nickname for his railroad. The moniker of "The Old Mullet Line" was discarded, and his new marketing campaign was to the call the A&EC the "Tobacco Route." The herald was a circular logo with the sun shining its rays down on a large tobacco leaf in its middle. From the start, Edwards served as general manager and supplied the operating knowledge, and Edward Buchan, served as the line's public relations person and chief salesman. Buchan had previously served as a member of the board of directors for the Edwards Railway Motor Car Company and was very familiar with Edwards and his management style. This venture began an eighteen-year partnership for the two men.

The A&NC offices had been located at Morehead City, but Edwards moved the offices and passenger service to New Bern and allowed Buchan to move the traffic and accounting offices to Kinston. J. A. Bolich, the third associate, served as vice president of operations and kept his office in Morehead City. In this organization of the management, all three major cities on the A&EC had the office of a major associate.

The early years were not easy for Edwards, and one has to wonder what was going through his mind during the first few months of his administration. The line experienced fourteen derailments the first ninety days of his management. War broke out in Europe three days after he signed the lease with the state of North Carolina. Then an English-imposed embargo on tobacco products nearly paralyzed the North Carolina tobacco industry, a primary revenue source for the railroad. In the first year the railroad posted a $3,975 net loss. However, the railroad was *never* operated in the red again under Harry P. Edwards's administration.

Just two years after Edwards took control of the A&EC, the country was plunged into World War II. In order both to facilitate training and to help secure the eastern Atlantic coast, a Marine Corp base was established along the line at Cherry Point, North Carolina. U.S. Representative Graham Barden was instrumental in convincing the Marine Corps to choose the site in Craven County. This location proved to be a tremendous boon to the line.

The entrance to the office of Harry P. Edwards **(top)** at the passenger depot in New Bern as it appeared in 1950. Baldwin built no. 101 **(above)** lasted less than a decade on the A&EC. It was acquired in 1936 from the ACL and scrapped in May 1943. ***Top, collection of William J. Edwards. Above, collection of Marvin Black.***

The necessary construction materials for the Marine expansion projects taxed the existing infrastructure, in regards to both the equipment and the tracks of the A&EC. The railroad had begun replacing light rail with heavier rail upon Edwards's gaining control of the line, but the pace would need to be accelerated due to the war effort. With the assistance of the U.S. Navy, a loan was secured to replace rail with relay rail. *Relay rail* is a term describing used rail; since the military effort commanded the entire country's steel production, salvage rail was the only source for securing heavier rail for the line. The line was also re-ballasted, with sand instead of the usual material, crushed gravel. Due to the construction of the military bases nearby and other high-priority projects, sand was the only material available in quantity and was therefore used until after the end of the war. At that time, the line was re-ballasted with gravel. In addition to providing heavier rail, the loan was used to repair and strengthen bridges and to purchase second-hand locomotives and rolling stock, particularly passenger coaches. The A&EC repaid the federal loan by deducting from freight and passenger rates items carried by the Federal government, primarily in the form of troop train movements.

The new Marine airfield at Cherry Point offered the A&EC fifty to seventy-five carloads of marl (a loam of clays and shells) a day, which were moved from Belgrade on the ACL line via the A&EC. This heavy traffic pattern held up unrelentingly every day over a period of several months in order to construct the airfield. After the airfield was completed, troop trains running from the base to other connections

As the A&EC geared up for moving war materials during WWII, Edwards was forced to purchase additional steam power, even though he was a strong proponent of diesel units. No. 102 **(top)** was originally built in 1907 for the ACL and came to the A&EC in 1944. No. 7 **(above)** was a GE 44 tonner and was produced during the war. After the sale of the A&EC to the Southern Railway in 1958, the unit became SR no. 403. ***Top, collection of Tom King. Above, collection of M.B. Connery.***

1350 H.P. DIESEL FREIGHT LOCOMOTIVE . . DESIGNED AND BUILT BY ELECTRO-MOTIVE DIVISION . . GENERAL MOTORS CORPORATION . . LA GRANGE, ILLINOIS. U. S. A.

became a part of the standard traffic pattern. In 1942, the A&EC boasted a personnel roster of four hundred employees.

Prior to construction of the airfield, the Civil Air Patrol served as spotters and looked for German submarines off the coast of North Carolina. Once the field was completed, B-25 bombers, carrying depth charges, took over the task of guarding the coastline. Tank cars carrying aviation fuel also became a major part of daily traffic over the line.

Because of the used rail, accidents were common. One accident in particular involved tank cars carrying highly flammable aviation fuel. The derailment occurred on the outskirts of Morehead City and involved several cars dumped over a two hundred foot area or more. The duty officer at Cherry Point was notified, and he confirmed the explosive nature of the cargo. The salvage crew in Norfolk was notified several times over several hours. Since the mainline was blocked, the standard procedure was to build a temporary spur or track around the derailment to allow the mainline to be reopened. The A&EC crew members gently placed the tank cars on their trucks and proceeded with the cleanup effort without assistance from the miltary. The cleanup took thirty-six hours from the first phone call until the time the main line was reopened for traffic. Bill Edwards was on hand to help with the clean-up

An EMD locomotive photo paster **(top)** showing an artist's rendition of A&EC no. 400, an F2A, decked out in colorful green and yellow livery with orange wings and the "Tobacco Belt Route" logo on the nose. No. 9 **(above)**, an SW-1 seen in 1950, three years after its delivery in 1947 from EMD. **Top, collection of the author. Above, collection of W. J. Edwards.**

efforts and never felt any strong feelings of fear. However, the Marines' reaction to news of the wreck was enough to instill a sense of urgency and caution in him and the crew handling the derailment. Since most civilians had never witnessed an aviation fuel fire, as the Marines had, most were unaware of the extreme explosive nature of the fuel.

As traffic continued to increase, Edwards caught the attention of *Time Magazine,* which carried a feature story on his career for the October 20, 1941 issue. It stated that "Edwards made money off the Old Mullet Line because he didn't know better." It further stated that "by using good common sense and by [being] willing to work for what he knew was a good thing, Edwards and Buchan have made their railway company an institution that will continue to serve its patrons in a progressive spirit."

To keep up with the increase of traffic, the A&EC acquired two large steam locomotives on a secondhand basis. The line was also able to secure two General Electric 44-ton locomotives, paying $ 38,633 for no. 7 and $ 37,759.75 for no. 8. The railroad once had a Porter diesel on the line but found the small locomotive inadequate to do much switching, much less mainline hauling. Edwards saw the savings and reliability the two GE units demonstrated, prompting him to look at securing two EMD diesels. These two units, along with two other diesels, made the A&EC one of the first railroads in the country to completely dieselize.

The A&EC has the distinction of having placed the first order for EMD's F-2A diesel-electric locomotives. With the war concluded, EMD rushed full-force into the diesel market and geared up its LaGrange, Illinois, factory to meet the many orders that had flooded in. With the success of the FT diesel-electric locomotive barnstorming tours across the country during World War II, EMD rushed new models to the production line. Edwards, always working at lowering operating costs and improving reliability, purchased the very first two F-2A units for the A&EC. The F-2A was a stopgap model between the FT's and the F-3 model and signaled the start of a decades long dominance by EMD over its rivals. The production included seventy-four F-2A cab units and thirty F-2B booster units.

As Edwards was very thrifty in his financial affairs, he ordered the two F-2A units to be built without steam generators. It must be noted that his family members remember Edwards always carrying

No. 501, an EMD GP7, was built new for the A&EC in 1951. No. 501 later became Southern no. 406 and later, Southern no. 8230. Retired in 1980, the unit was traded back to EMD. **Collection of William J. Edwards.**

a small ledger to record *every* transaction he made. Even a stop at the local soda shop prompted him to record the amount of the soda. So, when it came time to complete the order for the two units, he couldn't justify the additional costs of the generators. This decision came back to haunt the railroad because the military troop traffic to Cherry Point had not abated, even with the conclusion of the war. The A&EC mechanical department had to improvise a heating system and did so by building a steam generator car. This car was towed behind the diesels and in front of the coaches to provide heat when needed.

The first master mechanic was hired away from the Atlanta & St. Andrews Bay Railway, but he returned to that railroad after a short period of time. Harry Edwards soon hired another mechanic who had worked previously at the Southern Railway's Spencer Shops, then the principal steam shop for that railroad. Only after employing the mechanic did Edwards find out that he had a violent temper and a troubled past. While at the Spencer Shop, a fellow employee had refused to follow his order, and the mechanic responded by placing a pistol to the man's head and pulling the trigger. Fortunately for both of them, the "Saturday Night Special" failed to fire. This was probably the reason the mechanic was no longer employed by the Southern.

Harry Edwards ran the A&EC as a family business. His wife as well as his sister, married to his partner Edward Buchan, were employed by the railroad. Edwards's two sons, Bill and Winslow, were employed as well. Bill was an employee when the line began to dieselize and was sent to North Carolina State University, where he took a specialized course in diesel mechanics. Later, he undertook additional training in LaGrange, where he was instructed in the maintenance and care of the two diesels which were to appear shortly on the A&EC property. Bill Edwards later recalled remembering the complicated wiring diagram and schematic that went with the diesel engines. The wiring diagram was four feet by twenty feet and was nailed to a plywood sheet and mounted on a wall in the engine shop.

The new diesels posed a challenge for the shop crews more familiar with steam locomotives. Bill Edwards recalled a saying by the shop personnel. It went: "When trouble developed on a steam engine, it took five minutes to find it and five hours to fix it. With a diesel-electric locomotive, it takes five hours to find the

No. 400 **(top)** and its sister unit no. 401 **(above)** represented the very first orders for EMD of the new F2As. The locomotives were ordered in 1946 and were scrapped in 1961; No. 400 in Spencer, North Carolina, and no. 401 in Chattanooga, Tennessee. ***Both, collection of Marvin Black.***

problem and five minutes to fix it." As the upkeep of the diesels fell largely to Bill, the mechanics on the railroad were constantly in training in order to service the new diesel locomotives. On one particular day, an engineer was having a problem with one of the diesels, and Bill decided to ride down to Morehead City to learn what the problem was and to help the engineer understand how to fix it. On returning, Bill remembered he had not secured the permission of the master mechanic (with the violent temper) to make the trip and was met by this individual who promptly said, "You're fired!" Later the same day, Harry P. Edwards gave the master mechanic the same message.

The employee then demanded an appointment with the elder Edwards in hopes of re-securing his position. Later, Harry Edwards admitted to his sons and employees that a large envelope was on his desk when he talked to the disgruntled employee. Knowing the employee's history, Edwards had placed his .32 caliber revolver in the envelope in case he had to defend his life. As his son Bill recalled, "Dad was never a violent man, but he would not allow himself to be pushed around."

Edward had made employment on the A&EC a family affair and his other son, Winslow, was also involved with the railroad. Winslow worked in the Maintenance of Way Department, but his specialty was securing replacement railroad ties. After a tenure in the manufacturing field away from the railroad, Winslow returned to the MofW Department, where he eventually became its head and personally oversaw the replacement of the Trent River Trestle. The trestle had been destroyed by Hurricane Ione and forced the A&EC to utilize and pay the ACL for the use of their line.

Harry Edwards had a former employee of the Edwards Railway Motor Car Company on the A&EC payroll, Gates Huff. Huff was the chief draftsman for the ERwyMCC and was employed to develop a transfer table for the railroad. The transfer table was employed in conjunction with the new diesel repair shop. The shop was erected shortly after delivery of the two F-2A diesel-electric locomotives. The shop had an inspection pit and another level two feet up in order to work on the journals, batteries, and fuel tank. Above that was a wooden platform at the locomotive door level, which allowed the shop personnel to have access to the cooling fans and exhaust stacks located on top of the unit. The total cost for Edwards to completely dieselize the A&EC was $662,541.

Edwards's management of the A&EC had an immediate positive impact, making a profit for the lines as well as showing a profit for the state. A *Wall Street Journal* article in October 1940 reported that Edwards "turned a $16,465 net profit on his A&EC Railroad in his second year of operation." When Edwards took over operation of the line, the stock was selling for five dollars a share; two years later, it was selling for forty dollars a share, a seven hundred percent increase in value.

In 1949, Edwards petitioned the ICC to discontinue passenger service. Edwards, always analytical and methodical in his approach, had deduced that the passenger revenues did not justify the expenditure for passenger equipment. In 1950, the ICC approved the discontinuance of passenger service on the A&EC, the first time in ninety-two years that the passenger service was disrupted. In his petition to the ICC, Edwards presented as his case the fact that bus lines between Goldsboro and Morehead City generated two hundred thousand fares per year.

Soon after acquiring control of the A&EC in September 1939, Edwards placed an order for new rolling stock. One such car was no. 928, a forty ton capacity boxcar built in December 1939. **Collection of Marvin Black.**

The burning of a bond in Governor Kerr Scott's office symbolized the freedom from debt of the state owned A&NC. From left are M.G. Mann, A&NC president; E.R. Buchan, A&EC president; Governor Kerr Scott of North Carolina; and Harry P. Edwards, A&EC board chairman and general manager. Shortly before the ceremony it was discovered that the ICC had regulations governing the creation of a bond retirement committee, and so a couple of $1,000 bonds were burned in a symbolic gesture for photographers who had already been called in for the burning ceremony. **Collection of W.J. Edwards.**

This compared with only nineteen thousand fares collected on the A&EC for passenger service. He further cited in his report that 1948 brought with it losses of $31,900 for the passenger department, including a single loss of $10,000 on the rental of the Goldsboro Union Station.

After passenger service was discontinued, Edwards decided to revive a tradition he had started while general manager on the A&SAB in Panama City, Florida. He was going to sponsor a Santa Claus train to run the length of the A&EC trackage and provide gifts to the children of the employees of the railroad. The train consist in its first year of operation included the following equipment:

- One diesel locomotive
- One baggage car containing the Christmas tree and the presents.
- One baggage car equipped to serve free meals to all the volunteers and persons on board.
- Three passenger coaches to carry parents and the children.
- Edwards's private coach, "The Carolina," for the officers and special guests of the railroad.

The children were particularly thrilled and fascinated to see Santa travelling by train. During its second year of operation, the Santa Claus Train gained the notice of Governor Kerr Scott, who, along with several members of his entourage, rode the train on December 24, 1950.

This second Santa Claus train required six coaches just to carry the passengers. It was observed that the children insisted on getting on and off at each location that Santa made an appearance. Edwards noticed that this required considerable personnel to handle the children and to look after their safety. Anticipating that the Santa Claus train would only increase each year, Edwards sadly decided to cancel the Santa Claus train to avoid any potential accidents.

"The Carolina" fulfilled one of Edwards's many dreams. Having served on the A&W and the A&SAB without the privilege of a private car, Edwards had always set his mind on the fact he wanted one somewhere in the future. As the A&EC became more stable, he set about obtaining a private coach to take visiting dignitaries on a tour of the railroad. When the Norfolk Southern Railroad's office car burned, Edwards placed a bid on the car and was subsequently awarded it. Bill Edwards remembers that the car may have been owned by John Ringling at one time and was used as a traveling office for the Ringling Brothers Circus. The younger Edwards remembers that at least one North Carolina governor and a couple of USMC generals used the car to tour the coastal area of North Carolina.

Since Harry Edwards was very involved in the efforts of the local Chamber of Commerce to develop the area economically, he often used the "private car," as it was referred to, to haul prospective developers as well as high-level dignitaries. The Union Bag Paper Co., Weyerhauser and Stanley Tools all had representatives who took tours of the railroad in the private coach. Edwards went so far as to lend his private coach to the Union Bag Paper Co., who used it as their headquarters while they investigated the possibility of opening a plant in the region. Edwards had the car parked on a siding near Clarks, North Carolina, though his efforts at this time did not result in a plant being built because the company chose a different site for their plant. Through his tireless devotion to develop the local economic base, Edwards was also instrumental in helping to entice both Bosch and Tredegar as well as other manufacturers to locate near the tracks of the A&EC.

Facing increasing age and declining health, and knowing that his two sons were interested in other business ventures, Edwards met with Mason King, the vice president of the Southern Railway, in July 1953, to discuss transferring the lease of A&EC to the Southern. An agreement was reached in March 1954, and the details of the transaction were outlined. The transfer was to take place upon ICC approval with the Southern paying Edwards $525,000.

The ACL and Norfolk Southern railroads both protested the deal and the ICC held up its approval until February 1957. The final approval came with several drastic stipulations and restrictions placed on the Southern Railway which its management found highly objectionable. Only after persistent conversations with Edwards did the Southern Railway proceed with the transfer. Public sentiment ran strongly in favor of the Southern Railway's obtaining the lease over other nearby railroads.

Over his eighteen year tenure on the A&EC Railroad, the line had total gross revenues of $22 million. Wages had been at $.25 an hour for laborers and $.60 for skilled labor for years. Edwards slowly but steadily raised salaries during his management tenure to $1.00 for laborers and $1.85 for skilled workers.

Gross annual revenues increased from $350,000 to over $1,900,000 in the peak year of 1952. An additional eighty-one new industries and businesses located adjacent to the tracks of the A&EC Railroad. The Marine base at Camp LeJeune and at Cherry Point also helped contribute to the traffic base.

Harry McMullan, the Attorney General for the state of North Carolina, saluted Harry P. Edwards's accomplishments. A letter to Edwards's associate, Edward Buchan, reads in part, "I am glad to know that plans are progressing for the consummation of the sale to the Southern Railroad. The saving of the A&NC from destruction by you and Harry Edwards ought to be a lasting monument to your contribution to the welfare of the Eastern part of the state. I don't know what would have happened if you and he had not come along and leased it at the time you did." McMullan was the same individual who had drafted the original lease that Edwards had signed in 1939 with Governor Hoey. McMullan also had the distinction of attending every A&NC stockholders meeting as long as he was alive.

Appendix A - Abbreviations used in the text, maps & rosters

(Railroad abbreviations do not necessarily conform to A.A.R. assigned reporting marks.)

AF&G - Alabama, Florida & Gulf
ALCO - American Locomotive Company
ASARCO - American Smelting & Refining Company
Ap. Nor. - Apalachicola Northern
AAR - Association of American Railroads
AT&SF - Atchison, Topeka & Santa Fe
A&SAB - Atlanta & St. Andrews Bay
A&EC - Atlantic & East Carolina
A&NC - Atlantic & North Carolina
A&W - Atlantic & Western
ACL - Atlantic Coast Line
B&O - Baltimore & Ohio
B&SE - Birmingham & Southeastern
BR&L - Birmingham Rail & Locomotive Company
B&M - Boston & Maine
B&AP - Butte, Anaconda & Pacific
CN - Canadian National
C of G - Central of Georgia
CIRR - Chattahoochee Industrial
C&O - Chesapeake & Ohio
CB&Q - Chicago, Burlington & Quincy
C&S - Colorado & Southern
CYDZ - Conrad Yelvington Distributors
DL&W - Delaware, Lakawana & Western
D&RGW - Denver & Rio Grande Western
DOT - Department of Transportation (government)
D&S - Durham & Southern
ERCC - Edwards Rail Car Company (1998-)
ERwyMCC - Edwards Railway Motor Car Company
EMC - Electro Motive Corporation
EMD - Electro Motive Division (General Motors)
F de G - Ferrocarril de Girardot (Columbia)
FEGUA - Ferrocarriles de Guatemala
FNdeC - Ferrocarril Nacional de Chirigui
FMF&W - Ft. Madison, Farmington & Western
GE - General Electric
GAS&C - Georgia, Ashburn, Sylvester & Camila
GF&A - Georgia, Florida & Alabama
GSW&G - Georgia, Southwestern & Gulf
GMSR - Gulf & Mississippi
GM&O - Gulf, Mobile & Ohio
H&B - Hampton & Branchville
H&S - Hartford & Slocomb

IC - Illinois Central
ICG - Illinois Central Gulf
IMC - International Mining Consultants
IP - International Paper Company
IRCA - International Railway of Central America
ICC - Interstate Commerce Commission
LNP&W - Laramie, North Park & Western
LS&BC - LaSalle & Bureau County Railroad
LCL - Less than Car Load freight
L&N - Louisville & Nashville
MOW - Maintenance of Way
M&B - Marrianna & Blountstown
MCB - Master Car Builder
MATA - McKinney Avenue Transit Authority
MD&W - Minnesota, Dakota & Western
M&NF - Morehead & North Fork
NC&StL - Nashville, Chattanooga & St. Louis
NYNH&H - New York, New Haven & Hartford
N&S - Norfolk & Southern (pre 1910)
NS - Norfolk Southern (post 1910)
N&W - Norfolk & Western
NCRR - North Carolina Railroad
PAL - Paducah & Louisville
PC - Penn Central
P&LE - Pittsburgh & Lake Erie
P&W - Philadelphia & Western
RELCO - Railway Equipment Leasing Company
RSS - Rockdale Sandow & Southern
SF&W - Savannah, Florida & Western
SAL - Seaboard Air Line
SCFE - South Central Florida
SEPTA - Southeastern Pennsylvania Transportation Authority
SI&E - Southern Iron & Equipment Company
SLSF - St. Louis & San Francisco
UP - Union Pacific
UFC - United Fruit Company
USMC - United States Marine Corps.
USRA - United States Railroad Administration
VMV - VMV Paducahbilt (re manufacturer)
W&YR - Watauga & Yadkin River
WVC - West Virginia Central
WN&P - Wisconsin, Minnesota & Pacific

Appendix B - Edwards Railway Motor Car Company Roster 1917-1942

Compiled from original company documents with amplification by the author

Built	Original Railroad	#	Seating	Power Plant	Remarks
1917	Atlantic & Western	M-1	22	Kelly Springfield Gasoline	First unit, built by Atlantic & Western Railroad shop. Referred as the "Jitney" or "dinkey" by locals. Built on frame, transmission and engine manufactured by Kelly-Springfield. Referred to by Kelly-Springfield as K-50 Edwards Special.
1920	Atlantic & Western	M-2	22	Kelly Springfield Gasoline	Built by A&W shop. Appeared to have been coupled with a trailer. Referred to by Kelly-Springfield as K-50 Edwards Special.
1922	B&O	6000	22	Kelly Springfield Gasoline	Kelly-Springfield Model K-50. The car was soon returned to Edwards for major modifications. The original #6000 when returned was replaced instead by a Model 10, same number. The first #6000 may have been used as parts as the company slowly evolved to the Model 10.
1922	B&O	6100	34	Non-powered	Trailer, no power plant. Built with no platform, train doors only. Rebuilt by Perley Thomas and retired in 4/1936.
1922	CB&Q	500	42	Kelly Springfield Gasoline	Reportedly built by the Atlantic & Western shops. Perley Thomas Car Works submitted a proposal to built the car and the finished product matched the specifications submitted by this company. However, the CB&Q mechanical descriptions match those of a Kelly-Springfield K-50 Edwards Special. Perley Thomas' quote was for $3,887.50 and the car was sold to CB&Q for $11,550.00. Electric marker lights were installed at St. Joseph, MO in 2/1929.
1922	Maxton, Alma & SB		22	Kelly Springfield Gasoline	Built by Atlantic & Western shop. Referred to by Kelly-Springfield as K-50 Edwards Special.
1923	B&O	6000 (2nd)	25	Buda	Model 10. Original no. 6000 was returned for modifications and B&O was presented with one of the first Model 10s. Placed in service at Berkeley Springs, WV in late 3/32 and retired on 4/13/1936 and scrapped.
1923	Blue Star Coal		25	Buda	Model 10.
1923	Blue Star Coal		32	Non-powered	Trailer, no power plant.
1923	Ferrocarril de Caldas	1	20 or less	Probably Buda gasoline engine	Early Model 10 that was crank started. Ferrocarril de Caldas was a 3' line located in Colombia.
1923	Franklin & Pittsylvania	50	27	Buda 108 hp	Model 10. Later sold to the Central of Georgia Railroad.
1923	Laurinburg & Southern	4	25	Midwest 45 hp gasoline	Model 10.
1923	Laurinburg & Southern		36	Non-powered	Non-powered trailer.
1923	Mount Jewett, Kinzua & Riterville	10	25	Buda Gasoline	Model 10.
1923	Smoky Mountain Ry.		25	Buda	Model 10.

Edwards Railway Motor Car Company Roster 1917-1942, continued

Built	Original Railroad	#	Seating	Power Plant	Remarks
1923	St. Louis, Kennet & Southwestern	80	25	Buda 100 hp	To SLSF, 1927. Later converted to trailer in 1928 and scrapped 1931.
1923	St. Louis, Kennet & Southwestern	81	32	Non-powered	Non-powered trailer, to SLSF, 1927. Scrapped 1931.
1923	Sumter & Choctaw	500	25	Buda 100 hp	Model 10, later de-motored and used as a trailer.
1923	**Tennessee Central Railroad**	**16**	20	Non-powered	Non-powered trailer with large baggage compartment. Currently purchased and awaiting restoration by the ERCC (2005). Car was reportedly used as baggage or pay car.
1923	Tennessee, Kentucky & Northern		25	Buda 75 hp	Model 10.
1923	Tennessee, Kentucky & Northern			Buda 75 hp	Model 10.
1923	Virginia Central	M-2	25	Buda	Model 10.
1923	Virginia Central	M-3	25	Buda	Model 10.
1923	Virginia, Carolina & Southern	303	20	Buda 75 hp	Rebuilt from Birney streetcar body.
1923	Virginia, Carolina & Southern	300	32	Buda 75 hp	Model 10.
1923	Virginia, Carolina & Southern	301	32	Buda 75 hp	Model 10, unit later burned.
1923	Virginia, Carolina & Southern	302	32	Buda 75 hp	Model 10.
1923	**Washington & Lincolnton**	**500 on the B&SE**	22	Buda 60 hp	Model 10, later to Birmingham and Southeastern in 1929. Re powered in early 1980s with Chevy 350 engine. The unit has recently been refurbished by the ERCC.
1923	Wilmington Valley & Coast	1	25	Buda	Model 10.
1924	Atlantic & Western	M-3	24	Buda	Model 10.
1924	Atlantic & Western	M-4	30	Buda	Model 10.
1924	Blue Ridge Ry.		30	Buda	Model 10.
1924	Blue Ridge Ry.		30	Buda	Model 10.
1924	Cairo Northern		25	Buda 108 hp	Model 10.
1924	CB&Q	502	41	2 Buda 60 hp	Model 25, dismantled 9/34. Original sale price was $16,699. After dismantling, body was sold for $40.
1924	Crows Nest Coal, British Columbia		46	Non-powered	Non-powered trailer.
1924	Dansville & Mt. Morris Railroad		50	Buda 108 hp	Model 10.
1924	Morrisey, Fernie & Michael		34	Non-powered	Non-powered trailer.

Edwards Railway Motor Car Company Roster 1917-1942, continued

Built	Original Railroad	#	Seating	Power Plant	Remarks
1924	Morrisey, Fernie & Michael (Canada)		25	Buda Gasoline	Model 10.
1924	Nacional de Mexico	G-1	25	Buda Gasoline	Model 10.
1924	Nacional de Mexico	G-4	25	Buda Gasoline	Model 10.
1924	Nacional de Mexico	G-5	25	Buda Gasoline	Model 10.
1924	Nacional de Mexico	G-2	0	Buda Gasoline	Freight Motor (Motorman cab only).
1924	Nacional de Mexico	G-3	0	Buda Gasoline	Freight motor (Motorman cab only).
1924	Wilmington, Brunswick & Southern	11	28	Buda 75 hp	Model 10.
1924	Wilmington, Brunswick & Southern		40	Non-powered	Non-powered baggage-express trailer.
1924	Wilmington, Brunswick, & Southern			Non-powered	Used as a freight trailer.
1924	Yadkin, NC	100	25	Buda 75 hp	Model 10, this car probably went to Georgia Northern as their no. MC-12 in 1932.
1925	Argentine State Ry.		25	Buda	Model 10.
1925	Birmingham & Southeastern	501	28	Buda 108 hp	Model 10.
1925	Birmingham & Southeastern	502	36	Buda	Model 20, also had a 36-passenger trailer.
1925	Butler County (MO)	M-27	42	Buda 104 hp	Model 20, to SLSF in 1927. There is some thought this might be a Model 20 power unit and not a whole car since the sale price was only $5,077.
1925	**Butte, Anaconda & Pacific**	M-10		Buda 104 hp	Line inspection car. Platform on roof allowed easy access to work on electric catenaries. The car was marketed as a "locomotive" car, which could carry two standard passenger cars or four Edwards cars. The car is preserved at the World Mining Museum in Butte, MT. Only example built. There is some speculation was to whether just the chassis with motor and drive-chain was sold to the railroad, or if the sale incorporated a complete car.
1925	CB&Q	504	39	2 Buda 60 hp	Model 25. Later sold to Colorado & Southern 3/1926. Sold to Graysonia, Nashville & Ashdown in 9/1929, no. 600. Body later used as a diner in Hope, AR. Survives as mobile antique shop.
1925	CB&Q	503	40	2 Buda 60 hp	Model 25. Dismantled 9/34. Original sale price was $16,677. Body was sold to railroad employee for $40.
1925	CB&Q	552; 810; 530; 9530	42	2 Porter 100 hp gasoline	Referred to as Model 65 by CB&Q. The 65' length exceeded the length of the Edwards shops. Was built by H. K. Porter in Pittsburgh, PA. Rebuilt by EMC in 1929 with new power plant, traction motors and controls. Original price was $27,169.70, after refitting by EMC, total price was increased to $39,689.34. Seating capacity 42 with 27 in pass. section and 15 in smoker section.
1925	Crows Nest Coal, British Columbia		36	2 Buda gasoline	Model 25.

Edwards Railway Motor Car Company Roster 1917-1942, continued

Built	Original Railroad	#	Seating	Power Plant	Remarks
1925	Crows Nest Coal, British Columbia		25	Buda	Model 10.
1925	Ecuadorian St. Rys.			Buda	Model 10.
1925	Marion & Rye Valley		34	2 Buda 100 hp gasoline	Model 25, to Central of Georgia In 1934, later to Birmingham & Southeastern
1926	Alabama & Florida	500	16	Buda 50 hp	Model 10.
1926	Atlantic & Western	M-5	24	Buda 108 hp	Model 10.
1926	Atlantic & Western	M-6	30	Buda	Model 10.
1926	Atlantic & Western	6	30	Non-Powered	Non-powered trailer.
1926	Bonlee & Western		25	Buda 108 hp	Model 10.
1926	Cape Fear		30	Buda 108 hp	Model 10, one unit of this order later sold to the Winchester & Western.
1926	Cape Fear		30	Buda 108 hp	Model 10, one of the three Cape Fear cars had a center door and carried 42 passengers.
1926	Cape Fear		30	Buda 108 hp	Model 10.
1926	CB&Q	506	22	2 Buda 60 hp	Model 25, later sold to Laramie, North Park & Western in 3/1931 for $4,000. Original sale price was $18,295.
1926	CB&Q	507	22	2 Buda 60 hp	Model 25, de rostered 9/38 by CB&Q, body sold for $50 and served as private residence for fifty years. Currently in service on Ft. Madison, Farmington & Western Railroad, Iowa. Original sale price was $19,182.84.
1926	CB&Q	508	22	2 Buda 60 hp	Model 25. Later to Laramie, North Park & Western in 3/1931 for $4,000. Original sale price was $18,050.
1926	CB&Q	509	37	2 Buda 60 hp	Model 25. Partition was added for smoking section. De-rostered in 6/38. Body is currently preserved in Iowa awaiting restoration. Car body was originally given to a third party and paid through the Burlington Relief Fund for $50.
1926	Hampton & Branchville	M-200	42	Buda 108 hp, replaced before June 1, 1936 with a 108 hp Continental gasoline engine.	Model 20, preserved at North Carolina Transportation Museum, Spencer, NC. Represents the most intact original Edwards configuration to survive. Operated until Nov. 6, 1951 when a crankshaft problem sidelined the unit. It was stored in a windowless shed until 1998. While in service, it operated between Hampton and Cannadys, SC, a distance of 36 miles. Includes two toilets since this was a "Jim Crow" car.
1926	Morehead & North Fork	200	36	Buda 100 hp	Model 20, called "Blue Goose" by locals. Later to California Western no. M-100. Dieselized in 1954, extended and currently in service. Mid 1960s crash caused major damage and at that time the frame was extended on the rear and a school bus body applied to original frame.
1926	Morrisey, Fernie & Michael		40	Buda Gasoline	Model 20.

Edwards Railway Motor Car Company Roster 1917-1942, continued

Built	Original Railroad	#	Seating	Power Plant	Remarks
1926	Tucson, Cornelia & Gila Bend	401	30	Buda 80 hp	Model 10, now at Nevada State Railway Museum in Carson City, NV. In 1943 a White gasoline engine replaced a Continental gasoline engine. In 1997 the unit received a 75 hp Cummins diesel engine. In 1999, the unit was equipped with a fluid drive transmission and participated in Railfair '99. Operated as Washoe Zephyr no. 50 during the 1970s.
1927	FC Panama Nacional	200	20	Non-powered	Trailer, open platform.
1927	FC Panama Nacional	201	20	Non-powered	Trailer, open platform.
1927	FC Panama Nacional	202	20	Non-powered	Trailer, open platform. Preserved in town square of Boquete, Panama.
1927	FC Panama Nacional	203	20	Non-powered	Trailer, open platform.
1927	FC Panama Nacional	204	20	Non-powered	Trailer, open platform.
1927	FC Panama Nacional	205	20	Non-powered	Trailer, open platform.
1927	FC Panama Nacional	206	20	Non-powered	Trailer, open platform.
1927	FC Panama Nacional	100	30	Buda	Model 10, with Model 20 radiator mounted on the roof. Either no. 100 or no. 101. Was renumbered from no. 11 when the car left the Sanford, NC factory.
1927	FC Panama Nacional	101	30	Buda	Model 10, with Model 20 radiator mounted on the roof.
1927	FC Panama Nacional	102	39	2 Buda gasoline	Model 10, dual engines, center entrance. De-motorized and used as a trailer in mid 1950s. Reportedly still exists.
1927	FC Panama Nacional	103	39	2 Buda engines	Model 10, dual engines, center entrance.
1927	FC Panama Nacional	150		Buda	Freight motor. Purchased after a 1926 brochure featured the freight motors.
1927	FC Panama Nacional	151		Buda	Freight motor.
1927	Gainesville & Western		36	Buda 108 hp	Model 20, later to Chesapeake & Western.
1927	Panama Railroad	2	30	Buda Gasoline	Model 10. Scrapped 1938.
1928	Argentine State Ry.		42	Buda	Model 20.
1928	Argentine State Ry.		42	Buda	Model 20.
1928	A&SAB	500	28	Buda 108 hp	Model 10.
1928	A&SAB	501	28	Buda 108 hp	Model 10.
1928	A&SAB	503	20	Buda 108 hp	Model 10, originally built with air conditioning and 60' in length with baggage compartment, RPO compartment and 20 seats. Later sold to Tallulah Falls RR in 1939 and passenger section was removed. Used by TF as Post Office and express car. Served as private residence for several years in Georgia. Currently (2005) under restoration by the ERCC.
1928	A&SAB	510	28	Buda 108 hp	Model 10, no baggage compartment. No. 510 was later rebuilt into an observation/inspection car and renumbered 550. Was equipped with bedroom suite and kitchen.
1928	Panama Railroad	3	30	Buda 125 hp	Model 10.
1928	Panama Railroad	10	30	Buda 125 hp	Model 10.

Edwards Railway Motor Car Company Roster 1917-1942, continued

Built	Original Railroad	#	Seating	Power Plant	Remarks
1928	Rapid City, Black Hills & Western	6	12	Buda 123 hp	Model 10, large baggage compartment. Railroad referred to no. 6 as an observation car, and it was semi-permenantly coupled to a passenger coach. Scrapped.
1928	Rapid City, Black Hills & Western	5	28	Buda 123 hp	Model 10, burned 1947 and the line was abandoned in 1948. The car was coupled semi-permenantly to a passenger coach.
1928	Tranvia de Oriente de Medellin		0	Buda 80 hp	Freight unit (motorman cab only). Photographic evidence supports these units were later rebuilt as traditional passenger carrying motorcars. The line was a 1-meter gauge located in Colombia.
1928	Tranvia de Oriente de Medellin	704	0	Buda 80 hp	Freight unit (motorman cab only). Sold to Ferrocarril de Girandot in 1931. No. 704 was rebuilt by the Girandot shops in 1943.
1928	Tranvia de Oriente de Medellin	705; 700; 2700	0	Buda 80 hp	Freight unit (motorman cab only). Sold to Ferrocarril de Girandot in 1931. Later numbered 700, then 2700. Photographic evidence shows the 2700 survived into the 1980s as a hulk.
1928	Tranvia de Oriente de Medellin		0	Buda 80 hp	Freight unit (motorman cab only). See above.
1928	Panama Railroad	4	32	Buda 125 hp	Model 10, scrapped 1948.
1929	Ferrocarril de Girardot (Columbia)	700	24	Buda, 125 hp	
1931	Virginia, Carolina & Southern	304	40	Buda 108 hp	Model 20.
1934	Panama Railroad	5	46	Buda 125 hp	Model 21, streamlined. This was the second streamlined unit built. Equipped with open platform in rear of unit. Scrapped 1967.
1935	U.S. Navy		42	Buda Gasoline	Model 21, built as ERMCC no. 200, a demonstrator, and was the first streamlined unit produced by the company. Sold to U.S. Navy in 1938, then to Alaska RR (no. 212), retired 4/1954, scrapped in late 1959.
1935	Chilean State Railway	RT-1	32	Buda, replaced with Cummins model HRB-600; 165 hp.	Semi-streamlined Model 10. Operated on 1-meter line between La Calera and La Serena, a distance of 400 kilometers.
1936	Chilean State Railway	RT-2	32	Buda, see above	Semi-streamlined Model 10. See above.
1936	Chilean State Railway	RT-3	32	Buda, see above	Semi-streamlined Model 10. See above.
1936	FC Panama Nacional	104	30	Buda	Streamlined body, Model 10.
1936	FC Panama Nacional	105	30	Buda	Streamlined body, Model 10.
1936	FC del Estado	RT-1		Buda gasoline	Streamlined Model 10.
1936	Ferrocarril de Girardot	708	26	Two Buda gasoline engines; 128 hp each. Converted to dual Cummins diesel in 1938; 200 hp each.	Model 25. For many years these cars were erroneously labeled having gone to the "City of Medellin" due to a personally typed memo from Harry P. Edwards. He was trying to recall later in life where he had cars delivered and Medellin was one of the ports of entry for the motor cars. The line was a 36" or 914 mm gauge. The units purchased in the 1937 order were priced at $22,547.00.

Edwards Railway Motor Car Company Roster 1917-1942, continued

Built	Original Railroad	#	Seating	Power Plant	Remarks
1937	Ferrocarril de Girardot	709	26	See FdeG no. 708 above	Model 25. See FdeG no. 708 above.
1937	Ferrocarril de Girardot	710	26	See FdeG no. 708 above	Model 25. See FdeG no. 708 above.
1937	Ferrocarril Central del Norte	703			Model 10. Colombian railroad which later became Ferrocarriles Nacionales de Colombia. The FNdeC later purchased another Edwards car, the former no. 704 from the Ferrocarril de Girardot.
1938	Ferrocarriles Nacionales	704			Model 10. Car lettered as "Ferrocarriles Nacionales. Central Del Norte Seccion 1." Car survived into the early 1980s.
1938	Ferrocarriles Nacionales de Pacifico (Columbia)	707			Model 10. Unit owned by Ferrocarill de Girardot.
1938	Ferrocarril de Girardot	711	26	See FdeG no. 708 above	Model 25. See FdeG no. 708 above.
1938	Panama Railroad	6	46	Buda 125 hp	Model 21, closed rear platform. Trailer no. 6-A matched lead unit. Serviced as temporary station in 1964 when town's depot was burned during riots. Scrapped 1967.
1938	Panama Railroad	6-A	56	Non-powered	Non-powered trailer. Scrapped 1967.
1938	**United Fruit Co. (Guatemala)**	1150, later 150		Buda 125 hp	Model 10 Streamlined, used as an official's car. Body was later used as a pay-car by the IRCA and FEGUA Railroads. Car survives today in Guatemala awaiting restoration. Represents the last car constructed for international sales.
1942	U. S. Army, Newfoundland Base Company	P-40-1	35	Gasoline operated, power-plant unknown	Model 10, semi-streamlined. Represent the last units built by the Edwards Motor Car Company before converting over to wartime production. Two units each were shipped via two transports; one transport was sunk by a U-Boat. The surviving units were referred to as the "Toonerville Trolley" by soldiers operating the 9-mile spur. The line was a 42" gauge.
1942	U. S. Army, Newfoundland Base Company	P-40-2	35	See above.	See above.
1942	U. S. Army, Newfoundland Base Company	P-40-3	35	See above.	See above.
1942	U. S. Army, Newfoundland Base Company	P-40-4	35	See above.	See above.

Bold type indicates surviving car.

Appendix C – Atlantic & Western locomotive roster
Compiled by Ken Ardinger

Number	Type	Builder	Date	Drivers	Remarks
1	4-4-0	?	?	?	Built for Manhattan Ry. (New York Elevated) as no. 141, to no. 314. Sold to A&W on 9/10/1903. A&W records indicate last used 2/1920 and scrapped 2/18/1930.
1	Railcar	Edwards	1917	–	A nine ton highway truck with flanged wheels, which was powered by a Kelly Springfield gasoline engine.
2	2-4-6T	Mason	6/1885	54"	Built for Old Colony Railroad as no. 19, then to NYNH&H as no. 2101, to SI&E as no. 367, to A&W 2/26/1906 as no. 2 (may have served as first no. 10).
2	Railcar	Edwards	1920	–	A nine ton highway truck with flanged wheels and a Kelly Springfield gasoline engine, which seated 22.
3	4-4-0	McKay-Alders	4/1913	64"	Built for Central Railroad of New Jersey as no. 19, to no. 416, to no. 759. Sold to J.E. Bowen of Norfolk, VA, sold to A&W on 9/28/1913. Scrapped 1917.
3	Railcar	A&W	1924	–	Ten ton 31 ½ foot railcar with 30 seats and a Buda gasoline engine. Scrapped 2/18/1930. Edwards Model 10.
4	4-4-0	Pittsburgh B/n 25309 or 25310	7/1902	?	Built for St. Louis, Memphis & Southeastern RR as no. 23 or no. 24. Sold to A&W in 1912 and then to SI&E as no. 885, then on 2/1913 to Thomas & Edgar as no. 4.
5	2-8-0	Baldwin	6/1891	50"	Built for Western New York & Pennsylvania as no. 175, to PRR as no. 6301, to SI&E as no. 831, sold to A&W on 4/28/1913. Scrapped circa 1930.
5	Railcar	Edwards	1926	–	A ten ton 31 ½ foot railcar with 30 seats and a Buda gasoline engine. Edwards Model 10.
6	2-8-0	Baldwin	1891	?	Built for PRR and eventually sold to A&W 4/28/1913 and disposed of before 7/1923.
6	4-6-0	Rogers	1898	?	Built for the Mobile & Ohio RR as no. 161, to SI&E as no. 1829. Sold to A&W for $6,750, retired 5/28/1926, scrapped after 1930.
6	Railcar	Edwards	1926	–	A ten ton 31 ½ foot gasoline powered railcar with Buda engine. Scrapped in the early 1950s. Edwards Model 10.
7	4-4-0	Baldwin	?	?	Origin unknown. Rebuilt for Thomas & Edgar as no. 4 from 16x24 to 17x24 cylinders.
7	2-8-0	Roanoke B/n 98	5/1890	?	Built for N&W no. 236, then to Norfolk & Portsmouth Beltline as no. 15. To A&W 2/28/1927 and retired 8/30/1930. Scrapped after 1934.
7	Railcar	Brill	1927	–	Built for Long Island RR no. 1134 and had Cummins diesel engine installed in 1939. Sold to A&W 12/13/1939, Sold to a museum in Ohio in the mid 1960s. This car was purchased instead of an Edwards car.
8	4-6-0	Baldwin B/n 27415	2/1906	56"	Built as Cape Fear & Northern as (second) no. 103, to Durham & Southern RR as no. 106. Sold to A&W on September 1, 1930 after line had scrapped six other locomotives. Retired after 1936.
9	4-6-0	Baldwin B/n 26543	10/1905	56"	Built for Cape Fear & Northern as no. 106, then to D&S as no. 106. Purchased in 1934 for $2,000 and retired in 1936. Scrapped circa 1956.
10	0-4-4T	Mason	1885	?	Built for NYNH&H as no. ?, to Old Colony RR as no. 19. Sold to A&W 2/26/1906, disposition unknown.

Atlantic & Western locomotive roster, continued

Number	Type	Builder	Date	Drivers	Remarks
10	2-8-0	Baldwin	1911	?	Built for Elkin & Allegheny as (first) no. 100. To Georgia Car & Locomotive Co. as no. 430, to Kaul Lumber Co. as no. 15. To Birmingham Rail & Locomotive Co. as no. 811. To A&W on 6/2/1942. May be on display in Lillington, NC.
11	2-8-0	Richmond B/n 26831	2/1903	57"	Built for SAL as no. 652, renumbered 981. To Aberdeen & Rockfish as no. 45. To A&W circa 1947-1948. Wrecked in August 1948 and scrapped in 1950.
12	2-8-0	Baldwin B/n 37161	11/1911	50"	Built for Raleigh & Southport as no. 10, to Norfolk Southern as no. 99, renumbered 203. To A&W 6/8/1948, retired on 10/11/1950. Placed on display in Sanford, NC on 11/26/1966.
100	70-ton Diesel	GE B/n 30452	1950	–	The ONLY engine bought new for the A&W. On site, not active as of 2006.
101	80-ton Diesel	Porter B/n 7607	1/1944	–	Built for US Navy as no. 13, used in Norfolk, VA. Renumbered 65-00141. To Durham & Southern in 10/1962 as no. 500. To A&W in 1965, and scrapped in the late 1970s.
101 (2nd)	70-ton Diesel	GE B/n 29467	1/1948	–	Built as High Point, Thomasville & Denton as no. 203. To Superior Stone as no. 203, Rion, SC. To Martin Marietta, to Laurinburg & Southern as no. 102. To A&W as (second) no. 101. On site but not active as of 2006.
109	GP-10	EMD B/n 22074	7/1956	–	Built as GP-9 for D&RGW, no. 5940. Rebuilt as GP-10 in 5/1970. To ICG as no. 8323. To Meridian & Bigbee as no. 109. To A&W
1219	Sw 1200 RS	EMD	1956	–	Ex-CN no.1219. To A&W as no. 1590, then renumbered.

Appendix D - Atlanta & St. Andrews Bay locomotive roster
Compiled by Ken Ardinger

Number	Type	Builder	Date	Drivers	Remarks
101	4-4-0	Rogers B/n 3971	July 1888	64"	Built for SF&W as (second) no. 41. To ACL as no. 554. To A&SAB 1907, scrapped.
102	4-4-0	B&O (Mt. Claire)	?	69"	To A&SAB 1907.
104	4-4-0	Brooks B/n 1665	May 1890	?	Built for Winona & Southwestern as no. 3. To Winona & Western as no. 3, to Wisconsin Minnesota & Pacific as no. 1121. To Chicago Great Western as no. 1121. Acquired from Georgia Car & Locomotive Co. – Scrapped.
105	4-6-0	Baldwin B/n 32248	May 1907	56"	To Fuller Earth Co. – Marianna, Fla.
106	4-6-0	Baldwin B/n 32450	Dec. 1907	56"	To St. Mary's RR as no. 106 in 1935.
107	4-6-0	Baldwin B/n 33000	Oct. 1908	56"	Spent entire life on A&SAB before being scrapped.
110	4-6-0	Brooks B/n 2091	May 1892	56"	Ex-Ulster & Delaware no. 1, renumbered 17. To A&SAB, scrapped.
120	4-6-0	Baldwin B/n 39187	Jan. 1913	56"	To Sandersville RR as no. 120.
121	4-6-0	Baldwin B/n 17157	Oct. 1899	?	Built for Cape Fear & Northern as no. 99. To Durham & Southern as no. 99, to Greenville & Knoxville as no. 10. To A&SAB. To the Georgia, Southwestern & Gulf as no. 121 in 1917.
131	4-6-2	Schenectady B/n 57545	Sept. 1917	68"	Ex-Florida East Coast no. 131.
142	4-6-2	Richmond B/n 61763	May 1920	68"	Ex-Florida East Coast no. 142.
143	4-6-2	Richmond B/n 61764	May 1920	68"	Ex-Florida East Coast no. 143. To A&SAB. To Columbia, Newberry & Laurens as no. 143 in 1940.
145	4-6-2	Richmond B/n 61766	May 1920	68"	Ex-Florida East Coast no. 145. To A&SAB. To Georgia & Florida RR as no. 515 in 1946.
146	4-6-2	Richmond B/n 61767	May 1920	68"	Ex-Florida East Coast no. 146. To A&SAB. To FC Kansas City, Mexico y Oriente as no. 151 in 1948.
154	4-6-2	Schenectady B/n 63263	June 1922	68"	Ex-Florida East Coast no. 154. To A&SAB. To Columbia, Newberry & Laurens as no. 154 in 1940.
200	2-8-0	Baldwin B/n 29323	Oct. 1906	57"	Ex-Central of Georgia no. 1209, renumbered 209. To A&SAB. To Mississippi Export as no. 37 in 1936.
201	2-8-0	Baldwin B/n 29386	Nov. 1906	57"	Ex-Central of Georgia no. 1212, renumbered 212. To A&SAB. To Mississippi Export as no. 36 in 1936. To Gainesville Midland as no. 114.
202	2-8-0	Baldwin B/n 29364	Oct. 1906	57"	Built for Central of Georgia as no. 1211, renumbered 211. To A&SAB, sold in April 1945.

Atlanta & St. Andrews Bay locomotive roster, continued

Number	Type	Builder	Date	Drivers	Remarks
206	0-6-0	Richmond B/n 61023	May 1920	51"	Built for Florida East Coast as no. 140, renumbered 206. To Jacksonville City Docks as no. 206. To A&SAB. To Rockwood Alabama Stone Co., Russellville, Ala, about 1944.
208	0-6-0	Richmond B/n 63268	June 1920	51"	Ex-Florida East Coast no. 159, renumbered 208. To A&SAB. To Dominion Steel & Coal Corp. as no. 208 in 1944.
300	2-8-2	Brooks B/n 64145	Feb. 1923	51"	Ex-Minarets & Western no. 103. To A&SAB. To Chicago & Illinois Midland as no. 527, 12/1937.
401	2-8-2	Schenectady B/n 40995	Jan. 1907	63"	Originally 2-8-0 built for NYC as no. 2832. Rebuilt as 2-8-2, no. 3893. Rebuilt Reno NYC as no. 1342 in 1936 and acquired by A&SAB in 1937. Retired 5/1948.
402	2-8-2	Schenectady B/n 41849	Feb. 1907	63"	Originally 2-8-0 built for NYC as no. 2862. Rebuilt as 2-8-2 no. 3902. Rebuilt Reno NYC as no. 1350 in 1936 and acquired by A&SAB in 1937. Retired 5/1948.
403	2-8-2	Schenectady B/n 40987	Oct. 1906	63"	Originally 2-8-0 built for NYC as no. 2824. Rebuilt as 2-8-2 no. 3868. Rebuilt Reno NYC as no. 1324 in 1936 and acquired by A&SAB in 1937. Retired 5/1948.
404	2-8-2	Schenectady B/n 30797	Feb. 1905	63"	Originally 2-8-0 built for NYC as no. 2702. Rebuilt as 2-8-2 no. 3721. Rebuilt Reno NYC as no. 1247 in 1936 and acquired by A&SAB in 1938. Retired 5/1948.
500	Railcar	Edwards	1928	-	Model 10 car.
501	Railcar	Edwards	1928	-	Model 10 car.
503	Railcar	Edwards	1928	-	Model 25 car. Dual motors.
510	Railcar	Edwards	1928	-	Model 20 car. Later fitted as business/observation car.
550	Railcar	Edwards	1928	-	Former no. 510, Model 20. New number was adapted after the car was rebuilt as an inspection car.
500	GP7	EMD B/n 18416	5/53	-	Ex-Reading no. 616. To A&SAB. To SCFE as no. 9010, used as parts source by 2000.
500	GP38	EMD B/n 35176	8/69	-	Built for GM&O as no. 713, to IC as no. 9532 to A&SAB.
501	GP7	EMD B/n 15943	1/52	-	(Nose chopped). To SCFE as no. 9011, to Cape Cod Central as no. 1501, 3/2000.
501	GP38	EMD B/n 35170	8/69	-	Built for GM&O as no. 707, to IC as no. 9526. To VMV as no. 2000, to PAL as no. 2000. To A&SAB.
502	GP7	EMD B/n 15944	1/52	-	(Nose chopped). Renumbered as no. 511. To SCFE as no. 9012, to Cape Cod Central as no. 1502, 3/2000.
502	GP38	EMD B/n 35389	8/69	-	Built for PC as no. 7760, to CR as no. 7760. To GMSR as no. 7760, to A&SAB.

Atlanta & St. Andrews Bay locomotive roster, continued

Number	Type	Builder	Date	Drivers	Remarks
503	SD9	EMD B/n 21046	1/56	-	Wrecked 2/25/1978 and scrapped.
503	GP38	EMD B/n 35410	9/69	-	Built for PC as no. 7781, to CR as no. 7781. To GMSR as no. 7781, to A&SAB.
504	SD9	EMD B/n 21047	1/56	-	To Helm Lease as no. 505.
504	GP38	EMD B/n 35419	10/69	-	Built for PC as no. 7790, to CR as no. 7790. To GMSR as no. 7790, to A&SAB.
505	SD9	EMD B/n 24062	4/58	-	To Helm Lease as no. 505.
505	GP38	EMD B/n 35421	10/69	-	Built for PC as no. 7792, to CR as no. 7792. To GMSR as no. 7792, to A&SAB.
506	SD40	EMD B/n 31766	6/66	-	To Helm Leasing as no. 506.
506	GP38	EMD B/n 35440	10/69	-	Built for PC as no. 7811, to CR as no. 7811. To GMSR as no. 7811, to A&SAB.
507	GP39	EMD B/n 36312	7/70	-	To VMV as no. 507, to PAL as no. 8507.
507	GP38	EMD B/n 35448	10/69	-	
508	GP38-2	EMD B/n 72686-1	5/73	-	In service (as of 2005).
509	GP38-2	EMD B/n 72686-2	5/73	-	In service (as of 2005).
510	GP38-2	EMD B/n 75623-1	6/75	-	In service (as of 2005).
511	GP7	EMD B/n 15944	1/52	-	Re-numbered from no. 502, to SCFE as no. 9012. Then to Cape Cod Central as no. 1502 in 3/2000.
511	GP38	EMD B/n 35378	8/69	-	Built for Penn Central as no. 7749, to Conrail same number. To A&SAB.
512	GP7	EMD		-	Built for C&O as no. 6085, to RSS as no. 6085, renumbered 102. To A&SAB.
901	RS1	Alco B/n 69426	3/41	-	To US Army no. 8010 in 1/1943, received C-C trucks. To US Navy 65-00512. Assigned to McAlester, OK, now gone from Navy. No. 901 was from shop order S-1831, the first order of RS1s.
902	RS1	Alco B/n 69427	3/41	-	To US Army as no. 8011 on 1/1943. To Alaska RR as no. 1034 on 6/1951. Returned to Army as no. 8011, to DOT as no. 013, Avondale, CO on 9/1974. To Strasburg Railroad and repainted in Alaska RR lettering.

Atlanta & St. Andrews Bay locomotive roster, continued

Number	Type	Builder	Date	Drivers	Remarks
903	RS1	Alco B/n 69800	1/43	-	To US Army as no. 8012, then to US Navy, then to BR&L where it was scrapped.
904	RS1	Alco B/n 70810	4/43	-	Chopped nose, donated 1973 and is on display in Panama City, FL.
905	RS1	Alco B/n 70811	4/43	-	To Tennessee RR as no. 1, 7/1955, to SR, never lettered but numbered 1W. To South Carolina Port Railway as no. 1, to Maryland & Delaware as no. 22. To A&M as no. 22, then to St. Louis Transportation Museum.
906	RS1	Alco B/n 70821	4/43	-	To Tennessee RR as no. 2, to SR, never lettered but numbered 2H. To BR&L, to Peabody Coal as no. 16. Then to IMC as no. 203 and used at Kingsford, FL mine. Scrapped.
907	RS1	Alco B/n 70809	4/43	-	To BR&L, to Peabody Coal as no. 15. To IMC as no. 205, to CYDZ as no. 303 and in use at Orlando, FL 2/2003.
908	RS1	Alco B/n 70822	4/43	-	To Tennessee Central as no. 3, to SR, but never lettered. To BR&L, to MD&W as no. 15.
909	RS1	Alco B/n 72812	6/44	-	(Chopped nose). To Chattahoochee Industrial as no. 3. To CYDZ as no. 3, renumbered 275, used in Ocala, FL. While on CIRR it was named "The General."
910	RS1	Alco B/n 73332	4/45	-	(Chopped nose). To Interprovincial Steel Pipe, Regina, Saskatchewan, Canada, as no. 3, 9/1973.
911	RS1	Alco B/n 73333	4/45	-	(Chopped nose). To Chattahoochee Industrial as no. 118, 6/73. To CYDZ as no. 118, renumbered 294, used in Jacksonville, FL.
912	RS1	Alco B/n 75559	10/47	-	(Chopped nose). To Chattahoochee Industrial, 1984. Used as parts source.
913	RS1	Alco B/n 77848	2/50	-	(Chopped nose). To Hartford & Slocomb as no. 913, 2/1984. To Tennessee Railroad Museum, Chattanooga, TN.
1001	S2	Alco B/n 70276	11/42	-	Through G. Silcott, dealer, to Becker Sand & Gravel as no. 3. To Marlboro Plant, 1968. Probably scrapped once plant went to trucks.
1002	S2	Alco B/n 70277	11/42	-	Traded to EMD for SD40 no. 506, 1966.
1501	F3A	EMD B/n 5144	6/47	-	Traded to EMD for GP39 no. 507, 1970. Rebuilt by EMD to F7A.

Appendix E – Marianna & Blountstown Locomotive roster
Compiled by the author

Number	Type	Builder	Date	Drivers	Remarks
55	2-6-0	Rome B/n 284	7/1887	50"- 18x24	Built for West Virginia & Pittsburgh as no. 8. To B&O as no. 909, to Georgia Car & Locomotive as no. 74, to M&B on 3/2/1910.
70	4-6-0	Baldwin B/n 41463	6/1914	56"- 17x26	Built for Georgia Coast & Piedmont as no. 70. To Georgia Car & Locomotive Co. as no. 433, to M&B on 1/7/1920.
81	4-6-0	Taunton B/n 801	8/81	18x26	Built for UP as no. 999. To F. M. Hicks Co, 10/1903. To Natchez, Columbia & Mobile as (first) no. 4, 3/1904. Taken in trade by SI&E 10/25/1909 and assigned s/n 736. To M&B 3/12/1910. M&B paid $4,541.36.
97	4-6-0	Vulcan B/n 2461	12/1915	56"- 17x24	Purchased new.
101	4-6-0	Baldwin	7/1919	57"- 18x26	Built for Giles Bay Lumber Co. as no.1, to Georgia Northern 9/1925, to GAS&C 4/1937, to M&B.
113	4-6-0	Rogers B/n 2884	12/81		Built for NC&STL as no. 7. To Georgia Car & Locomotive Co. as no. 113, to Blountstown Mfg. Co. as no. 113, 7/1910, transferred to M&B by 1915. Purchased by M&B for $4,710.63 and sold by M&B on 1/1920 for $3,500.
444	4-6-0	Baldwin B/n 36174	3/1911	56"- 16x24	Built for Brinson Railroad as no. 444. To Savannah & Northwestern as no. 444, 3/1914. To Savannah & Atlanta as no. 444, 7/1917. To M&B in 1935. On display over original main line in Blountstown, FL.
11	600 hp	EMD B/n 1537	1941	-	Built for NC&STL as no. 20, renumbered 15. To L&N as no. 2115, renumbered 11 (second), sold 5/1970. Was M&B no. 1 in early 1970s.
44	300 hp	Whitcomb B/n 60198	1942	-	Model 45DE-27b. Built for General Steel Castings in Madison, IL as no. 2. To Standard Steel Spring Co., Granite City, IL, 2/1944. To U.S.Navy as 65-00218. For sale 1/1963 at Pensacola, FL by GSA. After M&B it went to CIRR and then to H&S by 7/1972. To Kaiser Chemical in Bainbridge, GA and then to RR Supply Corp. as no. 4774.
75	600 hp	GE B/n 29090	1947	-	To Whistler Equip. by 7/1966, to Iowa Terminal as no. 75. To Sisseton Southern in South Dakota as no. 75, lettered SSOR no. 75 and then to Dakota Southern, still as SSOR by 9/1992.
88	650 hp	Whitcomb B/n 60324	1941	-	Model 80DE-7. Built for U.S. Navy as no. 10 at Seawalls, VA, renumbered 65-0043. After M&B it went to Gary Yates Scrap and was still there as of 1997.
99	600 hp	GE B/n 3038	1949	-	Built for L&N as no. 126, renumbered 99. To CIRR 9/1969, then to M&B. To Inman Locomotive Service 2/1982. No. 99 may never have been officially on the M&B roster, but owned by individuals who managed the M&B as well as the CIRR.

Appendix F - Watuga & Yadkin River Locomotive roster
Compiled by the author

Number	Type	Builder	Date	Drivers	Remarks
101	2-8-0	Baldwin B/n 37895	1912	51"	Ex-Watauga Construction Co. of North Wilkesboro, NC. Cut up on site for salvage in early 1930s.
102	2-8-0	Baldwin B/n 38822	1913	51"	Ex-Grandin Lumber Co. of North Wilkesboro, NC. Cut up on site for salvage in early 1930s.

Appendix G – Georgia, Florida & Alabama Locomotive roster
Compiled by the author

Number	Type	Builder	Date	Drivers	Remarks
1	4-6-0	Baldwin	1897	50"	Built for Georgia Pine as no. 1. To GF&A as no. 121, used on Quincy branch due to light weight.
1	0-6-0	Baldwin	?	50"	To SAL as (second) 1000 in 1929.
2	?	?	?	?	
3	?	?	?	?	
4	?	?	?	?	
5	4-6-0	Baldwin	1901	50"	Wood burner renumbered 122.
6	4-6-0	Baldwin	1902	62"	Wood burner renumbered 123.
7	?	?	?	?	
8	4-6-0	Baldwin	1903	56"	Wood burner renumbered 124.
15	4-4-0	Pittsburgh	?		Wood burning locomotive.
16	?	?	?	?	Ex-Southern Pacific.
101	4-4-0	Baldwin	?	?	Ex-Logansport, Crawfordsville & Southwestern.
102	4-4-0	P&LE RR	1896	68"	Wood burner built for P&LE as no. 300. To Monongahela Ry. as no. 150, to SAL as (second) no. 100 in 1929.
103	4-4-0	Schenectady	?	?	Wood burner built for AT&SF.
104	4-4-0	Baldwin	1905	62"	Wood burner, to SAL as (third) no. 101 in 1929.
105	4-4-0	?	?	?	
106	?	Rhode Island	1897	?	To SAL as (third) no. 102 in 1929.
120	?	B&O - Mt. Clare Shops	?	?	
121	4-6-0	Baldwin	1897	?	Built for Georgia Pine as no.1, to GF&A as (first) no. 1, then to SAL as no. 684 in 1929.
122	4-6-0	Baldwin	1901	50"	Renumbered from 5. To SAL as no. 684 in 1929.
123	4-6-0	Baldwin	1902	62"	Renumbered from 6. To SAL as no. 685 in 1929.
124	4-6-0	Baldwin	1903	56"	Renumbered from 8. To SAL as no. 686 in 1929.
125	4-6-0	Baldwin	1905	62"	To SAL as no. 687 in 1929.
126	2-8-0	Baldwin	1906	62"	To SAL as no. 688 in 1929.
128	2-8-0	Baldwin	1906	56"	Renumbered 200.
129	2-8-0	Baldwin	1906	56"	Renumbered 201.
200	2-8-0	Baldwin	1906	56"	Renumbered from 128. To SAL as no. 920 in 1929.
201	2-8-0	Baldwin	1906	56"	Renumbered from 129. To SAL as no. 921 in 1929.
202	2-8-0	Baldwin	1907	56"	To SAL as no. 922 in 1929.
203	2-8-0	Baldwin	1913	56"	To SAL as no. 923 in 1929.
204	2-8-0	Baldwin	1913	56"	To SAL as no. 924 in 1929.
300	2-10-0	Baldwin	1918	56"	Russian Decapod, to SAL as no. 521 in 1929.

Georgia, Florida & Alabama Locomotive roster, continued
Compiled by the author

Number	Type	Builder	Date	Drivers	Remarks
301	2-10-0	Baldwin	1918	56"	Russian Decapod, to SAL Ry. as no. 522 in 1929.
400	2-10-0	Baldwin	1924	56"	To SAL Ry. as no. 523 in 1929.
401	2-10-0	Baldwin	1924	56"	To SAL Ry. as no. 524 in 1929.
402	2-10-0	Baldwin	1926	56"	To SAL Ry. as no. 525 in 1929.
403	2-10-0	Baldwin	1926	56"	To SAL Ry. as no. 526 in 1929.
404	2-10-0	Baldwin	1926	56"	To SAL Ry. as no. 527 in 1929.
405	2-10-0	Baldwin	1926	56"	To SAL Ry. as no. 528 in 1929.

Appendix H – Atlantic & North Carolina/Atlantic & East Carolina Locomotive roster

Compiled by Ken Ardinger

Number	Type	Builder	Date	Drivers	Remarks
name	4-4-0	Rogers, Ketchum, & Grosvenor	1/1856	60"	Named "Governor Bragg." In service 3/15/1856.
name	4-4-0	Breese, Keeland & Co.	?	60"	Named "Charles F. Fisher." In service 11/26/1856.
name	4-4-0	Rogers	?	60"	Named "John Baxter." In service 5/13/1857.
name	4-4-0	Breese, Keeland & Co.	?	60"	Named "John Stanly." In service 7/1857.
name	4-4-0	Norris	?	?	Named "Dr. Hawks." In service 7/1858.
name	4-4-0	Norris	?	?	Named "William Gaston." In service 7/1858.
name	4-4-0	Baldwin	1862	54"	Named "Vulcan." Ex-US Military "Vulcan."
name	4-4-0	Breese, Keeland & Co.	1856	60"	Named "Scout." Ex-U.S. Military "Scout," formerly "Eclipse." To N&S no. 20 in 1905.
name	4-4-0	Baldwin	1855	?	Named "Blue Bird." Originally Philadelphia & Reading "Blue Bird," Purchased form US Military 11/30/1865. Rebuilt with new boiler in 1881, renamed "A.M. Scales," Retired by NS RR in 1911.
10	4-4-0	Richmond	1891	60"	To NS as no. 22, retired 1925.
11	4-4-0	Richmond	1891	60"	To NS as no. 23, retired 1925.
11	2-6-0	Montreal	1911	50"	Acquired 1935. Ex-Carolina Southern no. 101, originally McDonnell & O'Brien no. 25.
12	4-4-0	Richmond	1905	?	To NS as no. 25, retired 1925.
12	4-6-0	Baldwin	12/1912	51"	Ex-East Carolina no. 12.
13	4-6-0	Richmond		48"	To NS as no. 25, retired 1925.
14	4-4-0	Baldwin	1898	60"	To NS as no. 37.
15	4-4-0	Pittsburgh	12/1894	62"	To NS as no. 48, retired 1922.
16	4-4-0	Pittsburgh	2/1900	62"	To NS as no. 49, retired 1922.
17	4-4-0	Pittsburgh	4/1900	62"	To NS as no. 50.
18	4-4-0	Baldwin	2/1901	60"	To NS as no. 70, retired 1932.
19	4-4-0	Baldwin	2/1901	60"	To NS as no. 41, retired 1932.
30*	0-6-0	Baldwin	11/1905	50"	To NS as no. 3, A&EC no. 3, assigned to B&M 1935-39.
4*	0-6-0	Schenectady	1900	51"	Ex-NS no. 4, acquired 1935.
5*	0-6-0	Baldwin	4/1901	51"	Ex-NS no. 5, scrapped 1942.
6*	0-6-0	Baldwin	4/1901	51"	Ex-NS no. 6.
7*	2-6-0	Baldwin	10/1907	?	Built for Louisiana Ry as no. 5. To Big Sandy Lumber Co, Hull, Al. To Tremont & Gulf as no. 21, to BR&L and then to A&EC.

Atlantic & North Carolina/Atlantic & East Carolina Locomotive roster, continued

Number	Type	Builder	Date	Drivers	Remarks
102*	4-6-0	Baldwin	5/1907	64"	Ex-ACL no. 976, acquired 1936.
103*	4-6-0	Baldwin	1907	64"	Ex-ACL no. 919, acquired 1936.
601*	4-6-0	Baldwin	10/1922	?	Ex-Wis. & Mich. no. 601, acquired 1937.
602*	4-6-0	Baldwin	10/1922	?	Ex-Wis. & Mich. no. 602, acquired 1937.
785*	2-8-0	Schenectady	1908	?	Ex-DL&W no. 785.
792*	2-8-0	Schenectady	1908	?	Ex-DL&W no. 792.
797*	2-8-0	Schenectady	1908	?	Ex-DL&W no. 797.
1031*	4-6-0	Baldwin	1931	?	Ex-ACL no. 1031, to Virginia & Carolina Southern RR as no. 1031. On display in Florence, SC.
?*	4 wheel gasoline	Plymouth	?	-	Probably second Plymouth on line.
6	44-tonner	GE	5/1943	-	Ex-US Army no. 7088, sold to Laurinburg & Southern in 1947. Renumbered 102, to A&EC 2/18/57. Renumbered 402 on 7/30/58 and retied 1969. To BR&L to RELCO, scrapped 8/10/1970.
7 (2)	44-tonner	GE	2/1943	-	Renumbered 403, 9/12/1958. To BR&L 9/1966, to U.S. Railway Equipment Leasing in Dolton, IL. To scrap company in Blue Island, IL, 1/1971.
8	44-tonner	GE B/n 18145	11/1943	-	Sold in 1955 to Pan American Engineering. Rebuilt 6/57 by GE to ASARCO no. 44 in Mexico.
9	SW1	EMD	4/1947	-	To SR and renumbered 404 and then 1007. To NS as no. 1007 on 6/1/1982 and retired 1/1996.
400	F2A	EMD	7/1946	-	First order of F2As for EMD. Retired 8/7/1961 and scrapped at Spencer, NC.
401	F2A	EMD	7/1946	-	Retired 12/20/1961 and scrapped at Chattanooga, TN.
500	RS1	ALCO	4/1951	-	Renumbered 405 by SR. Retired 1972 and traded to GE 6/28/1972.
501	GP7	EMD	5/1951	-	To SR and renumbered 406 and then 8230. Retired 1980 and traded to EMD.

Locomotives identified with an asterisk were carried over to the new lease, which formed the Atlantic & East Carolina Railroad. The lease went into effect September 1, 1939.

Bibliography

Abdill, George B., *Civil War Railroads; Pictorial Story of the Iron Horse 1861 Through 1865*, Superior Publishing Co., Seattle, WA, 1961.

Anderson, Andy, The Rapid Canyon Line, *Model Trains*, May 1955, pages 30-33.

Brill, Debra, *History of the J.G. Brill Company*, Indiana University Press, Bloomington, IN 2001.

Bumgarner, Matthew C., *Legacy of the Carolina & North-Western Railway*, Overmountain Press, Johnson City, TN, 1996.

Cline, Wayne, *Alabama Railroads*, The University of Alabama Press, Tuscaloosa, AL, 1997.

Collias, Joe G., *Frisco Power: Locomotives and Trains of the St. Louis-San Francisco Railway, 1903-1953*, Sekan Printing, Ft. Scott, KS, 1997.

Davis, Burke, *The Southern Railway: Road of the Innovators*, University of North Carolina Press, Chapel Hill, NC 1985.

Drury, George H., *The Historical Guide to North American Railroads*, Kalmbach Publishing, Waukesha, WI, 1988.

Drury, George H., *The Train-Watcher's Guide to North American Railroads*, Kalmbach Publishing, Waukesha, WI, 1988.

Duke, Donald and Edmund Keilty, *RDC: The Budd Rail Diesel Car*, Golden West Books, San Marino, CA, 1990.

Edwards, Harry Powell, personal correspondence regarding Atlantic & Western Railroad, March 27, 1923. Duke University, Special Collections, Perkins Library.

Edwards, William, personal correspondence covering various subjects, various dates.

Fick, Dean K., *The Lakeside and Marblehead Railroad*, Montevallo Historic Press, Columbus, OH, 2000.

Foster, Norman T., Railroading on the Yadkin, *The State*, September 1981, pages 16-19.

Gilbert, John and Grady Jefferys, *Crossties Through Carolina; the Story of North Carolina's Early Day Railroads*, Helios Press, Raleigh, NC 1969.

Greensboro Daily News, April 21, 1946.

Interstate Commerce Commission Report, June 1915.

Interstate Commerce Commission, Finance Docket No. 9032, June 4, 1932, July 25, 1932, August 12, 1932.

Interstate Commerce Commission, Finance Docket No. 10205, February 17, 1934.

Johnson, Robert Wayne, *Through the Heart of the South; the Seaboard Air Line Railroad Story*, Boston Mills Press, Erin, Ontario, Canada, 1995.

Kaminski, Edward S., *American Car & Foundry Company, 1899-1999*. Signature Press, Wilton, CA, 1999.

Keilty, Edmund, *Doodlebug Country: The Rail Motorcar on the Class 1 Railroads of the United States*, Interurban Press, Glendale, CA, 1982.

Keilty, Edmund, *Interurbans Without Wires: the Rail Motorcar in the United States*, Interurban Press, Glendale, CA, 1979.

Keilty, Edmund, *The Short Line Doodlebug: Galloping Geese and Other Railcritters*, Interurban Press, Glendale, CA, 1988.

Lawson, Tommy, Jr., *Logging Railroads of Alabama*, Cabbage Stack Publishing, Birmingham, AL, 1996.

Lewis, Edward A., *American Shortline Railway Guide*, Kalmbach Publishing, Waukesha, WI, 1996.

Lenoir (NC) News, January 23, 1912, May 31, 1912, August 15, 1916, December 14, 1918, July 17, 1933.

Liljestrand, Bob, *Alco Reference no. 1*, The Railroad Press, Hanover, PA, 1998.

McDonald, Charles W., *Diesel Locomotive Rosters*, Kalmbach Publishing, Waukesha, WI, 1992.

Miller, Jeff and Jim Vaughn, *The Winston-Salem Southbound Railway: Including the High Point, Thomasville & Denton Railroad*, Private Publication, Winston-Salem, NC, 1996.

Mischke, James, *Baltimore & Ohio Railroad Diesel Locomotive Roster, Second Edition*, Panther Hollow Press, Albuquerque, NM, 1998.

Mulhearn, Daniel J. and John R. Taibi, *General Motors F-Units: the Locomotives that Revolutionized Railroading*, Quadrant Press, New York City, NY, 1982.

Mutschler, Charles V., *Wired for Success - the Butte, Anaconda & Pacific Railway, 1892-1985*, Washington State University Press, Pullman, WA, 2002.

Nickell, W. Lynn, *Riding the Blue Goose With Stops at Wrigley and Lenox: A Pictorial History of the Lenox and Morehead & North Fork Railroads in Kentucky*, W. Lynn Nickell, West Liberty, KY, 1993.

Pacific Rail News, April 1976, page 19. December 1978, pages 6-7. April 1988, page 41.

Poole, Cary F., *A History of Railroading in Western North Carolina*, The Overmountain Press, Johnson City, TN, 1995.

Prince, Richard E., *Central of Georgia Railway and Connecting Lines*, R.E. Prince, Millard, NE, 1976.

Prince, Richard E., *Norfolk Southern Railroad Old Dominion Line and Connections*, R.E. Prince, Millard, NE, 1972.

Prince, Richard E., *Seaboard Air Line Railway, Steam Boats, Locomotives and History*, Indiana University Press, Bloomington, IN, 2000.

Reck, Franklin M., *On Time: The History of Electro-Motive Division of General Motors Corporation*, Electro-Motive Division of General Motors Corporation, 1948.

Reed, Jay, *Critters, Dinkys & Centercabs*, Rio Hondo Publishing, Santa Rosa, CA, 2000.

Southern Lumberman, December 14, 1911, February 26, 1918, December 24, 1918.

Reevy, Tony, The Atlantic & Western Railway, *National Railway Bulletin*, NHRS, Vol. 66, No. 4, 2001.

Sanford (NC) Herald, Feb. 24, 1922; Aug. 17, 1923; Dec. 21, 1928; Sept. 19, 1970; 1974 Souvenir edition and various undated issues.

Shortline, The, Atlantic & East Carolina Ry, Vol. 2, No. 6, pages 2-5, Vol. 3, No. 1, pages 2-4.

New Bern (NC) Sun Journal, October 12, 1971.

Southern Railway, *The Floods of July, 1916: How the Southern Railway Organizations Met An Emergency*. The Overmountain Press, Johnson City, TN, 1995.

Tallahassee Democrat, September, 1971.

Jacksonville Times-Union, May 13, 1972.

Trelease, Allen W., *The North Carolina Railroad: 1849-1871*, The University of North Carolina Press, Chapel Hill, NC, 1991.

U.S. Pike in Newfoundland, *Railroad Magazine*, December, 1945, pages 127-128.

Walker, R. Douglas, The Wautauga Route, *Blue Ridge Stemwinder*, 1995.

Withers, Paul K. and Tom L. Sink, *Southern: A Motive Power Pictorial*, Crusader Printing, Hatfield, PA, 1987

Withers, Paul K., *Diesels of the Southern Railway, 1939-1982*, Withers Publishing, Halifax, PA, 1997.

Index

Railroad names are spelled out in full in their main listing with their abbreviation, if used, in parenthesis. In order to conserve space, if the railroad is listed in a sub category, only the abbreviation is used. (A listing of abbreviations can also be found in Appendix A.) Standard two digit postal abbreviations are used for states. Where photographs are found in the text, they are listed as "Photos" in entries with sub listings, or with a "(P)" in shorter entries. Appendixes are not indexed.

Agasote, 35, 52, 92, 100
Agasote Millboard Company, 52
Agriculture, 3, 5-6, 81, 117, 133, 135, 147
Alabama, Florida & Gulf Railroad (AF&G), 5, 132-35
Alabama, Florida & Southern Railroad, 132-33
Alaska Railroad, 76
ALCO, 6, 128
Allison transmission in ERCC cars, 93-95, 97-98
American Car & Foundry Co., 68
American Locomotive Co., 6, 128
American Railway Express, 116
Americans With Disabilities Act (ADA), 102
Apalachicola River, 129, 135
Ardilla, Alabama, 132
Argentine Railway, 66(P), 73(P)
Arlington, Georgia, 145
Army, U.S., 75-76(P), 80-81
Asheville, NC, 141, 143
Askew, Governor Ruben, 136
Atchison, Topeka & Sante Fe Railroad, 12
Atlanta & St. Andrews Bay Railway (A&SAB)
   AF&G, opposition of sale to M&B, 133
   Bay Line Railroad, LLC, reorganized as, 120, 128
   Commodities shipped, 128
   Construction, 121, 123
   Dieselization, 128
   Edwards, H.P.
      Designing first steel bulkhead pulpwood car, 5, 126
      Diversification of industrial base, 126-27
      International Paper Co., 5, 126-27
      Markets cultivated in Central and South America, 71
      Resignation, 127
      Vice president and general manager, 4, 65, 124-27, 152
   ERwyMCC, and, 57, 88, 105, 127
   ERwyMCC photos, 30, 88, 108, 125-26
   First train, 123
   Genesse & Wyoming, ownership of Bay Line, L.L.C., 120, 128
   Graceville, FL to Campbelton, FL branch, 128
   Interchanges, 123
   International Paper Co. gains control, 126-127
      see also International Paper Co.
   Interstate Commerce Commission, 127
   Logging along the line, 121-23, 126, 128
   Lynn Haven spur, 123
   Passenger service discontinued, 128

Atlanta & St. Andrews Bay Railway (A&SAB) *(continued)*
   Rail Management & Consulting Co., 119-20, 128
   St. Andrews Bay Holding Co., 127
   St. Andrews Bay Transportation Co., 4-5, 126-27(P)
   Santa Claus train, 159
   Southwest Paper Industries, 128
   Stone Container Co., 128
   United Fruit Co. gains control, 123-24
      see also United Fruit Co.
Atlantic & East Carolina Railway (A&EC)
   Carolina (private business car), 159-60
   Debt, retiring of, 159(P)
   Dieselization, 6, 70, 156, 158
   Discontinues passenger service, 158
   Edwards, H.P. leases, 6, 78, 152
   Interstate Commerce Commission, 127, 158-60
   Santa Claus train, 159-60
   Tobacco Route slogan adopted, 152-53(P)
   WWII, 153-57
Atlantic & North Carolina Railroad (A&NC), 149-52
Atlantic & Western Railroad, *see* Atlantic & Western Railway
Atlantic & Western Railway (A&W)
   Abandonment of Jonesboro to Lillington segment, 118-19
   Atlantic & Western Corporation, 119
   Atlantic & Western Railway, L.P., 119-20
   Atlantic & Yadkin Railway, acquiring the south end of, 120
   Construction, 113, 115
   Crops, encouraging the diversification of, 117
   Edwards, H.P. and the A&W
      Early work, 3
      General manager, 3-4, 113, 119
      Receiver, 68
      Relationship with during second tenure at ERwyMCC, 76
      Resignation, 4
   ERwyMCC and the A&W, *see under* ERwyMCC
   Edwards, William Joseph, 1, 13, 113, 115
   European investors, 113
   Genesee & Wyoming Incorporated, 120
   Incorporation, 113
   Interstate Commerce Commission, 119
   Lease of freight cars, 120
   Maintenance of way, 117
   Passenger service discontinued, 118
   Rail Management & Consulting Corporation, 119-20
   Receivership, 68, 117

Atlantic & Western Railway (A&W) *(continued)*
   Reorganization, 117
   Roundhouse (P), 119
   Shops, 116
   Tie replacement, 115
Atlantic & Yadkin Railway, 120
Atlantic Coast Line Railroad (ACL)
   A&EC rerouted over ACL after hurricane Ione, 158
   Interchanges with A&EC, 154
   Interchanges with AF&S, 132-33
   Opposition to lease of A&EC by Southern Railway, 160
   Opposition to sale of AF&S to M&B, 133-35
Atomic Weapons, production of parts for, 81

B-24 Liberator bombers, production of parts for, 81
B-25 bombers, 155
Bainbridge, GA, 145, 147
Baker, Lorenzo, 124
Baltimore & Ohio Railroad
   Baltimore & Ohio Magazine, 27-29
   ERwyMCC cars built for, 16, 25-30, 34, 116
   Photos, 20, 26-27, 32
   Railway Age article, 25-26
Bananas, 124, 126
Bank of Maxton, 1
Bank of Sanford, 1, 3
Bay Line, *see* Atlanta & St. Andrews Bay Railway
Bayou George, Florida, 123
Beaufort, NC, 149
Belmont Abby College, Belmont, NC, 3
Belvedere & Delaware excursion train, 88-89
Berkshire Partners, LLC, 13
Birmingham, Alabama, 79-80
Birmingham & Southeastern Railroad
   ERCC restores no. 500, 85-87, 103
   Photos, 42-43, 85-87, 103
Birmingham Rail & Locomotive Company, 115
Birney streetcar, 33
Black River & Western Railroad, 88
Blountstown, FL, 129, 132, 138-40
Bolich, J.A., 152-53
Bonanno, Joseph C., 136-38
Boquete, Panama, 105
Bosch magneto, 36, 49
Branch lines, 11, 13, 26, 28, 35, 40, 64, 127
Breese, Kreeland & Co., 149
Brill Co.
   Brill car restored by ERCC, 88-89
   Brill cars rebuilt into Edwards cars, 83
   Early history, 12-13
   Edwards, H.P. compares Brill with ERwyMCC, 79
   Photo, 116
Broadway, NC, 113, 117
Bucaramanga depot, Colombia, 72(P)
Buchan, Edward, 152, 157, 159(P), 160
Buda engine, 40, 42, 48-49(P), 56, 59, 62, 104
Buda motor car, 48
Budd Co., 66
Bus lines, 13, 15, 105, 125-26, 158
Butte, Anaconda & Pacific Railway, 60(P), 107(P)

Caldwell & Northern Railroad, 141
Caldwell County, NC, 5
Caldwell, Joseph, 149

California Western, 64, 103-4, 104(P)
Callao-Lima Railroad, Peru, 124
Camp LeJeune (Marine Base), 160
Campbellton, FL, 128
Cape Fear & Yadkin Valley Railway, 113
Cape Fear Railway, 20(P), 31(P)
Carolina & North-Western Railroad, 141
Carolina & Northern Railroad, 1
Carolina Central Railway, 1
Carolina Railroad Company, 1
Centenary lines, 107
Central of Georgia Railroad, 80, 123, 128, 135
Chandler, Asa G., 123
Charlotte, North Carolina, 149
Cheat Mountain Salamander, 87, 106(P), 109(P)
   see also West Virginia Central Railroad
Chenille sewing machine, manufacture of, 82
Cherry Point, NC (Marine base), 153-157, 160
Chevrolet gasoline engine in ERCC cars, 92-95, 98
Chicago, Burlington & Quincy Railroad (CB&Q)
   ERwyMCC cars built for, 30-31, 57, 60-63
   ERwyMCC cars restored or waiting for restoration, 83-84, 103
   Photos, 20, 29, 61-63, 84
Chipola River, 138(P)
Chrysler, production of parts for, 81
Civil Air Patrol (WWII), 155
Civil War, 149-51
Clayton, Georgia, 88
Clayton Equipment, Limited, 91
Colorado & Southern Railroad, 61(P)
Continental engine, 60, 106
Convict laborers, 141, 143(P)
Corsicana, Texas, 89
Cotta transmission, 36, 39
Cottondale, FL, 121, 123, 128, 134-35
Cottonwood, AL, 133
Cowarts, AL, 133
CSX Railroad, 128
Cummins diesel engine, 92-95, 97-98, 104, 106
Curtis Write Hell Diver plane, production of parts for, 81
Cuthbert, Georgia, 145

Dahlgreen Proving Grounds, VA (U.S. Navy), 75-76(P)
Dakota Southern Railroad, 131
Dallas, Texas, 87-89, 102
Darby, NC, 141, 144
Denby, Alton, 135
Dieselization, 6, 11-12, 128, 131, 156, 158
Dogner, P.J., 121
Doodlebug, *see* Motor Car
Dothan, AL, 4, 5, 121-23, 126-28, 132-35
Dothan National Bank, 133
DuPont, A. Felix, 131
DuPont Co., 53
Durden, K.E. "Earl," 119-20
Durham & Southern Railway, 118

East Troy Electric Railroad, 89
Edwards, Harry P.
   Alabama, Florida & Gulf Railroad, 5, 132-135
   Atlanta & St. Andrews Bay Railroad, see under A&SAB
   Atlantic & East Carolina Railway, 152-60
   Atlantic & Western Railway, *see under* A&W Railway
   Attire, 2-3(P)

Edwards, Harry P. *(continued)*
  Birth, 1
  Boosterism, 7
  CB&Q, correspondence with, 62
  Chambers of Commerce, and, 1, 5, 7, 126, 160
  Consulting Engineer, employment as, 5, 132-35, 144, 147
  Death, 7
  Education, 3
  Edwards Railway Motor Car Co.
    Central American sales, 6, 65, 71, 76
    Early experimentation, 3-4
    Early Years, reminiscence of, 15-16
    Organization (of company), 4, 16, 24
    Resignation, 4, 68, 70
    Resignation, second, 78
    Return to, 71
    South America, sales to, 6, 65, 71, 76
    Vice president for sales, 71
  Freeman & Co. investment bankers, employment with, 5, 147
  GF&A, consulting engineer for, 147
  International Paper Company, 5
  Interstate Commerce Commission, 5, 127, 132-35
  Knights of Columbus, and the, 7
  Marianna & Blountstown, consulting engineer for, 5, 132-35
  Marriage, 3
  NC Resettlement Administration, employment with, 5-6
  W&YR, consulting engineer for, 5, 144
Edwards Hell Divers baseball team, 81
Edwards Railway Motor Car Co. (ERwyMCC)
  Atlantic & Western Railway
    Cars built for the A&W described, 16-17
    Experimentation on the A&W, 15, 16, 25, 34, 76, 116
    Maintenance cost of Edwards cars on A&W, 21
    Operating cost of Edwards car on A&W, 14
    Photos of A&W Edwards cars, 15, 17-18, 33-34, 40
  Birmingham, Alabama, proposed move to, 79, 80
  Boxcars, manufacture of, 78-79(P)
  Central American sales, 6, 59-60, 65, 70-71, 74, 76, 80, 90, 107
  Competition, 12-13, 63, 65-68, 70, 74, 83
  Customizing of cars, 33-34
  Demonstrator unit, 73(P)
  Early experimentation, 3-4, 12-18, 116
  Edwards Bulletin, 17, 19, 21-22
  Factory
    Construction, 4
    Detailed description of structures and function, 24
    In house/outsourcing broken down, 33-34
    Great Depression, 70
    Option on factory, 80
    Photo and layout, 22-23
    Post ERwyMCC production, 80-82
    Workforce, 24-25
  Freight Motors, *see* ERwyMCC, Model 10, Special Fast Freight and Express
  HSG (higher than standard gauge) described, 40
  Huff, John Gates, see Huff, John Gates
  Incorporation, see ERwyMCC, Organization (of company)
  Interior (of Edwards cars),
    Described, 35, 52-54, 92-93, 95-97, 99-101
    Interior photos, 36, 54, 56-57, 86, 105-106
  Line Inspection Car, 60(P), 77-78, 125(P) 107
  LMG (lower than meter gauge) described, 40
  Maintenance costs, 21
  Model 5, 36, 97, 107

Edwards Railway Motor Car Co. (ERwyMCC) *(continued)*
  Model (no designation, early photos), 15-18, 20, 26-27
  Model 10
    Advertisement, 10, 39
    Birth of standard Model 10, 33-34
    Detailed description, 35-36, 92
    Elevation plans, 10, 32, 39, 40, 42, 78, 92, 93
    Hybrid leading to Model 10, 31-33
    Identifying characteristics, 40, 42
    LMG/HSG designations, 40
    Operating cost, 10, 37-38, 41-42
    Photos, 20, 30-34, 38, 65-67, 71, 73, 75-76, 85-87, 92-93, 103, 106, 108, 119, 125-6
    Photos, component parts, 35-36
  Model 10 Special Fast Freight and Express
    Description, 59
    Elevation Plans, 60, 78, 98
    Photos, 59-60, 66, 72
  Model 20
    Cost, 42
    Described, 42
    Detailed description, 49-55, 93-95
    Dimensions, 36, 42
    Elevation plans, 43, 61, 93-95
    Mounting prime mover on front truck, 12, 42, 44-47
    Operating cost, 64-65
    Photos, 43, 49, 64, 68, 72, 84, 105
    Photos, component parts, 49-52
  Model 21
    Described, 56, 95-96
    Elevation plans, 71
    Photos, 65, 74, 96
  Model 25
    Described, 36, 56
    Elevation plans, 61, 88, 95
    Photos, 56-58, 61-62, 70, 75, 77, 84, 89, 100, 104, 106, 108-9, 126
    see also, United Fruit Company, no. 150
  Model 45, 36, 57
  Model 65, 36, 57, 62
    Elevation plans, 62-63
    Photos, 62
  Model 199, 31
  Model K-35, 21-22
  Model K-50 "Edwards Special," 17, 19, 34
  Mounting prime mover on front truck, 12, 42, 44-47
  Officers, list of, 24
  Operating cost of Edwards cars
    1921, on Atlantic & Western Railway, 14-15, 21
    1922, on Baltimore & Ohio Railroad, 28
    1925 (circa), on unknown, 36-37
    1926 (circa), on Chicago, Burlington & Quincy Railroad, 62
    1926, on Morehead & North Fork, 64
    1933, Central of Georgia (hypothetical), 79-80
    1936 (Panama Railroad), 65
  Operation of cars described, 63
  Organization (of company), 4, 16, 24
  Receivership, 68, 70
  Resignation of H.P. Edwards, 4, 68, 70
  Patents, 4, 3, 42, 44-47, 51, 67
  Plant, see ERwyMCC, Factory
  Sales Brochures
    1921 Sales bulletin, 17, 19, 21-22
    1922 Advertisement, 39

Edwards Railway Motor Car Co. (ERwyMCC)
  Sales Brochures *(continued)*
    1923 Catalog, 34-36
    1924 Marketing brochure, 38
    1925 (circa) operating cost notes, 37
    1926 Catalog sparks sales of "freight Motors," 59-60
    Operating costs from M&NF used in advertisements, 64
  South America, sales to, 6, 59-60, 65, 70-71, 74, 76, 80, 90, 107
  Special Fast Freight and Express models, *see* ERwyMCC, Model 10, Special Fast Freight and Express
  Trailers
    Described, 57, 100-101
    Elevation plans, 25, 39, 42-43, 100-101
    Photos, 15-16, 26, 32, 59, 65, 76
  Workforce, names of, 25, 69
Edwards Railcar Company (ERCC, 1998-)
  2005 Company catalog reproduced, 90-102
  Dinner Trains, ERCC cars manufactured and used as, 89, 94-95
  Mechanical system of Edwards cars, 91
  Model 5 condensed Specifications, 97
  Model 10 condensed specifications, 92
  Model 10-C condensed specifications, 92
  Model "1938 Special," *see* United Fruit Company, no. 150
  Model 20 condensed specifications, 93
  Model 20 diner car condensed specifications, 94
  Model 21 condensed specifications, 95-96
  Model 25 modified hybrid, 87
  Model 30 condensed specifications, 96-97
  Model ES 700 series Peter Witt streetcar, 102
  Model ES standard series streetcar, 103
  Model FM 10 condensed specifications, 98
  Model S 10 condensed specifications, 98-99
  Model T 10 trailer car condensed specifications, 100
  Model T 20 trailer car condensed specifications, 100-101
  Model T 21 trailer car condensed specifications, 101
  Propulsion systems, 91
  Replica Edwards cars, 83
  Streetcar replicas, manufacture of, 90
  Torrico, Steven, 83, 85, 90
Edwards, William Joseph, 1, 3, 13, 113, 115, 152
Edwards, William Joseph "Bill," 4, 6-7, 116-117, 155-158
Edwards, Winslow, 6, 116-117, 157-158
Eisemann magneto, 39
Electric block signals, 64
Electro Motive Company, 13, 60, 62-63, 74
Electro Motive Division, 6, 128, 156-157
Elkville, NC, 141
EMC, 13, 60, 62-63, 74
EMD, 6, 128, 156-157
Esporanza hotel, la (Colombia), 70(P)
Excellence in War Production award, 80-81
Excite storage batteries, 36

Fabrikoid, 36, 53
Fare, Fredrick, 144
Farming, *see* Agriculture
FBI, 136-138
FC Panama Nacional Railroad, 59(P), 105
Federal Bureau of Investigation, 136-138
Federal Railroad Administration, 128
Ferrocarril de Caldas Railroad, 41(P)
Ferrocarril de Girardot Railroad, 66(P)
Ferrocarril Nacional de Chiriqui Railroad
  Photos, 41, 57, 76

Ferrocarril Nacional de Chiriqui Railroad *(continued)*
  Superintendent praises ERwyMCC, 76
Ferrocarriles Nacionales de Pacifico Railroad, 71(P)
  see also Ferrocarriil de Girdot Railroad
Ferrocarriles Nacionales de Colombia Railroad, 66(P), 72(P), 74(P)
Ferrocarriles del Estado Railroad, 66(P), 73(P)
Fidelity Trust Company, 117
First National Bank of Fayetteville, 1
Fish cars (for transporting fish packed in ice), 151
Floods, 5, 138(P), 143-144
Forbs, Tom, 82
Ford, manufacture of tractor parts for, 82
Fort Pepperrell, St. Johns, Newfoundland, Canada, 45-76
Four Wheel Drive Auto Company, 12
Frank, J.H., 127
Freeman & Company investment bankers, 5
Ft. Madison, Farmington & Western Railroad, 83-84(P), 103

Gary, A.J, 123
General Electric components, 13
General Electric locomotives, 6
General Motors, 13
Genesse & Wyoming incorporated, 120
Georgia, Florida & Alabama Railway, 145-47
Georgia Northern Railroad, 32(P)
Georgia Pine Railway, 145
German-American Lumber Company, 121, 123
Golden Peanut processing plant, 128
Goldsboro, NC, 13, 113, 149, 158-59
Goldsboro, NC, Union Station, 159
Gulf Coast Development Company, 121
Graceville, FL, 128
Grandin, W.J., 141-44
Grandin, NC, 141-44
Grandin Lumber Company, 141-44
Graustein, A.R., 135
Graysonia, Nashville & Ashdown Railroad, 61(P)
Great Depression, 5, 70, 74, 83, 118, 131-32
Green County, NC, 1
Greenbriar Equity, LLC, 13
Greenwood, FL, 133, 135
Guatemala City, Guatemala, 77(P)
Gulf Line Railway, 1
Gurney ball bearings, 36

H.K. Porter Locomotive Works, 36, 57, 62, 156
Hampton & Branchville Railroad (H&B), 68(P), 87, 103, 105(P)
Hansen, Rick, 85
Harnett County, 3
Harrihan, W.J., 3
Hoey, Governor Clyde R., 151-52, 160
Hoke, Robert, 141
Homasote, *see* Agasote
Howeland Improvement Co., 151
Huff, John Gates
  A&NC, and, 78, 158
  Background, 67
  Constructs moonshine still, 70
  Designs Perley A. Thomas trolley car, 67
  ERwyMCC, employment with, 25, 67, 69-70(P)
  Post ERwyMCC, 70, 81-82
Hurricane Ione, 158
Hurricanes, 1916, 143
Hyatt roller bearings, 36, 40, 50

ICC, *see* Interstate Commerce Commission
International Paper Co., 5, 126-28, 133, 135
International Motor Truck Company, 70
International Railways of Central America, 99, 124
Interstate Commerce Commission
    AF&G, and the, 5, 132-35
    A&SAB, and the, 127
    A&EC, and the, 127, 158-60
    A&W, and the, 119
    Edwards, H.P., and the, 5, 127
    Edwards Railway Motor Car Company, and the, 28
    M&B, and the, 132-37
    W&Y, and the, 144
Interurbans, *see* Streetcars
Irwin Car & Equipment, 87, 91
Isthmus of Panama, 64

Jenkins, C.E., 144
J. G. Brill Company, *see* Brill Company
Jonesboro, NC, 113, 118-19

Keith, Minor C.
    Appoints H.P. Edwards vice president and general manager of A&SAB, 4, 124
    Background, 123-24
    Death, 5, 126
    H.P. Edwards makes contacts through, 6, 65, 71, 74
Kelly-Springfield
    Chassis used for early ERwyMCC cars, 15-17, 19, 21, 116
    Edwards transitions away from, 25, 29-31, 53
Kershaw, Royce, 85, 89
Kershaw Manufacturing, 89-90
King, Mason, 160
King, W.H., 3, 134
Kinston, NC, 149-51, 153
Knights of Columbus, 7

LaGrange, IL, 156-57
LaSalle & Bureau County Railroad, 136
L&L Truck Co. and H. P. Edwards employment with, 5
LCL (less than car load freight), 48, 59
Landon, H.C., 143
Laramie, North Park & Western Railroad, 62(P)
Laurinburg, NC, 1
Lee County, NC, 70
Leece-Neville Co. (electrical equipment), 36, 49
Lenoir, NC, 141
Liberty Furniture Co., 82
Light Rail, 90
Lillington, NC, 113, 116-18, 118(P)
Logging
    A&SAB, along line, 121-23, 126, 128
    M&B, along line, 129-33
    W&YR, along line, 141-44
Louisville & Nashville Railroad, 121-23, 129-35
Lumber mills, 131, 141-43, 147
Lynn Haven, FL, 123, 128

Mack Truck Co., 12, 63
Malaria, 64
Malone, FL, 132
Mann, M.G., 159(P)
Marianna, FL, 4, 5, 126, 129, 133-35, 138

Marianna & Blountstown Railroad (M&B)
    Abandonment of line, 138
    Alabama, Florida & Gulf, efforts to acquire, 5, 132-35
    Bonanno, Joseph C. purchases line, 136-38
    Condition of roadbed, 129, 136-38
    Crushed rock as revenue source, 136
    DuPont, A. Felix gains control, 131
    Edwards, H.P. as consulting engineer for, 5, 133-35
    First train on line, 129
    Incorporation and construction, 129
    Interstate Commerce Commission, and the, 132-37
    Logging along line, 129-33
    Memorial to M&B created, 138-40
    Scotts Ferry to Blountstown section abandoned, 131
Marbury, E.L., 132
Marine Corps, 156, 160
    see also Camp LeJeune
    see also Cherry Point
Marl, 154
Master Car Builder (MCB) trucks, 91, 96, 102
MATA, 87, 102
Maxfield, Ron, 89
Maxton, Alma & Southbound Railroad, 16, 18(P), 25, 27, 33
McCallum, General D.C., 149
McDonald, Bill, 83, 89
McKeen Jr., William R., 12
McKeen Car Co., 12, 53
McKinney, R.L., 121
McKinney Avenue Transit Authority, 87, 102
McMullan, Harry, 160
McNeil, FL, 132
Meddendorf, William & Co., 113
Miami, FL, 5
Midwest Motors, 39
Miller, O.O., 131, 135
Millville Junction, FL, 123
Miner, Dave, 83-84
Mobile, Alabama, 80, 103
Montgomery, Alabama, 89
Moonshine, 70
Morehead, Governor John Motley, 149
Morehead & North Fork Railroad, 64(P), 103
Morehead City, North Carolina, 149, 153, 155, 158
Motor car (railroad), gasoline, early development of, 11-13
Mt. Dora, FL, 83, 85, 89
Mt. Dora, Tavares and Eustis Railroad, 83-85(P), 89
Mt. Jewett, Kinzua & Riterville Railroad, 38(P)
Myrob, FL, 132

Nacionales de Mexico Railroad, 41(P), 67
Narrow Gauge, 35, 77-79
    see also, ERwyMCC, LMG
Naval Stores, 121, 131
Navy, U.S., 74-76, 80-81, 128, 154
    A&SAB and countermeasures station Panama City, FL, 128
    A&EC gets loan from Navy for relay rail, 154
    Dahlgreen Proving Grounds, VA, 75-76(P)
    Edwards plant produces bilge pumps for, 81
    ERwyMCC sells cars to, 74-76(P), 80-81

Nevada State Railroad Museum, Carson City, NV, 40, 105-6
Neversweat & Washoe, 107(P)
New Bern, NC, 149-51, 153(P)
New Holland farm co., manufacture of equipment for, 82

New Jersey Locomotive & Machine Workings, 151
Norfolk & Southern Railway (pre 1910), 151
Norfolk & Western Railroad, 141
Norfolk-Southern Corporation (Modern), 120
Norfolk Southern Railroad (1910-1974), 12(P) 116, 118, 151, 160
North Carolina Railroad, 149
North Carolina Resettlement Administration, 5-6
North Carolina Transportation Museum, Spencer, NC, 68, 87, 103, 103(P), 105(P)
North Wilkesboro, NC, 141, 144

Oil City Trust Co., 144
Official Guide of Railways, 119
Orange Blossom Dinner Train, 89
   see also: Mt. Dora Tavares and Eustis Railroad
Oreja Railroad, Peru, 124
Osgood Bradley Co., 13

P-40 Tomahawks, production of, 81
Packard, J.C., 131
Page, Henry, 152
Page Trust Co., 1
Panama Canal Railway, 79, 90
Panama City, FL, 4, 5, 121-24, 126-128, 134
Panama City, Panama, 65(P)
Panama Railroad
   Buys ERwyMCC cars, 64-66
   History, 64
   Photos, 40, 52, 65, 72, 74
Parrish, William F., 81-82
Pearley A. Thomas Co., 29(P), 31, 67
Penn Central Railroad, 136, 138
Pennington & Evans Co., 131
Pensacola, FL, 4, 126
Peter Smith Heater Co., 26
Peter Witt streetcar, 102
Philadelphia & Western Railroad, 83
Platt Co., 82
Platt Saco Lowell Co., 82
Port of Los Angeles, 124
Porter Locomotive Works, 36, 57, 62, 156
Preston, Andrew, 124
Pullman Co., 13, 147
Pulpwood car, first steel bulkhead, 5, 126
Pumps, production of, 81-82(P)

R.J. Reynolds Co., manufacture of machines for, 81(P)
Rail Car, see Motor car
Rail Management & Consulting Corporation, 119-120, 128
Railbus, see Motor car
Railway Age, 25-26
Railway Express, 116
Raleigh & Gaston Railroad, 149
Rapid Canyon Line, 65-66(P)
Rapid City, Black Hills & Western Railroad, 65-66(P)
Redstone Arsenal, production of parts for, 81
Regulation of railroads, 11
Relay rail, 154
Remington Arms factory, 88
Richland, Georgia, 145
Ringling, John, 89, 160
Ringling, John and Mabel Museum, 89
Ringling Brothers Circus, 160
Rogers, Ralph B., 80

Rogers Diesel and Aircraft Corporation, 80-81

Saco-Lowell, 70, 82(P)
St. Andrews Bay Holding Co., 127
St. Andrews Bay Transportation Co., 4, 126-127(P)
St. Johns, Newfoundland, Canada, 45-46
St. Joseph, MO, 30
St. Louis Car Co., 13, 89
Sanford, NC
   Edwards, H.P., 3, 6
   Edwards, William Joseph, 1, 3
   ERwyMCC, 16
   A&W, 13, 113, 117, 119-120
   see also ERwyMCC, factory
Santa Fe Railroad, 12
Scott, Governor Kerr, 159(P)
Scotts Ferry, FL, 129-32
Seaboard Air Line Railroad, 3, 5, 117, 145-47
SEPTA, 83
Sheppards Point, North Carolina, 149
   see also Morehead City, North Carolina
Sherman, W.C., 124
Sierra Railroad, 64, 103-4(P)
SKF bearings, 50-51
Skunk Train, 64, 103-4(P)
Smith, Jim, 139
Snow Hill, NC, 1
Southeastern Express, 116
Southeastern Pennsylvania Transportation Authority, 83
Southern Kraft Co., 135
Southern Railway
   A&W defers, then pays debt to, 117
   Negotiates (unsuccessfully) to purchase cars from ERwyMCC, 67
   1916 Hurricanes, 143
   Refuses to lease, then leases A&EC, 151-52, 160
   W&YR interchanges with, 141
Southern Traction Co., 89
Southwest Paper Industries, 128
Sperry Rail Car Co., 88
Steele, A.B., 121, 123
Stone Container Corporation, 128
Strayer, A., 127
Streetcars, 11, 33, 67, 87-88, 90, 102-3
   Background, 11
   ERCC manufactures Replica streetcars, 90, 102-3
   ERCC restores streetcars, 87-89
   ERwyMCC refurbishes streetcar into Motor Car, 33
   Huff, John Gates, designs, 67
Stromberg carburetor, 39
Sumter & Choctaw Railway, 31(P), 78-79(P)
Swansboro, NC, 115

Tallahassee, FL, 145-47
Tallulah Falls Railroad, 57-58(P), 88, 105, 108(P)
Tapper, George, 135
Tennessee Central Railroad, 105
Texas Electric, 89
Time Magazine, 151, 156
Tobacco, 6, 81, 147, 152-53
T.O.F. (Trailer On Flatcar), 128
Train wrecks, 103-4, 123, 155-56
Trammell, Robert, 140
Trans Iranian Railroad, 128

Tranvia de Oriente (de Medellin) Railroad, 59(P), 66
Traveltown, Los Angeles, CA, 106
Trolley car, *see* Streetcar
Tropical Trading and Transport Co., 124
Tucson, Cornelia & Gila Bend Railroad, 40, 105-6, 106(P)
Turpentine Industry, 131
    see also, Naval Stores

U-boat, 75-76, 155
U.S. Army, 75(P), 76, 80-81
U.S. Corps of Engineers, 135
U.S. Marine Corp, 156, 160
    see also Camp Lejeune
    see also Camp Lejeune
U.S. Military Railroad (Civil War), 151
U.S. Navy 74-76(P), 80-81, 128, 154
    see also Dahlgreen Proving Grounds
Union Pacific, 12
United Fruit Co.
    Edwards, H.P., makes contacts through, 65, 71
    History, 123-24
    No. 150 (renumbered 1150)
        Described 78, 99-100, 107
        Photos, 77, 99-100, 108
    see also Keith, Minor C.
United States Railroad Administration (USRA), 3, 134
Ussery, E.T., 116-19

Valley Railroad, 88
Virginia & Carolina Southern Railroad, 17(P), 33, 43(P)

Wainwright ship yards, Panama City, FL, 128
Walker, R. Douglas, 117-18
Wall St. Journal, 158
Washington & Lincolnton Railroad, 85
Wasson Manufacturing Co., 13
Watauga & Yadkin River Railroad (W&YR), 5, 141-44
Watauga & Yadkin Valley Railroad, 141-43
Waukesha Motor, 36
Wellington bomber (British), production of parts for, 81
West, G.M., 121
West Virginia Central Railroad, 87(P), 89, 106(P), 109(P)
Western Guatemala Railroad, 124
Western North Carolina Railroad, 141, 149
Westinghouse air brakes, 19, 21, 26, 35-36, 51
Westinghouse electric starter, 22, 39
Westinghouse generator in ERCC Cars, 96
Westinghouse pneuphonic horn, 55
White Motor Co., 12, 106
Whitsitt, W.B., 27-29
Wilkes & Western Railroad, 144
Williams, J.P., 145
Wilmington & Raleigh Railroad, 149
Wilmington & Weldon Railroad, 149
Wilson, FL, 133, 135
Wilson, Woodrow, 3
Wilson, W.S., 132
Winton Engine Co., 13
Witt, Peter, 102
Woolf, H.W., 134
Women in workforce during WWII, 81
World Mining Museum, Butte, MT, 107
World War One, 11, 48, 129
World War Two

A&SAB, 128
A&EC, 153-157
    Civil Air Patrol, 155
    Diesels acquired during war, 128, 156
    Edwards plant turns out war materials, 80-81
    ERwyMCC cars sunk when transport hit by U-boat, 75-76
    M&B, 135
    Oil Trains, 128
    Women in workforce, 81

Yadkin Railroad, 33(P)
Yadkin River (NC), 141-44
Yellow Fever, 64
Youngstown, FL, 123

Zenith carburetor, 36, 49

Still avalible from Hot Box Press:

Featuring: 176 pages with 139 photographs by Jack Delano, Walker Evans, Dorothea Lange, Russell Lee, Carl Mydans, Arthur Rothstein, Ben Shahn, John Vachon, and Marion Post Wolcott

An American Journey
Images of Railroading During the Depression

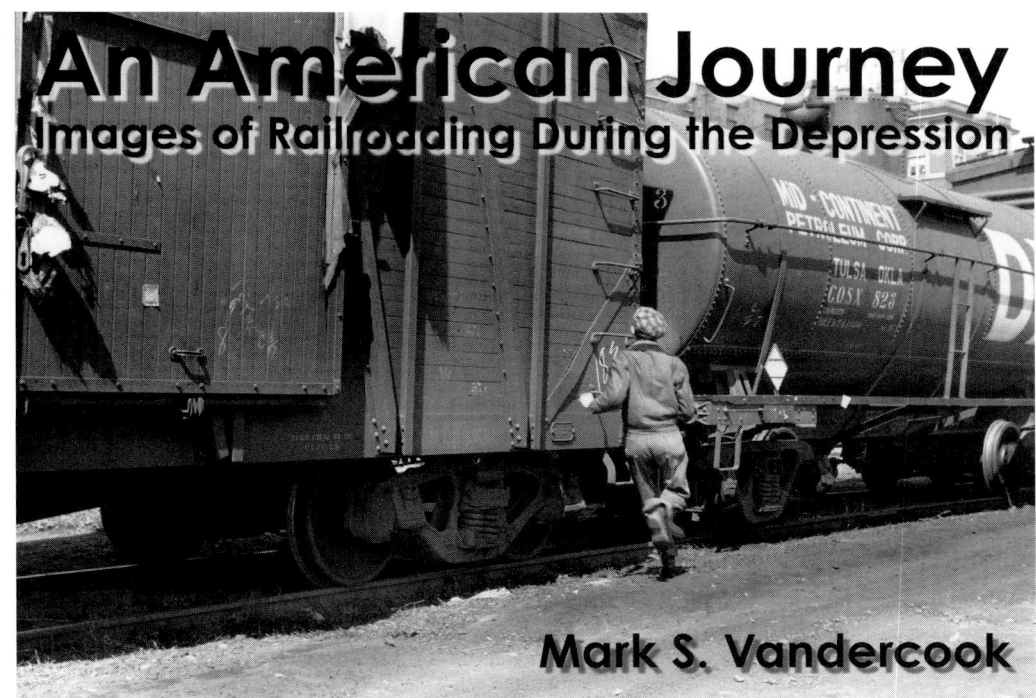

By: Mark S. Vandercook isbn 0-9703544-4-4 **$24.95**

At the height of the Great Depression, the Farm Security Administration (FSA) set out to document, in photographic form, the state of America and its people. The FSA photographers, regarded today to be among the best of the 20th century, amassed a collection of more than 270,000 negatives. "The work of the photographic section of the Farm Security Administration," declares the Encyclopedia of Photography, "stands as the high-water mark of social documentary in this country." Forever frozen in time, these photographs have captured a significant point in American history that will never be forgotten.

Upon observing these photographs it becomes obvious that during this time in American history it was almost impossible to separate the American people from one thing that bound them all together: the railroads. How else can one account for the number of railroad related photographs in the collection if, by their very nature, the railroads were not tied in some fundamental way to American society? The railroads were, in fact, essential to the life and livelihood of countless Americans.

This book then, is a snapshot of what could be called the "railroad culture," a culture that has long since vanished. So sit back and take a photographic journey through time. These photographs cover a wide range of subjects, each with an underlying railroad theme. The linear journey begins in 1935 and concludes just before our entry into the war in 1941. With the diversity of subjects and situations presented, the more enlightening journey will be that into the paradigm of the "railroad culture."

"it's one of the most impressive railroad books I've ever seen" - Jim Boyd, August 2001 Railfan & Railroad "Camera Bag" review

"This is a facinating look at American life, during the Depression." - Trains Magazine, March 2001

"It's exciting to see how nine creative photographers treated railroads and railroad people in the 1930's. Vandercook presents a significant review of a time when railroads were a part of everyday life. . . " - John Gruber, Center For Railroad, Photography and Art

---

$24.95 + 4.00 domestic S/H. Log onto www.HotBoxPress.com to purchase, or ask for it at your favorite Hobby Shop/Bookstore, or send check to HBP, PO Box 161078, Mobile, AL 36616

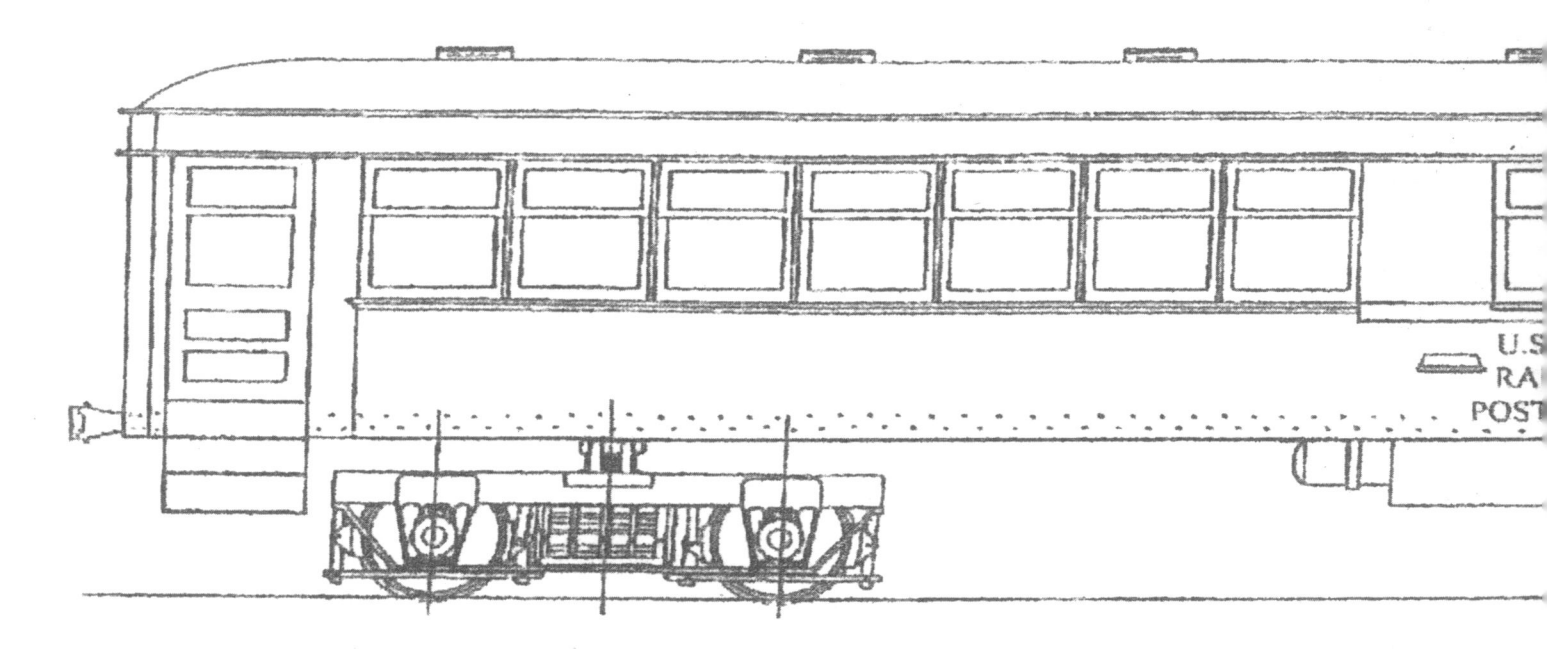

U.S.
RA
POST

LENGTH
WI

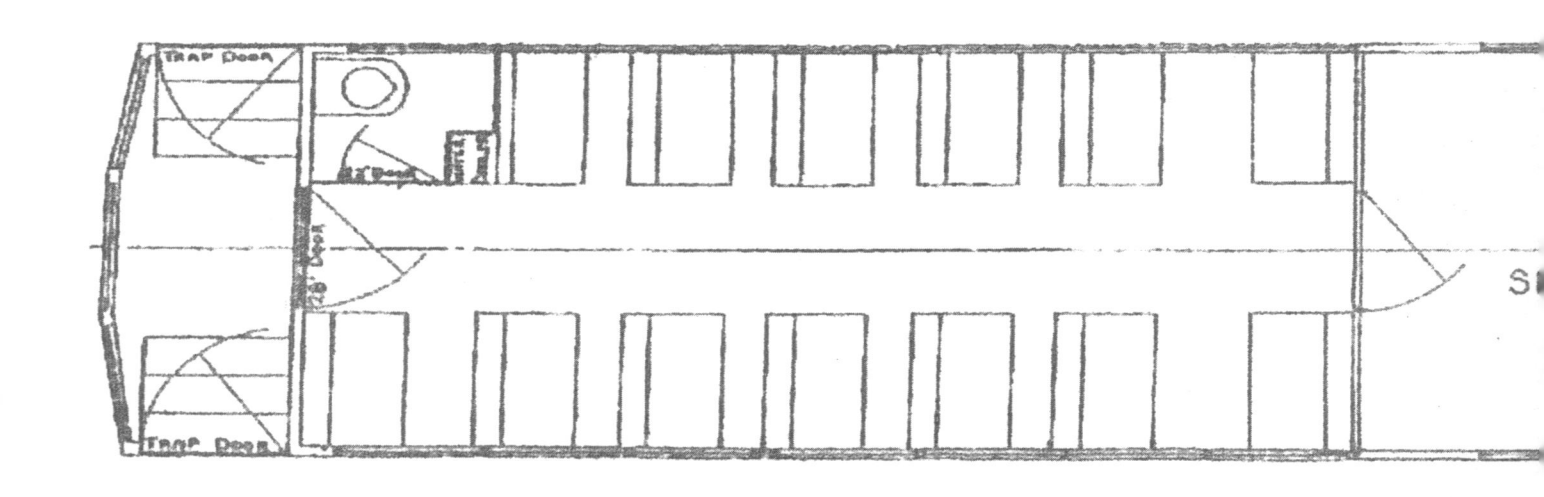

TRAP DOOR

S